31,50

More Praise for *Imago Relationship Therapy*

"Imago Relationship Therapy (IRT) is a major contemporary approach to helping couples in trouble, and in this book Harville Hendrix and his collaborators show us why. An intriguing and important contribution, the book describes the evolution of IRT principles and practice, clarifying both its theoretical and applied potential. These eminently practical essays, by an impressive panel of contributors, will expand the thinking of novice and seasoned practitioners alike."
—Jeffrey K. Zeig, director,
The Milton H. Erickson Foundation

"Some of the very best thinkers and clinicians offer their insights into the importance of relationship. The book will help one to become a more effective therapist and a better partner! Well worth reading for anyone involved in the helping professions."
—Jon Carlson, distinguished professor,
Governors State University

Imago Relationship Therapy

Imago Relationship Therapy

Perspectives on Theory

Harville Hendrix, Ph.D.,

and Helen LaKelly Hunt, Ph.D., Series Editors

Mo Therese Hannah, Ph.D.,

and Wade Luquet, Ph.D., Volume Editors

Foreword by Randall C. Mason, Ph.D.

Imago Series, Volume 1

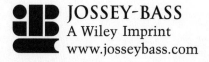

JOSSEY-BASS
A Wiley Imprint
www.josseybass.com

Published by Jossey-Bass
A Wiley Imprint
989 Market Street, San Francisco, CA 94103-1741   www.josseybass.com

Jossey-Bass books and products are available through most bookstores. To contact Jossey-Bass directly, call our Customer Care Department within the U.S. at 800-956-7739 or outside the U.S. at 317-572-3986, or fax to 317-572-4002.

Jossey-Bass also publishes its books in a variety of electronic formats. Some content that appears in print may not be available in electronic books.

Library of Congress Cataloging-in-Publication Data

Hendrix, Harville.
    Imago relationship therapy : perspectives on theory / Harville Hendrix, Helen LaKelly Hunt, Mo Therese Hannah.
      p. cm.
    Includes bibliographical references and index.
    ISBN 0-7879-7828-0 (alk. paper)
    1. Imago relationship therapy. I. Hunt, Helen LaKelly. II. Hannah, Mo Therese. III. Title.
    RC488.5.H465 2005
    616.89'156—dc22   2004021980

Printed in the United States of America
FIRST EDITION
HB Printing 10 9 8 7 6 5 4 3 2 1

Contents

Foreword: My View of Imago   ix

Randall C. Mason, Ph.D.

Acknowledgments   xv

Introduction: A Theory of Relationality   1

Wade Luquet, Ph.D.

Part One: Perspectives of the Founders   11

1   The Evolution of Imago Relationship Therapy:
    A Personal and Professional Journey   13

Harville Hendrix, Ph.D.

2   Relationship as a Living Laboratory   35

Helen LaKelly Hunt, Ph.D.

3   Conscious Marriage as Covenant   48

Helen LaKelly Hunt, Ph.D.

Part Two: Perspectives on Comparisons
with Other Models   61

4   Family Systems Theory and Imago Therapy:
    A Theoretical Interpretation   63

Randy Gerson, Ph.D.

5   An Exploration of Imago Relationship Therapy
    and Affect Theory   91

Joseph Zielinski, Ph.D.

6   Relationship Knowing: Imago
    and Object Relations   108

Stephen R. Plumlee, M.Div., Ph.D.

7   **Contemporary Psychoanalytic Relational Theories and Imago: Concepts for Relational Healing**   122
Mona R. Barbera, Ph.D.

Part Three: Perspectives on Clinical Theory   137

8   **Imago, Relationships, and Empathy**   139
Randall C. Mason, Ph.D.

9   **Imago, Relationships, and Empathy: A Response to Mason**   162
Ted Smith, D.Min.

10   **Imago: A Theory and Therapy of Connectivity**   177
Randall C. Mason, Ph.D.

11   **The Relationship Nightmare as an Expression of Disconnection**   193
Randall C. Mason, Ph.D., Margaret Mason, Ph.D., and Mo Therese Hannah, Ph.D.

12   **Envy's Manifestation in Individuals and Couples: Implications for Imago Therapy**   201
Bernard J. Baca, Ph.D.

13   **The Conscious Self in a Creational Paradigm**   213
Sophie Slade, Ph.D.

About the Editors   221
About the Contributors   223
Index   225

Foreword: My View of Imago

Randall C. Mason, Ph.D.

My journey began with my serving as the mediator between my father and my mother. My father was a clergyman; my mother was an invalid from rheumatoid arthritis. During an extended period of my childhood, my father lived on the second floor of our home while my mother lived on the first. I went from floor to floor, carrying out the role of mediator and serving as a persuasive advocate for each parent. These experiences left me puzzled about relationships and generated a lot of troubling questions, which eventually led me into the field of couples therapy.

Even with my interest in marital dynamics, I didn't know much about marriage back then. Only after my first marriage of sixteen years ended did it finally dawn on me how dependent I was and what the relationship rupture had done to me. Emotionally, I barely survived that situation. But ironically, my professional functioning improved dramatically. I had become a self psychologist during the second half of those years, and the pain of my divorce enhanced my understanding of self psychology and its application to my own life. I realized that I had been doing and teaching psychotherapy for years without any real sense of what emotional pain was like. I now felt empathy for what my clients were going through.

I went through six years of a second marriage, but I still didn't get it. In retrospect, I realize that I married someone who was too

This essay was derived from a segment of Randy Mason's clinical instructor's manual and was published posthumously with the permission of Margaret Mason. The editors deeply appreciate her cooperation in facilitating the publication of this writing.

much like me and not a real imago match. Then I met Margaret. She was the loveliest and sweetest person I'd ever known, and she was also a tough lady. For a while, we rode the roller coaster of ecstasy and catastrophe.

Shortly after Margaret and I were married, Harville Hendrix and Helen LaKelly Hunt invited us to join them for supper. From that point on, my thinking has been dominated by Imago. At last I'd found a marital theory that made sense to me. I also discovered that self psychology and Imago theory and therapy were mutually illuminating.

The Beginnings of the Intentional Relationship

Imago Relationship Therapy (IRT) starts with the overall guiding assumption that nature is in the process of healing itself and that our work with relationships is intrinsic and assistive to that process. Part of the healing process involves an increase in consciousness.

Since the Industrial Revolution, which ushered in the phenomenon of choice, civilization has been moving toward a new view of relationships. People began to belong to themselves rather than to a superior, and so they became able to make choices about such things as moving away from the town where they were born or divorcing their spouse. Women's suffrage opened up options for women. People began to choose their own marital partners instead of entering into arranged marriages, and the difficult marriage became changeable or even terminable.

I once asked a colleague who had lived in India whether, given the prevalence of arranged marriages there, couples had difficulties similar to ours. She indicated that perhaps they did, but that "they didn't make such a big deal out of it." Relationship difficulties were a part of life, similar to a physical illness that a person "comes down with" and can do nothing about. If one ended up with a lousy spouse, well, those were the breaks: one person has a bad marriage; another is born blind.

We do not take such a fatalistic approach to marriage. We now think about what a relationship means to us and how our relationship adds to or detracts from the quality of our life. With this shift in thinking, we can create a good marriage through becoming aware of the ingredients of a desirable spouse and intentionally planning to find, and to be, such a person. Growth is an even newer choice: we can choose to use consciousness and intentionality.

Threads of the New Paradigm

Many believe that Imago is a completely new theory coming out of nowhere. Quite the opposite is true: Hendrix drew from and combined into a new system some of the best elements of classical psychotherapy.

Hendrix received his psychoanalytic training at the University of Chicago during the time when Rogerian theory was prevalent. In the late 1960s, Hendrix conducted empathy training as developed by Truax and Carkhoff. Then came his immersion in Transactional Analysis and Gestalt therapy, along with his experiences undergoing Jungian analysis and Bioenergetics.

Hendrix wove various elements of these theories into a new paradigm that transformed the dynamics of couple work. Let us look at some of the attributes of this new paradigm.

First of all, in this new paradigm transference is considered an intense force for change. People understand that transference is the transfer onto the therapist of thoughts and feelings related to the client's early life experiences, but the power of such transference experiences is often underestimated. I use the word *experiences* to indicate that we are not dealing with intellectual issues arising from scintillating conversations between analyst and client, leading to brilliant insights by the all-wise analyst. Rather, any insights that emerge are helpful and germane only to the extent that they relate to the pain and struggle of the transference experience.

Just as we might describe a couple's marriage as a "parallel relationship," many analytic situations could also be labeled as such. In both types of transference experiences—marriage and the analytic relationship—there ought to be an intensity to the transference, as it is that intensity which provides a powerful potential for change. This is not to imply that either marital or analytic relationships need be devoid of happiness or even of joy.

When I was in therapy with a psychoanalyst during my breakup with my first wife, we talked about my divorce as being comparable to an empathic break between an analyst and patient. A colleague related to me that his analytic experiences were of such intensity that, some mornings, he felt he could not get up and go on with his daily life because he'd experienced an empathic break with his analyst.

Hendrix recognized that similar transference experiences exist in romantic relationships. The term *Imago* and, in fact, the entire theory center around the transference experiences of couples and explain how such experiences provide an opportunity for change. IRT capitalizes on the transferences that already exist in the couple relationship. Unlike with the transference between analyst and patient, between romantic partners there's no need to wait for the transference to develop.

This transferential characteristic of romantic partnership leads to the second feature of the paradigm shift. The transference of interest is that which takes place between the two partners, not between the couple and the analyst. Previously, in the old paradigm, as one analyst suggested, a couple in analysis would develop positive transferences with the analyst, and those transferences would then shift from the analyst to the spouse.

The third characteristic of the new paradigm is a marked change in the roles of therapist and client. When I went to an Imago couples workshop for the first time, I got the impression that the couples were doing their own diagnostic work. Although some might argue against a couple's capacity to do diagnostic work, my experience is that their work often compares favorably with that of many therapists. I should clarify that this does not imply any approval of codependent behavior or of the fixing of one partner by the other. Rather, it means that each partner works to understand the other, which eventually leads them to experience empathy at its very best. On the basis of an empathic understanding of oneself and one's partner, relating in a new way becomes possible.

The Imago Therapist

What does this imply for us as therapists? When working with a couple, the therapist provides a containing or holding environment while avoiding any intrusion on the primary transference experiences of the couple. Many have described the therapeutic role of the Imago therapist as one of a coach, although such coaching must be devoid of any shaming. Perhaps the term *supervisor* is more accurate; the therapy supervisor provides a holding environment for the supervisee, helping him or her understand transference-countertransference issues and develop alternative ways of relating to the client.

The primary underlying assumption of IRT is that nature uses committed relationship to achieve its own healing. This invites us, first, to stand in awe of the mystery we are witnessing in our work with couples. Granted, very often that mystery seems nothing other than demonic; yet if we were to pause long enough to grasp the depth of the mystery, our only possible response could be one of awe.

Second, I would urge you to view the couple with respect and reverence. Sometimes, to let off a little bit of steam, we may need to talk about the "couple from hell" we just saw, but we must never let such perceptions linger. Having made the comments we have made, we need to shift our focus toward the recovery of our respect for the couple and their relationship.

Third, I would encourage you to embrace the new insights that each couple can bring to you. Sitting with a couple with curiosity instead of dogma advances our theory and, even more, our own growth.

My final invitation is to shed yourself of any idea that you are the Director of Healing or even a healer for the couples you work with. Healing is a process that occurs within the couple relationship, and we merely assist in that process. We do not heal; the couple does. A way of testing our fidelity to this stance is to ask ourselves, at the end of a session, whether our helpful interventions involved giving an interpretation or assisting the couple in their own healing process.

All of this is much easier to talk about than it is to actualize. But I hope that you will eventually be able to experience the joy that comes from assisting nature in its work of healing itself through relationships.

This book is dedicated to the memory of several departed Imago relationship therapists whose theoretical and conceptual contributions continue, to this day, to influence Imago theory and practice. These individuals, who were respected within the Imago community for their seamless integrity as much as for their incisive intellect, include Randy Mason, Robert Elliott, Randy Gerson, Joan Lankin-Marantz, and Ted Smith. We also commemorate the many Imago relationship therapists who have passed on unknown to us but who, in perhaps equally remarkable ways, enriched the lives of many.

Acknowledgments

Imago Relationship Therapy rests on the foundation of Imago theory, and to do Imago therapy, you need to understand Imago theory. This book gives voice to those who best know Imago Relationship Therapy—leading Imago clinicians, thinkers, and writers.

Each chapter of this book was originally published in the *Journal of Imago Relationship Therapy*. The *Journal of Imago Relationship Therapy* was born out of the energy of two Imago relationship therapists, Rony Berger and Lisa Kelvin-Tuttle, who served as the journal's first editors. We thank this talented pair for the immense amounts of energy they dedicated to shaping a high-quality journal. Thanks also are due to Margaret Emery of International Universities Press and to her predecessor, George Zimmar, for ensuring the perfection of each issue. Gratitude is due to the Jossey-Bass staff, including Alan Rinzler, who embraced immediately, and enthusiastically, this book of essays on Imago theory, and to Seth Schwartz, who walked us through the intricate details of this project from beginning to end. The editors wish to express appreciation to Siena College student Lauren F. Stack for her generous editorial assistance. We also thank Siena College professor Joe Marrone for his numerous contributions to, and support of, the theory and spirit of Imago. Finally, appreciation is due Barney Karpfinger and Josseline Charas for their careful attention to the contract details.

Imago Relationship Therapy

A Theory of Relationality

Wade Luquet, Ph.D.

> *The man who first saw the exterior of the box from above*
> *later sees its interior from below.*
> THOMAS KUHN, *THE STRUCTURE*
> *OF SCIENTIFIC REVOLUTIONS*

It is almost certain that when, in 1962, science historian Thomas Kuhn wrote about paradigms and paradigm shifts, he had no idea how often his ideas would be misused. Many theorists, researchers, and visionaries claim that their ideas represent a paradigm shift, a new way of seeing things. In reality, most new ideas are no more a paradigm shift than the new car that is hailed as a paradigm shift when in fact, like all other cars, it consists of four tires, a metal frame, and a gas engine.

According to Kuhn (1962), those who create true paradigm shifts have two characteristics: "Their achievement was sufficiently unprecedented to attract an enduring group of adherents away from competing modes of scientific activity. Simultaneously, it was sufficiently open-ended to leave all sorts of problems for the redefined group of practitioners to resolve" (p. 10). What you are about to discover in this book is how adherents to an emerging paradigm—*the relational paradigm*—have attempted to apply this new paradigm to such unresolved problems.

Paradigm in Mental Health

Mental health professionals have made several paradigmatic shifts over the past 150 years. Prior to Sigmund Freud, mental illness was thought to result from spiritual deficiencies and thus was God's punishment for immorality. One hundred years ago, Freud's work emphasized the intrapsychic realm; with the help of a psychoanalyst, people could gain insight into the depths of the psyche and thereby master the unconscious forces that led to destructive behaviors. Next the pendulum swung toward behaviorism, which ignored the unconscious and instead focused on overt behavior change.

In the 1970s, as family therapy found adherents in the mental health community, a new paradigm emerged. This paradigm shifted the focus away from individuals toward systems. Practitioners and theorists began to examine how patterns of relationships within families caused individual dysfunction. Systems theorists proposed that families maintain an equilibrium by designating one family member as the "identified patient." The symptoms displayed by the identified patient are seen as stemming from the dysfunction within the family system. Systems theorists maintain that when the family system is restructured so that it functions in a healthier manner, the identified patient no longer needs to express symptoms. Thus such family therapists as Minuchin, Whitaker, Satir, Bowen, and Haley trained therapists to become manipulators and changers of systems.

The Relational Paradigm

Over the last several decades, the gap between what present-day couples need in order to save their relationships and what the individual paradigm is able to offer has steadily widened. As a result, theorists and therapists have started to develop a new paradigm for understanding couples dynamics and for designing clinical strategies. The relational paradigm, instead of focusing on either the individual or the system, focuses on the *relationship* as a unit of analysis.

The relational paradigm may seem foreign to those who are steeped in Western culture, in which rugged individualism has been the predominant value. Following the myth of the self-made person, we are taught to take care of ourselves, to put ourselves first; if we let go of our own needs, we lose our selves. The relational paradigm argues that quite the opposite occurs. In one of the most paradoxical statements ever uttered, the contemporary philosopher Pierre Teilhard de Chardin wrote, "Union differentiates" (Teilhard de Chardin, 1999/1955, p. 186).

The relational paradigm is based on the findings of quantum physics, cosmology, and contemporary philosophy. According to quantum physics, atomic particles operate in relationship with one another—emerging, disappearing, reappearing, and merging in relationship to other particles. "To tell the full story of a single particle we must tell the story of the universe, for each particle is in some way intimately present to every other particle in the universe" (Swimme & Berry, 1992, p. 29).

Likewise, because the microcosm is a reflection of the macrocosm, human beings operate in relationship. In an effort to explain this new way of thinking, Judith Jordan of the Stone Center for Women (1988) stated, "Moving from Aristotelian logic and Newtonian physics to quantum physics, we begin to see reality defined by relationships, continuities, and probabilities, rather than by discrete objects and dualities" (p. 1). In short, we find our true *selves* in relationship.

In her now classic book *In a Different Voice* (1982), Carol Gilligan proposed that women have a different developmental trajectory than men: women's development occurs within relationship, whereas men's development hinges more on their individuation from others. Gilligan's colleagues at the Stone Center for Women at Wellesley College expanded on her work to suggest that women develop through mutuality in their relationships and that they discover "self-in-relationship" (Jordan, Kaplan, Miller, Stiver, & Surrey, 1991). More recently, these authors suggested that men's development ought to incorporate the feminine emphasis on relationality and mutuality (Shem & Surrey, 1999). Jean Baker Miller (1993) described mutuality's effect on individual functioning: "Each person feels a sense of 'zest' (vitality, energy). Each person feels more able to act, and does act. Each person has a more accurate picture of himself/herself and the other person(s). Each person feels a greater sense of worth. Each person feels more connected to the other person(s) and feels a greater motivation for connection with other people beyond those in the specific relationship" (p. 30).

Mutuality and empathy have taken a back seat in much clinical work, however. Many therapists tell clients to take care of their own needs first; people should follow their own bliss, and everything else will follow. Clients are instructed to "find themselves" and to learn to "love themselves" so that they will be able to love another.

Martin Buber (1958) expounded against this theme in his seminal work *I and Thou,* in which he discussed how understanding the other is a way of understanding ourselves. He advised us to appreciate the "otherness of the other," which requires us to let go of our ego and step into another's shoes. When we do so, we move out of our usual I-It position and move into an *I-Thou* relationship. The I-Thou relationship is deeper, richer, more connected, and more spiritual. According to Buber, it is within the space "between I and Thou" that the spirit emerges (Buber, 1958, p. 39).

Cosmogenesis

In actuality, everything we see in the universe has been created through a union from which evolved differentiation. According to a principle known as *cosmogenesis,* or universe in process, everything in the universe is constantly evolving into something more complex. In cosmogenesis, elements are formed through a three-stage interactive process involving differentiation, subjectivity, and communion. In this process, everything becomes differentiated from everything else: "Evolution is in part a self-transcending process; it always goes beyond what went before. And in that novelty, in that emergence, in that creativity, new entities come into being, new patterns unfold, new holons issue forth" (Wilber, 1996, p. 24).

According to the new cosmology, in the beginning everything was one (Ferris, 1997; Filkin & Hawking, 1997). The universe consisted of tiny, searing-hot particles that did not distinguish themselves one from another. Then parts of the universe began to cool, creating an environment that allowed the particles to work together, first as nuclei of atoms, then as the hydrogen atoms that came to fill the universe. It was at this point that differentiation began: hydrogen particles differed from particles that preceded them. This is when subjectivity began: because hydrogen differed from both the particles that created it and those that followed it, hydrogen had its own *interiority*. Here, with the particles working together to form hydrogen, communion also occurred. Gravity then pulled the hydrogen atoms together and formed different elements, such as helium, lithium, and all the other elements that constitute the universe.

Thus each element was *differentiated* from all the other elements; each had its own interiority or *subjectivity*. Yet each of the elements also worked together, in *communion,* to form all that we see and all that we are: the communion of two distinct elements, hydrogen and oxygen, creates water, and twenty-eight elements work together to form the human body. "Everything in the universe is made by union and generation—by the coming together of elements that seek out one another, melt together two-by-two, and are born again in a third" (Teilhard de Chardin, cited in Lubac, 1971). Water and organic materials formed plant cells and one-celled creatures, which evolved into different plants, fish, reptiles, mammals, and, about two million years ago, into the early human being.

Cosmogenesis proceeded toward higher levels of complexity. Humans developed a larger brain that had the capacity for artistic achievement, logic, the use of tools, a sense of time, and eventually the development of culture, laws, rituals, and the appreciation of beauty. Humans entered into what Teilhard de Chardin called the *noosphere,* the thinking layer of the earth. The cosmogenic process of differentiation, subjectivity, and communion continues to operate as human beings develop into higher levels of consciousness.

Human relationships develop and operate according to the same cosmogenic process. We need the subjectivity that comes with our own individual personality and point of view. We need differentiation, an awareness of how we are different and distinct from others. We also need communion, which helps us understand and appreciate our oneness with others.

Imago Relationship Therapy

For those who subscribe to the relational paradigm, and Imago relationship therapists are among them, *relationship is the vehicle for growth.* Therefore, if the relationship is healthy, so too will be the individuals who are in that relationship. Long-term committed relationship is seen as another emanation of the cosmogenic process:

through dialogue, couples engage in communion and emerge into a higher level of *differentiation within connection.*

The primary goal of Imago Relationship Therapy (IRT; Hendrix, 1988; Luquet, 1996; Luquet & Hannah, 1998) is to help couples recapture and maintain safety and passion in their relationship. IRT's central process, the Couples Dialogue, is a three-step exercise that includes mirroring (reflecting) of the partner's message, validation (of the partner's point of view), and the expression of empathy toward the partner's feelings. Serving as a facilitator, the therapist guides the couple through the dialogue process, in which partners take turns sharing their own subjectivity regarding an issue, typically one that is painful or conflictual. The structure of the dialogue creates an umbrella of safety that encourages partners to reveal who they really are and what they truly feel. Such authentic sharing allows each partner to recognize and accept the subjectivity of the other— a critical component of differentiation. It is only when two people are sufficiently differentiated that true communion can occur between them: "The more intimately we become acquainted with anything, the clearer our recognition of its difference from everything else" (Swimme & Berry, 1992, p. 73). From the vantage point of IRT, then, intimate partnership becomes a place of discovery, growth, and change; marriage becomes, to coin a term, *marriagenesis,* marriage constantly giving birth to itself (Luquet, 2000).

IRT also contains a psychoeducational component in which couples are taught the principles of romantic partnership. For example, couples learn that each of us carries within our psyche an unconscious image of our early caretakers. This image, referred to as the imago, is the model that guides romantic attraction. We are drawn to a partner who matches this image, who is a facsimile of our early caretakers, so that we can re-create the childhood scenarios in which we were wounded and, in the context of adulthood romantic love, effect our healing. Healing occurs as we receive from our partner what our parents did not sufficiently provide to us as children. And as we give to our partner what he or she lacked during childhood, we receive the opportunity to mature, to grow characterologically, in the ways we most need to.

Thus, for IRT, committed partnership is intended to do no more, and no less, than bring about true healing and true growth.

About This Book

This book will not teach the nuts and bolts of conducting IRT. For those who are interested in learning about the processes of IRT, Harville Hendrix's books *Getting the Love You Want: A Guide for Couples* (1988) and *Keeping the Love You Find: A Guide for Singles* (1992) are recommended as basic texts. Wade Luquet's *Short-Term Couples Therapy: The Imago Model in Action* (1996) is a detailed, session-by-session manual on conducting short-term IRT. Applications of IRT to a variety of couple types can be found in Luquet and Hannah's *Healing in the Relational Paradigm: The Imago Relationship Therapy Casebook* (1998).

This book is the first to explicate the relationship between Imago theory and preceding schools of thought, such as psychoanalytic theory, family systems theories, affect theory, and self psychology. Each chapter was written by a clinician who, although viewing couples through the lens of the relational paradigm, is thoroughly schooled in related theoretical viewpoints and is able to articulate the similarities and differences between those perspectives and Imago theory.

The book is divided into three parts. The first consists of three chapters written by the founders of IRT, Harville Hendrix and Helen LeKelly Hunt. In the first chapter, Hendrix traces the history of IRT, beginning with his first inklings of the theory, which stemmed from his students' questions about romantic relationships, continuing through the early development of the theory and of the Couples Dialogue, and culminating in the growth of IRT into an international movement involving more than two thousand practitioners. In Chapter Two, LaKelly Hunt reveals how she and Hendrix mastered a difficult period in their marriage by using IRT skills and construing their own relationship as a living laboratory. In Chapter Three, Dr. Hunt explicates the psychospiritual underpinnings of Imago's concept of the conscious marriage.

As is true of any new paradigm, IRT attracted those who had originally adhered to other treatment models. In the second part are four chapters in which the authors discuss the overlaps and differences between Imago theory and other models. In Chapter Four, Randy Gerson, one of the early developers of the genogram in the family systems model, addresses the overlaps and distinctions between family systems theories and Imago theory.

In Chapter Five, Joseph Zielinski begins his exploration of the parallels among IRT, affect theory, and script theory by explaining the two primary modalities of affects, which are innate hard-wired emotional responses to situations, and scripts, or repeatable responses that typically follow the affect. According to Zielinski, IRT techniques can assist couples in replacing maladaptive scripts with new and more adaptive ones.

In Chapter Six, "Relationship Knowing: Imago and Object Relations," Stephen Plumlee describes two different types of knowing: separate and connected. Plumlee goes on to propose that connection and differentiation, which are the goals of both IRT and object relations therapy, occur as each partner learns about his or her self through the Imago process.

In Chapter Seven, "Contemporary Psychoanalytic Relational Theories and Imago: Concepts for Relational Healing," Mona Barbera compares Imago with contemporary psychoanalytic relational theories and finds compelling similarities between the two, especially in terms of the primacy of the relationship and its potential for healing. She reminds the reader that the transference that often takes months or years to develop in analytic work is immediately accessible when a couple engages in couples therapy.

The book's third part presents the ideas of prominent Imago thinkers whose writings expanded on Imago's original theoretical proposals. One author, the late Randall Mason, contributed three chapters to this part. In Chapter Eight, Mason borrows from the work of the Stone Center for Women and the writings of self psychology to address the importance of empathy in couples relationships. He reminds us that although empathy is the connective tissue of relationships, couples should be cautioned that too much of a good thing, even empathy, is not helpful. Chapter Nine is the late Ted Smith's response to Mason's chapter. Here, Smith explores the interactions between the self and the relationship, asking whether a relationship causes problems for the individuals who are in it, or vice versa, and recommending that we be flexible in how we conceive such cause-and-effect relationships.

In Chapter Ten, Mason addresses the meaning of connectivity in committed relationships. Following the principles of self psychology, Mason points out that self-expansion occurs through the person's connection to a self-object—most notably, to a partner in a committed relationship. According to Mason, differentiation requires not disconnection but connection.

Chapter Eleven is based on an Imago clinical training Mason gave in Philadelphia and was written posthumously through a collaboration between his wife, Margaret Mason, and Mo Therese Hannah. Here the authors provide a colorful description, complete with case examples, of Randy Mason's successful clinical approach to untangling a notorious clinical knot, which Mason called the *relationship nightmare*.

In Chapter Twelve, "Envy's Manifestation in Individuals and Couples: Implications for Imago Therapy," Bernard Baca contends that envy is the source of conflict in couples. One partner perceives the other partner as having what he or she lacks, and this perception is projected onto the other in the form of envy. Baca shows the various ways in which envy manifests in relationships and urges that it be identified and managed, lest it become destructive to the relationship.

Chapter Thirteen is Sophie Slade's inspiring commentary, "The Conscious Self in the Creational Paradigm." Slade calls on the reader to recognize that to be relational is to be creational: when we relate effectively with others, we help them create who they are, and likewise they help us create who we are.

As all theories are lies in search of the truth, Imago theory, too, is imperfect in both theory and practice; it is a still evolving school of thought. What you will read in this book is the work of only a few of the two thousand clinicians who are practicing IRT throughout the world. We are confident that Imago work will evolve into something truer and more complex, and thanks to our confidence in the evolving nature of all things, we look forward to the future with curiosity and hope.

References

Buber, M. (1958). *I and thou*. New York: Scribner.

Ferris, T. (1997). *The whole shebang*. New York: Simon & Schuster.

Filkin, D., & Hawking, S. (1997). *Stephen Hawking's universe*. New York: Basic Books.

Gilligan, C. (1982). *In a different voice*. Cambridge, MA: Harvard University Press.

Hendrix, H. (1988). *Getting the love you want: A guide for couples*. New York: Henry Holt.

Hendrix, H. (1992). *Keeping the love you find: A guide for singles*. New York: Pocket Books.

Jordan, J. V. (1988). Relationship development: Therapeutic implications of empathy and shame. *Work in Progress,* No. 39. Wellesley, MA: Stone Center Working Paper Series.

Jordan, J. V., Kaplan, A. G., Miller, J. B., Stiver, I. P., & Surrey, J. L. (Eds.). (1991). *Women's growth in connection: Writings from the Stone Center.* New York: Guilford Press.

Kuhn, T. S. (1962). *The structure of scientific revolutions*. Chicago: University of Chicago Press.

Lubac, H. (1971). *The eternal feminine: A study on the poem by Teilhard de Chardin, followed by Teilhard and the problems of today.* London: Collins.

Luquet, W. (1996). *Short-term couples therapy: The Imago model in action.* New York: Brunner/Mazel.

Luquet, W. (2000). *Marriagenesis: The evolution of marriage.* Unpublished dissertation, Union Institute, Cincinnati, Ohio.

Luquet, W., & Hannah, M. T. (Eds.). (1998). *Healing in the relational paradigm: The Imago Relationship Therapy casebook.* New York: Brunner/Mazel.

Miller, J. B. (1993). What do we mean by relationships? *Work in Progress,* No. 22. Wellesley, MA: Stone Center Working Paper Series.

Shem, S., & Surrey, J. L. (1999). *We have to talk: Healing dialogues between men and women.* New York: Basic Books.

Swimme, B., & Berry, T. (1992). *The universe story.* San Francisco: HarperSanFrancisco.

Teilhard de Chardin, P. (1999). *The human phenomenon: A new edition and translation of Le phenomene humain* (S. Appleton-Weber, Trans.). Brighton: Sussex Academic Press. (Original work published 1955)

Wilber, K. (1996). *A brief history of everything.* Boston: Shambhala.

Part One

Perspectives of the Founders

The Evolution of Imago Relationship Therapy

A Personal and Professional Journey

Harville Hendrix, Ph.D.

When does anything begin? Each of us is an energy pulse that began around ten billion years ago with the creation of the universe. Most of who we are—our DNA, genetic code, instinctual defenses, IQ—came into being before we were born. The rest is experience, and some, but not much, of that is remembered. And all of it contributes to the creation of our personal and collective history. And some of that is remembered. Here is what I remember.

Imago Relationship Therapy (IRT) is a synthesis of the genetic and personal history of myself and my wife Helen. The source of the impulse that gave it birth is our similar yet quite distinct childhoods: the death of my parents and the absence of Helen's father, motivators of our primal search for healing through reconnection. Our divorces are another source, the aftermath of which led us to reflect on what happened to our marriages, to inquire into the nature of committed partnerships, and to resolve to find a way not to repeat the past.

The Beginning of Imago Relationship Therapy

In a more formal sense, IRT began on the morning after I received my divorce papers. When I returned to teach a class on psychotherapy at Perkins School of Theology, Southern Methodist

University, a student questioned me regarding the difficulty men and women have relating to each other and the mystery of the male-female relationship. I admitted that I did not know the answer, but I committed to finding the answer to that question for personal and professional reasons, not knowing that such a resolve would lead to an altered career and a new lifestyle. All these factors constitute the roots of IRT.

In addition to these roots, IRT owes much of its form and content to the dynamics of Helen's and my relationship as a couple, including our years of courtship. Although the contribution each of us made is a function of our unique gifts, needs, resources, and personal history, IRT is in all respects, like any child, a cocreation. And paradoxically, the dynamics of our relationship are largely a product of the experiments we developed to improve them, which in turn gave birth to the Imago system.

Childhood Influences

Although Helen and I come from opposite ends of the social and economic spectrum and did not meet until we both were parents of two children and had divorced, the similarities in our childhood experiences formed a bridge for our personal and professional partnerships. When I was born, my father was dying, and my mother was situationally depressed. When I was six, my mother died, leaving me an orphan cared for by older siblings, who became my surrogate parents. Helen saw little of her father for her first seven years; thereafter, both of her parents were preoccupied with events outside the home, leaving her virtually an emotional orphan cared for by household staff, who became *her* surrogate parents. Our first relationship lesson was thus identical: "No matter what you do or don't do, you can't get the attention you need." I grew up feeling valueless and powerless; Helen, powerless and invisible. Hence our mutual interest in and difficulty with primary relationships was, if not primordial, at least primitive, and our search for stable partnerships somewhat obsessive!

The spiritual tone and missional qualities of the Imago system have their roots in our teenage involvement with religion, specifically the Baptist Church. I grew up in a small town and became active in a relatively small First Baptist Church; Helen grew up in a city and became involved in the world's largest First Baptist Church. In those religious communities, we unconsciously sought a supportive context in which to feel valuable and visible in a way that compensated for what was missing in our homes. Helen became active in the church choir and dreamed of becoming a missionary or a minister's wife. I became a preacher–boy evangelist and considered the mission field. Both of us had a vision of making a difference in the world. Helen's vision took shape as a community activist and philanthropist, committed to the visibility and empowerment of women, yet always invested in creating an intact home with family members closely bonded and reliable for each other. My vision took form, first as a minister, then as a pastoral psychotherapist and later as a professor of pastoral care and advocate of children, with an interest in personal healing and a deep commitment to a secure family. These activities have now become for us a shared vision of a society transformed by conscious marriages and conscious parenting, producing healthy, empathic children who will create a world whose essential texture is personal freedom and universal equality, empty of any emotionally underprivileged and disenfranchised persons.

An Early Hypothesis

My answer to the student at Perkins School of Theology who asked "Why do men and women have so much trouble being together?" began the construction of the theoretical system that became IRT. Responding immediately with "I haven't the slightest idea," I continued with some intuitive, though random, thoughts about a possible connection to unresolved childhood issues. Promising to think more about it, I came back to the class the following week and put forth this tentative hypothesis: "It appears that we tend to marry people who are similar to our parents, with whom we struggle over issues that were unfinished in childhood." This became a tenet of IRT. One of the students in that class invited me to elaborate on those remarks to a singles' group in his church. As there were several weeks before the lecture date, I spent a lot of time reading and thinking about the functions of projection, transference, and unconscious perception in the selection process. In that lecture, titled "Love or Illusion," I developed the thesis that romantic love was a response to the unconscious perception of the similarity between certain traits in the personalities of one's parents and the selected partner. Many people in the audience, although expressing discomfort with the idea, admitted that it made sense of their experience. It was much later that I discovered the parallel role of projection and the limited role of transference in the selection process.

Over the next several months I was invited to repeat the lecture in several contexts: churches, public conferences, and professional associations. The response that it "made sense" was so consistent that I began to feel I had stumbled on a key to the mystery of romantic love, which I soon began to understand as a "selection process." Invitations to repeat the lecture over the next several months encouraged my confidence in the thesis and spurred me on toward what was eventually to become the Imago system.

In 1977, two years after the classroom event, Helen and I met at a party and began a personal relationship. Our mutual interest and training in psychology, personal experience of divorce, and skeptical attitude toward remarriage sparked a conversation about relationships, which we continue to this day. In addition to our graduate psychology training, both of us had studied Transactional Analysis and Gestalt therapy with Bob and Mary Goulding, which provided us with a common perspective for conversation. To complete an internship for her degree, Helen chose to become a cotherapist in one of my groups, thus beginning our professional work together.

Needless to say, our relationship became very complex and conflicted, providing the perfect but unplanned laboratory in which we incubated ideas and invented behavioral processes, which we tried to practice with each other. The result of the many hours we spent talking about our childhoods, trying to figure out our mutual vulnerabilities, was the development of the concept of the wounded child, which, we theorized, had to be healed in relationship. For many months we debated the issue of whether this healing could occur in therapy or whether it could happen only in a committed partnership. We finally came to the conclusion that because the *wounding* occurred in relationship with one's parents, logic required that the *healing* could occur only in a context that reactivated the wounds. The idea was born, though not then named, that marriage, conducted with the aim of mutual healing, is the most effective form of therapy; thus evolved the phrase *marriage as therapy*.

The Evolution of IRT

One day, sometime during 1978, Helen made a suggestion that led to the development of two procedures that later became foundational in IRT. The first, which we called *mirroring,* is essentially the Rogerian reflective listening technique. In a heated argument in which both of us were talking and neither was listening, Helen stopped the argument and proposed that we take turns, one of us talking while the other listened. We agreed to the rule that one of us could talk only after reflecting what had been heard, but not before. Because both of us remembered a childhood in which we were not listened to, that process had such a significant effect on our relationship that I began to teach it to the couples in my practice. In my work with these couples, it soon became clear to me that no one seemed to have been listened to as a child, especially when they were upset or angry. Reciprocal listening had such a healing and bonding effect that couples experienced immediate improvement in their relationship.

Helen's second suggestion was about managing our anger, and that led to the development of the Container exercise. Both of us had been exposed to a rage-reduced process by our mutual therapist, John Whitaker, a psychiatrist who used Transactional Analysis and Gestalt methods in his practice. In one of his workshops he had demonstrated a process that he called "The Four R's: Rage, Rest, Rub, and Relaxation." Helen suggested we use this process to deal with our anger toward each other. Over time we modified it into the seven-step structure of the Container exercise, adding the Behavior Change Request process, which I had learned from Richard Stuart, a social learning theorist who wrote the excellent book *Helping Couples Change* (1980), and the Holding exercise, which was suggested by *Holding Time* (1989) by Martha G. Welch, M.D. We added the Belly Laugh component of the exercise after we learned about the ability of laughter to replace adrenaline with endorphins.

Helen also made a contribution to the theoretical explanation of the power of the Container exercise to de-energize projections. She had written a paper on Jung's theory of projection in which he developed the concept of "holding," rather than reacting to, the projections of others as a means of de-energizing these projections. We found that the regular use of the Container exercise helped us (and the couples with which we experimented) eventually withdraw and own our projections and distinguish partners from parents. The Container exercise became the "flagship" procedure for dealing with couples' anger and the centerpiece of the couples workshop.

Marriage and Childhood Connection

In the meantime, I continued to work with my therapist to figure myself out and get a grip on why I was divorced. I also started a systematic reading program on marriage literature, increased the number of couples in my part-time private practice, and started to study them. Up until that time, I had never been interested in marriage intellectually, and the literature on marriage did little to whet my appetite, but I was driven by confusion, curiosity, and pain.

In rereading the writings on love and marriage by Sigmund Freud, Carl Jung, Eric Berne, and Fritz Perls (my psychological mentors at the time, although their relationships were abysmal failures, as was the marriage of my theological mentor, Paul Tillich), I discovered that for the most part they all viewed marriage as a transferential experience of infantile expectations, directed toward one's spouse, which had to be resolved. Resolution from their point of view consisted of obtaining insight, differentiating one's spouse from one's parents, and surrendering one's childhood expectations. I understood from this that in order to mature, we must wean ourselves from the yearning of childhood, grieve the loss of unmet childhood needs, and get on with the business of adulthood. Then we could have a happy marriage. Yet my own experience in working with couples over the years led me to the conclusion that resolution by analysis and weaning was the opposite of what actually worked. Helen and I reframed the wish of partners for need satisfaction as an indicator of what they truly needed, and their reenactment of the childhood scene in the relationship as an attempt to heal the childhood trauma, not a repetition compulsion of the familiar. Therapeutically, we helped partners honor and empathize with each other's childhood wounds, give full expression to their anger and sadness in the Container, and stretch to meet one another's needs. This program seemed to restart their arrested childhood development and help them achieve emotional adulthood. Now they could have a happy marriage.

Revelations as Both a Client and a Therapist

My own therapy, at that time, focused on understanding my childhood by mentally reconstructing my relationship with my parents, regressing to recover the early script decisions, working through all my feelings, and making new decisions based on adult reality. I would like to credit my therapist, John Whitaker, for contributing another healing component to the Imago process. Using Gestalt methods, he sought to help me heal my childhood wounds by assisting me to imaginatively recreate my parents into ideal images from whom I received what I did not receive in actuality. He also assigned me to group therapy where I could augment this healing process with surrogate help from other group members, and simultaneously figure out my unconscious attitudes toward women and marriage in general. Although I did not experience healing or characterological growth in therapy, I did eventually become aware of the way I had lived unconsciously in my previous marriage. In retrospect, my experiences in this marriage matched the dynamics of my childhood—yearning for attention but not taking initiative out of fear of my ex-wife's emotional unavailability. That inaction, I now speculate (given my knowledge of my ex-wife's childhood), probably triggered her fear of abandonment, which she acted out by emotionally withdrawing from the relationship. The emotional void between us restimulated our mutual abandonment fears, which we eventually legalized through divorce.

During this time in my clinical practice, I started listening to couples phenomenologically—that is, suspending my theoretical assumptions. I had learned of this approach from Maurice Merleau-Ponty, a student of Husserl, to whom I had been introduced by Eugene Gendlin, a philosopher of phenomenology who had been a student of Carl Rogers. Merleau-Ponty (1973) took issue with his German Idealist mentor, who believed in the possibility of a "pre perception" by arguing that the best we can do is "bracket" our beliefs, not suspend them, in the process of perception. While listening in a sort of reverie of suspended thinking as couples described their frustrations with each other, I began to have images of them as children crying about unmet needs, complaining about their partners as they had complained about their parents. Even though I had attempted to suspend my assumptions, the transferential theory seemed validated by my observations. No longer was it necessary to develop the transference with me, the therapist; the transferential links between partners became the rich field for exploration.

My first interventions were to interpret this awareness, provoke insight into the couples' parental transferences, attempt to wean them from their infantile expectations of each other, and help them reparent themselves imaginatively by using Gestalt exercises. I also put partners into separate groups for experiential reparenting by the group members—just as my therapist had done for me—all to no avail. Most couples terminated joint therapy in about five sessions, but many of them continued their work in separate groups.

Understanding the Needs of Marriage

During this time, Helen was completing her internship as my co-therapist in the groups. We shifted our procedure and began to ask partners what they needed from each other that, were they to receive it, would create their dream marriage and end their frustration. The answers were unequivocal: they all wanted their partner to change while they remained the same. And what they wanted from each other reminded me of the needs of children: someone who could be counted on, who would be available when he or she was needed, and who had no needs of his or her own. Their complaints about their spouses were similar to, and in most cases the same as, complaints they had about their parents; it soon became clear that each partner wanted his or her spouse to act as an ideal parent, not like the ones they had in childhood.

I began helping couples negotiate around those needs. From Stuart's *Helping Couples Change* (1980), I understood that change occurs more rapidly when partners ask for specific, measurable behaviors from each other and respond with positive reinforcement. When I began experimenting with these procedures, I encountered the problem of helping couples understand the importance of changing their own behaviors and creating positive experiences for each other that addressed one another's childhood issues. In sheer frustration, I decided to invite all the couples in my practice to spend a weekend with me. This was the inauguration of my first couples workshop. Twelve couples accepted the invitation. I took them to a Methodist camp, which had simple rooms and plain food and was located in a wooded setting. For two days I lectured to them about how their childhood needs were influencing their relationship, exhorted them that they must learn to meet those needs in specific ways, and experimented with ways for them to create positive experiences for each other. The only experimental exercise I used in that workshop was mirroring. When they returned to their private sessions, all the couples were more motivated to work, and ten of them began to make progress. Of the remaining two, one left therapy and the other decided to divorce.

IRT Practice Grows

In 1979, Helen moved to New York, while I remained in Dallas. We both thought our relationship was over, as neither of us wanted a long-distance relationship, but we kept in contact long distance and occasionally visited one another. Our conversations continued, and our relationship seemed to endure the separation. I developed the workshop for couples, using some of the behavioral procedures I had learned from Stuart, the mirroring exercise, the Container, and some guided imagery based on some work I had done in graduate school on the use of the imagination. Some therapist couples began to attend the workshops and became interested in what I was doing. One therapist, Gay Jurgens, now a workshop presenter, insisted that I teach her what I was learning. She, along with Robert Elliott, my senior faculty partner at Perkins, offered to pull together a group of therapists for what became the first training seminar. Although I did not know where I was headed with this work, this format gave me a context within which to begin articulating my insights and to receive feedback from interested and competent professionals. This serendipitous event led eventually to a formal training program, although the content and structure changed with each new insight. Pat Love joined the second training program and began teaching the theory in the Graduate Department of Marriage and the Family at East

Texas State University, thus giving the system an academic foundation. The couples workshops, which soon became a monthly event with around fifteen couples, offered me another context in which to explore my theories.

Around this time several people began encouraging me to write a book. Initially I resisted because I felt I did not yet understand my subject and had limited time and increasing activity. Later, with Helen's encouragement, I undertook the project and secured the services of a writer to help organize the structure of the book and translate my opaque, academic language into recognizable prose. IRT as a system, however, was *in utero* and not ready to be born until ten years later.

In 1982 Helen and I married, and I moved in with her in New York. With her financial generosity and emotional support, I took a semisabbatical (returning to Dallas twice a month to see my clients) to complete the book. In 1984 we decided to turn the Dallas practice into the Center for Relationship Therapy, staffing it with trained Imago therapists and developing it as a model for the creation of other centers across the country. That same year, we created the Institute for Imago Relationship Therapy in New York, where Imago therapists Robert and Joan Thorne introduced me to the New York professional community and helped me establish a training program and clinical practice.

With these organizational structures in place, I traveled to Dallas monthly to meet with the board and supervise the staff of the Center, conduct a workshop and a training program, and do publicity and public relations. The nonprofit Center soon attracted the attention of the community, and with Helen's help secured an excellent board of directors and received a $50,000 grant by the Meadows Foundation. During this time, Helen was involved in establishing the Dallas Women's Foundation, actively supporting the Center and the Institute, and covering all family duties while I was away. And we continued to engage in conversations (we had not yet discovered "dialogue") about Imago theory and practice, actively using our relationship (out of necessity) as a practicum. In 1986, after staff resignation jeopardized its financial status, and sacrificial efforts to maintain the Dallas Center exhausted available funds and energy, we made the decision to close it and transfer the name and remaining equipment to my dear friend Robert Elliott, who operated it as the umbrella of his practice.

Getting the Love You Want

Meanwhile, I continued to work on the book, which did not yet have a working title, literary agent, or publisher. My secretary at the time had a contact at Holt Publishers, whom she told about the book and gave a two-hour audiotape of a lecture I had given at the annual meeting of the Southeastern Transactional Analysis Association. Some Holt editors who had listened to the tape invited me to meet with their editorial board; the result was that Holt bought the book on the basis of the tape and the interview. I then secured the services of an agent, Julian Bach, to complete the contract. Jo Robinson, a freelance writer from Oregon, signed on to assist me, and she and I put together a proposal, which was accepted. The book now had everything it needed except a title. After we had completed the book in 1988, we decided to assign the term *conscious marriage* to the type of relationship that could be created by couples who used the process. The first title of the book was *The Conscious Marriage: Journey to Wholeness*. After completing all the edits, Helen and I took a trip to Indonesia. While we were in Bali, the publisher called with a request to change the title, as they had done market research and discovered the title would make it a poor seller. In desperation I said, "Well, call it *Getting the Love You Want*," but did not mean it. They thought it was a good idea, did market research on that title, and found it to be a potential bestseller. Jo Robinson suggested we add *A Guide for Couples* as a subtitle. The book now had a title and went to press.

Holt's publicity department sent the book to *The Oprah Winfrey Show*. According to Debbie DeMaio, the show's executive producer, Debbie put it on a stack of other books on relationships without having any intention of reading it. After her fiancé read it and suggested they use it to improve their relationship, she read it and invited me to be a guest on the show. The response to that show prompted Oprah to contact me later and suggest we film the workshop and air excerpts on the show. The 1989 airing of that two-hour series, which won Oprah an Emmy for its "socially redeeming value," put *Getting the Love You Want* on the *New York Times* best-seller list. In 1992, *Keeping the Love You Find: A Personal Guide* (originally *A Guide for Singles*) was published by Simon and Schuster, Pocket Books division, and became a *New York Times* best-seller also. Later that year, the certified workshop presenters and I launched *Keeping the Love You Find: A*

Workshop for Singles. In 1994, Helen and I jointly authored *The Couples Companion: Meditations and Exercises for Getting the Love You Want.* By that year couples workshop attendance reached 100 to 150 couples, and singles workshop attendance reached 100 attendees. In the meantime, the number of certified Imago therapists, who in 1990 had formed the Association for Imago Relationship Therapy, reached close to eight hundred in number. Eighty-plus workshop presenters were presenting an average of four hundred workshops annually, including some international workshops; eighteen clinical instructors were annually training two hundred therapists nationally and internationally. A seven-hour home-study version of the workshop was broadcast over more than two hundred public television stations, resulting in the growth of the Institute's database to about sixty-five thousand names. A revised version of this series was broadcast over the VISN cable network. By 1993, the staff of the Institute had grown to nine full-time persons.

IRT's Continued Evolution

The theory and practice of IRT continued to evolve and mutate. Mirroring evolved from a one-level exercise to the three-stage Couples Dialogue/Intentional Dialogue process comprising mirroring, validation, and empathy. Theory developments included a metatheoretical proposition of human essence as essentially pulsating energy, influenced by quantum theory and the psychological work of Core Energetics, developed by John Pierrakos (1987). I also developed a systematic, detailed description of the stages of human development by synthesizing the theories of Margaret Mahler (1975), Daniel Stern (1985), Harry Stack Sullivan (1953), and Erik Erikson (1963). This led to the development of the new characterological profiles, a clarification of the meaning and function of symbiosis, and the recognition that IRT concepts and processes reflect an emerging paradigm shift from an ontology of separation to an ontology of connection.

The New Paradigm

Because I have not discussed the new paradigm in previous writings, I will briefly elaborate on its meaning and significance here.

Ontology of Separation

In an ontology of separation, reality is composed of discrete, essentially self-contained entities, composed of a density called matter, which interact with each other along a continuum of positive and negative valance but which have no intrinsic connection. This view is reflected in the Newtonian and atomistic view of reality, which posits objects as closed although interactive, views space and time as absolutes, and posits an absolute point of reference. In this ontology, the relationship between these entities is secondary to their delineation and to the preservation of their welfare and boundaries. In the human species, this is reflected in the primacy given to the individual and the secondary valuation of context and relationship. The central valuation of the individual makes autonomy the goal of development, and independence and self-sufficiency the indicators of maturity. In the healing professions, this view is reflected in the status of psychotherapy as the reigning model of treatment, and in conflict-free intrapsychic functioning as the goal of therapy. Connection and relationship are seen as problems to be solved, but they can be solved only after successful resolution of intrapsychic functioning and clear, firm delineation of self boundaries.

Ontology of Connection

In an ontology of connection, reality is viewed essentially as a tapestry in which everything is intrinsically connected. There are no entities as such except as distinguishable points, or nodes, in the tapestry of being, and these nodes, which appear as matter, are essentially energy present in various and distinct densities. Because the energetic nodes are essentially made up of other nodes, relationship is their primary reality. The tapestry of being thus comprises the connectional, energetic points and their interaction, both of which have equal ontological status. Entities exist in a context that influences their structure and function, and they in turn influence the dynamics and valences of the context. Each in some sense cocreates the other. This view of reality is expressed in physics by relativity theory and quantum mechanics, and in psychology by Core Energetics, developed by John Pierakos, with whom I have done considerable personal and intellectual work. The energetic, relational theory views entities as open, essentially connected, and mutually influencing each other; views time and space as a continuum; posits no absolute point of reference; and views all things as in motion. In this view, connection, relationship, and constantly changing interaction are ontological; the perception or experience of separation and inaction have no ontological support and are therefore illusory. What this suggests is a vision of the universe as truly a uni-verse, a dynamic, constantly changing cosmic oneness, a unitary organism, essentially alive and thus conscious, with no independent parts. This cosmic oneness is expressed in every perceived part, in galaxies, solar systems, and planets. The earth as an ecosystem is a living, conscious organism in which all animate and inanimate parts are conscious, interdependent, essentially connected, and dependent on the whole.

For the human species, an ontology of connection means that a human being is essentially a unitary, vitally alive, conscious organism with no mind-body split. In addition, all human beings are connected, interdependent, and mutually influential and cannot become immune to contextual influence. For therapy, this means that the focus is placed on the interactive "in-between" of Martin Buber and also on the internal world of individuals, both of which constitute the context. IRT, dependent on and expressing this worldview, is therefore a "relationship" therapy that views marriage partners as conscious, energetic interactors with constantly fluctuating boundaries, constituting an interdependent whole, which is itself an instance of the cosmic process. The quality of the marriage is a function of the couple's actual interactive relationship, which includes the projections of the intrapsychic subjectivity of the two individuals, and is dependent on their congruence with the cosmic process. Developmental processes are contextually determined, character structure is fluid and context-dependent, and effective exchanges are responses to contextual stimulation. Partners are unable *not* to influence each other; there is no such thing as a static state, self-sufficiency, or independence. The goal of therapy is to become self-reflectively conscious, consciously intentional, differentiated, and accepting of one's dependency. At the same time, one strives to become aware of oneself as both a cocreator and a creature of context. This is the basis for the position that because wounding occurs in relationship, healing and growth can occur only in the context of a relationship.

Developing Dialogue and a Theory of Symbiosis

Given this view of reality, dialogue becomes the intervention of choice. Dialogue was explained in *Keeping the Love You Find,* but the process of its development was not described, so I will do so here, as well as present an outline of my theory of symbiosis, which has evolved since the publication of that book.

Beyond Mirroring and Validation

In 1988, when *Getting the Love You Want* was published, the therapeutic focus of IRT was on facilitating couples through a series of five exercises: reimaging the partner, restructuring frustrations, resolving rage, reromanticizing, and revisioning the relationship. The only therapeutic tool was mirroring. Helen suggested that I reread Buber's *I and Thou* (1958), which she saw as an example of the relational paradigm and thus a resource for helping to reframe IRT and a potential resource for understanding how to help couples create an I-Thou relationship.

After revisiting Buber's thought, I became aware of the need to go beyond teaching communication exercises as a therapeutic tool. Mirroring clarified the message of the other, but it often led to further polarization. Stretching to meet one's partner's needs offered an opportunity to grow, but it was often a purely cognitive decision motivated by the hope for change in one's partner, and it lacked an emotional component. What seemed needed, in addition, was an altered perception, attitude, and affect toward one's partner. To achieve that degree of change would require a deeper level of contact. Buber clarified for me that a "Thou" relationship with others required honoring their "otherness" as an "I" distinct from me and any concepts I might have of them. This required a willingness to look at the world of another through his or her eyes.

In addition, the constructivist's view that there is no such thing as pure perception and that every percept is a construct, and the relativist's view that all aspects of reality are intrinsically related and that there is no absolute position, contributed to clarifying that there is no position from which one could possibly perceive an "objective" world, free from interpretation. Thus all perceptions are relative to the perceiver. From these sources I finally put together the concept of validation as the necessary second step in the dialogical process. Validation requires one to look through the eyes of the other, to see the other's world as it appears to him or her, and to understand the logic of the other's point of view. Furthermore, it requires suspending judgment about the sensibility of the other's world and the accuracy of his or her logic, and accepting that the other's perception of the world is as valid as one's own.

Mirroring and validation made the world of the other accessible as information and demonstrated the logic in each partner's perspective, thus creating equality, but the process still lacked affect and compassion. To address this I recalled my earlier years of empathy training based on Carl Rogers's work (1961) and that of his students Truax and Carkhuff (1967), as well as other students of empathy, such as Heinz Kohut (1977, 1978) and Martin Hoffman (1990). The concepts of cognitive and participatory empathy helped the third step in the three-part process fall into place.

The Beginning of Dialogue in Therapy

I felt it would be impossible in the early stages of therapy to expect aggrieved partners to empathically "participate" in the affective world of the other, but it might be possible to help them "imagine" the emotions of their partner and achieve cognitive empathy. I put these three steps together as the structure and progression of the dialogue process and began to experiment with couples, with much success. In the meantime, Imago therapist and clinical instructor Maya Kollman was experimenting with arousing empathy in the Behavior Change Request process by having couples add the phrase, "and that reminds me of . . ." (referring to childhood wounds) after expressing the pain created by a particular relationship frustration and before making three specific requests for behavioral change from the partner. This addition of eliciting the childhood wound behind the frustration before making the Behavior Change Request aroused empathy in the receiving partner and transformed this stretching process into a powerful motivation for action. Mirroring, validation, and empathy were now integrated into all "exercises." That is, although each exercise, from Holding to the Container, is a discrete procedure, they are all modifications of dialogue.

The outcome of these experimentations was my awareness that the process of dialogue itself produced a change in perception, attitude, and affect as well as increased connection and bonding. This insight required a reconceptualization of training and therapy. The focus of the therapeutic process was changed from that of making a commitment, learning a skill (dialogue), and engaging in five procedures (reimaging, restructuring, resolving, reromanticizing, and revisioning) to "dialogue as process," which incorporated the five procedures. I elevated dialogue to a central place in IRT and sought to eliminate any nondialogical transactions in the therapy sessions.

While experimenting with this focus and trying to make the process as pure as possible, I observed an interesting phenomenon. No matter what couples talked about or what exercises were used, if they did not become "dialogical," nothing changed in the relationship. If they achieved dialogue—that is, made contact through mirroring, saw the logic of the other's point of view through validation, and achieved some level of empathy—they began to lose interest in their "problems," became empathic with each other, and expressed compassion rather than frustration. I concluded that the content of the dialogue was irrelevant to the outcome of the process. To check this out, I decided to do an experiment by giving several couples a neutral subject, one that did not arise out of their relationship, such as the weather or pets, and facilitated their dialogue about it until they reached a level of empathic contact. For instance, I asked a couple to discuss cats in the dialogue format. I observed that the process of engaging in dialogue about a neutral subject altered their relationship so much that most of the energy bound in the problem they brought to therapy began to dissipate like air escaping from a balloon. I concluded from this that the safety of the dialogue process allowed the defenses to relax. This experience of safety and the consequent improvement of the relationship appeared to be the couple's the unconscious goal, which, once achieved, made their problems no longer relevant.

Dialogue and Paradoxical Problems

From these observations, I deduced that problems in relationship stem from the partners' fears of disconnection—their fear of losing contact with one another, with original aspects of themselves, and thus with their own original wholeness. They are also, paradoxically, an unconscious attempt by partners to reestablish contact without losing their identity, and to recover a sense of wholeness. The following scenario is an illustration of this dynamic:

> George complains about Mary's criticism of his use of time, his overworking, and his emotional and physical unavailability on weekends. Mary wants more emotional and physical contact time. She agrees with George's perception of her frustrations and adds that the more she complains, the less cooperative he becomes.

> Their conscious impasse is over time and space. George's complaint and his increased distance as a response to her criticism reflect his intuition of her wish for fusion. If he did not keep his distance, he would be absorbed and thus lose himself by trying to be what she wants him to be. In his unconscious, the loss of himself to her physically would mean not only psychic death but physical death, for the unconscious does not distinguish between the two. In addition, to not be himself would mean that he would risk losing his connection with her. And because her desire for closeness reflects his denied need for closeness, he, through losing contact with her, also loses contact with the projection through which he maintains contact with his wholeness. George's experience of this global loss of control over his time and space, and the resulting "deaths," is a fear that he would disappear from the universe.

> For her part, Mary experiences her partner's distance as a loss of contact and connection, which threatens her physical and psychic safety by arousing her fears of abandonment. Unconsciously, such abandonment means her physical death and the loss of cosmic connection. Her complaints, however, function to maintain distance in order to block her fears of fusion and loss of her psychic self. They also serve to maintain contact with George, which she intuits is essential for her survival, and to maintain contact with her Denied Self projected on him—that is, her unconscious and prohibited need for distance.

Essentially, problems such as these appear to be maintained by partners' attempts (fueled by their reciprocal needs and fears) to differentiate from their spouse without allowing the spouse to differentiate in turn. Paradoxically, this means that what appears to be dysfunctional behavior at the conscious, interpersonal level in committed partnerships is actually, at the unconscious level, functional; it serves the survival directive, which is to remain connected to context. Projection is therefore a form of connection to the other and the self, and the denial of perceived negative self-traits are an attempt to remain connected to the disapproving other. Interpersonal problems, especially impasse issues, are therefore a defense against disconnection and its consequences. If safety can be established and connection restored, then the problems that served the survival directive are no longer necessary.

Therapist as Coach

Having drawn these conclusions, I felt that the therapeutic process and the role of the therapist had to change drastically. Diagnosis, analysis, history taking, and all forms of therapists' authority and expertise seemed irrelevant if couples, caught in the power struggle, were trying unconsciously to restore connection and recover wholeness without losing themselves through fusion with one another. Instead of needing from the therapist such "expert" functions as interpretation and confrontation, couples needed to be helped to cooperate with what their unconscious was trying (but failing) to do through interpersonal conflict. For me, this meant that the role of the therapist was analogous to a coach, a facilitator of the dialogue process. The task of the therapist should be to manage the interaction between partners so that no nondialogical transactions could occur in the session. This would make dialogue a safe structure that allowed for the relaxation of defenses and the restoration of contact. Achieving contact and freedom from the fear of losing oneself through fusion would allow for the true discovery of the other and, through that, the discovery of the self. If it were successful, the dialogical process would allow partners to restore contact, achieve self-differentiation, and become "interior" to and empathic with their partner's subjectivity. Were this to happen, it would make sense that "problems" would disappear, for the intentions of the unconscious would have been served.

The most exciting and unexpected consequence of the dialogical process that I have observed is that the creation of safety, the achievement of differentiation, and the restoration of contact and connection appear to restart the psychological development for both partners that was interrupted in childhood. The defenses that were activated in response to childhood wounding and that had been energized by the core self were able to relax, thus returning the core energy to the original functions of the self.

A Theory of Symbiosis

Experiencing these therapeutic outcomes led me to explore the role of symbiosis in conflict between partners. When our daughter Leah was born, Helen and I witnessed a phenomenon that made us question the extant theory of symbiotic fusion with the mother as the natural condition of the infant at birth. We experienced Leah as attached and relational, even protoempathic within minutes of her birth. Her immediate connection to us prompted us to propose a revision of symbiosis theory. We postulated that symbiosis is a condition created by the trauma of the birth process itself, not a condition of nature, as traditionally viewed. The birth trauma is elicited by the difficulty of birth, the attitude of the parents, and often by the mother and child's being drugged by medication. Leah was born in a warm room within three hours of the first contraction; her umbilical cord was cut by me; she was not spanked; she was placed immediately in my arms and then on Helen's chest for a full hour. In addition, Helen had received no painkilling medication. Thus Leah's birth was devoid of the usual traumatic trappings. As Leah grew, she exhibited great interest in and sensitivity to other persons' experience, a high degree of empathic connection to her surroundings—people, animals, and plants—and a chronic exhibition of intense and joyful aliveness. Just recently, at age eleven, she reported walking down the hallway at her school and spontaneously breaking into a dance. At first, she felt some self-consciousness and interrupted her dance. Then she thought, "I have no one to impress," and returned to her dance, with others joining her.

When I reviewed the research on child development over the course of ten years, I observed that developmental researchers have discovered behavior in newborns that appears empathic, which they call "protoempathy," and empathic responses to others around the eighth month that matched our experience of Leah. Not only have protoempathic responses been observed at birth, but true empathic responses have been observed at three months, and clearly empathic responses at eight months. This suggested a need for revising Margaret Mahler's view (1975) of attachment as being the first developmental task, to the view that the first developmental impulse is the maintenance of attachment.

My next question was, "If empathy, rather than symbiosis, is the natural condition at birth, how is empathy lost and symbiosis acquired?" The answer lay in the meaning of symbiosis. I began to define symbiosis as the unconscious fusion of objects with the self, meaning that others and things in the external world are constructed in such a manner as to serve the survival needs of the self. These survival needs are intensified because of physical and emotional wounding along the developmental continuum, which results in a level of self-absorption in which one's perception of the external world is altered and reconstructed in the service of the self. The self, responding to the pain and threat of wounding, needs the outside world to be a certain way in order for the self to maintain a sense of security. When security is threatened by the actuality of the other, the self goes into an alarm state. This is the source of all frustration.

In response to the threat of the loss of need gratification and ultimately survival, the self acts to restore the homeostasis by symbiotic construction that attempts to quiet the survival directive— in childhood by a cry, and in adulthood by criticism, both aimed at a fusion of the symbiotic image with the objective other. For instance, the cry is an attempt to force the objective other (mother) into behaviors that match the symbiotic image of the "mother who brings me food," thus quieting the survival alarm turned on by hunger. In adult criticism, the infliction of verbal and emotional pain on the objective other (spouse) is an attempt to encourage or force one's spouse to surrender his or her self existence and conform to one's symbiotic image of the spouse as "one who meets my needs" (for example, the need for one's spouse to be on time so one can avoid experiencing the childhood abandonment fears triggered by his or her lateness). The failure to achieve this homeostasis creates panic.

I postulated that symbiosis was the single source of the power struggle. With this perspective, I saw the function of dialogue as a safe process of discovering the spouse as the objective other seemed the only essential therapeutic process. The desired therapeutic outcome appeared to be a reciprocal dialogical exchange that enabled partners to release each other from their symbiotic prisons, communicate their own needs, and stretch to meet one another's needs. I had already clarified that stretching to meet the spouse's need produced characterological change that activated psychological growth toward a short-circuited adulthood. Now I conclude that the dialogical process is the means not only of deep communication but also of growth essential to achieving healing and wholeness. Such reciprocity between two differentiated and separate, yet ontologically connected, persons is the beginning of true love.

References

Berne, E. (1985). *Games people play.* New York: Ballantine.

Buber, M. (1958). *I and thou.* New York: Scribner.

Erikson, E. H. (1963). Eight stages of man. In *Childhood and society* (pp. 247–284). New York: Norton.

Hendrix, H. (1988). *Getting the love you want: A guide for couples.* New York: Henry Holt.

Hendrix, H. (1992). *Keeping the love you find: A guide for singles.* New York: Pocket Books.

Hendrix, H., & Hunt, H. (1994). *The couples companion: Meditations and exercises for getting the love you want.* New York: Pocket Books.

Hoffman, M. (1990). The contribution of empathy to justice and moral judgment. In N. Eisenberg & J. Strayer (Eds.), *Empathy and its development.* New York: Cambridge University Press.

Kohut, H. (1977). *The restoration of the self.* New York: International Universities Press.

Kohut, H. (1978). *The search for the self: Selected writings of Heinz Kohut: 1950–1978* (Vols. 1–2; P. H. Ornstein, Ed.). New York: International Universities Press.

Mahler, M. (1975). *The psychological birth of the human infant.* New York: Basic Books.

Merleau-Ponty, M. (1973). *Adventures of the dialectic: Studies in phenomenology and existential philosophy.* Evanston, IL: Northwestern University Press.

Perls, F. S. (1969). Projection. In *Ego, hunger and aggression: The beginning of Gestalt therapy.* New York: Random House.

Perls, F. S. (1970). The rules and games of Gestalt therapy. In J. Fagan & I. L. Shephard (Eds.), *Gestalt Therapy now: Theory, techniques, applications* (pp. 140–149). Palo Alto, CA: Science and Behavior Books.

Pierrakos, J. C. (1987). *Core energetics: Developing the capacity to love and heal.* Mendocino, CA: Life Rhythm Publications.

Rogers, C. (1961). *On becoming a person.* Boston: Houghton Mifflin.

Stern, D. (1985). *The interpersonal world of the infant.* New York: Basic Books.

Stuart, R. B. (1980). *Helping couples change: A social learning approach to marital therapy.* New York: Guilford Press.

Sullivan, H. S. (1953). *The interpersonal theory of psychiatry.* New York: Norton.

Truax, C. B., & Carkhuff, R. R. (1967). *Toward effective counseling and psychotherapy: Training and practice.* Chicago, IL: Aldine-Atherton.

Welch, M. G. (1989). *Holding time.* New York: S & S Trade.

Chapter Two

Relationship as a Living Laboratory

Helen LaKelly Hunt, Ph.D.

Two years ago, Harville and I stood before the Imago community and told them that we were not living the Imago process. Our marriage was in jeopardy because we were not living in private what we were preaching in public.

This was a surprise to others and to us. Harville and I had started our journey together with a common value: relationship. On our first date twenty-three years ago, we mused about the significance of love as we eagerly dissected Buber's concept of the in-between. We both were intrigued by the unarticulated power of committed partnership. Soon, with our four children and extended families, we found ourselves living the complexity of relationship firsthand. We both believed fervently in the healing power of relationship, and we looked forward to experiencing it in our lives. But we failed to actualize it in our daily living.

Slowly I began to realize that my hopes for a marriage and family with safety and connection were not materializing. I had lived for many years feeling that we were just about to turn the corner and get there. As my denial began to crumble, I realized that I was living an existence vastly different from my image of it. Although I knew intimately every aspect of Imago theory and was married to the man who was key in generating it, we had not integrated the theory into our lives. I began to feel as though we were living a split existence.

At times, in my relationship with Harville, we dialogued endlessly without either of us taking in what the other was saying. We were both so full of ourselves that we lacked negative capability, so we pushed our own thinking on one another. Because we both came from difficult backgrounds, neither of us had much capacity for self-empathy.

I needed to unravel the mystery of what had happened and to uncover the meaning and purpose of it all. So I began to think of myself as a *living laboratory*. How did our lives become so divided? How was it that we had answers for problems in other people's marriages, but when it came to our own, we were clueless? What did this say about me? I entered this personal laboratory and tried to look at myself more carefully. I began to study each transaction we had. I knew that if I could understand what was happening to *us*, others might benefit from our self-observation and our conclusions.

Harville and I became students. We entered into dialogue with the Imago community and became transformed in the process. We moved from saying what we were supposed to say to what we needed to say. We left behind the stock characters and the stereotypes and reached deeper into our humanness. Hoping to discover some new tonic, I explored formulas using data derived from epistemology, feminist psychology, and Imago theory. My new serum began to bubble up, causing some interesting chain reactions. What I am about to describe is a chemistry of personal narrative, psychology, and epistemology that I hope will have meaning to others.

Six Theorems from the Living Laboratory

My lab work led me to the six theorems that I discuss in this chapter. I believe that these theorems apply directly both to my own marriage and to the Imago community, which is continuing to evolve a fresh and true description of relationship theory and practice. The six theorems are as follows:

1. The epistemological distinction between separate and connected knowing is important for relational theory.
2. Extreme separate knowing can lead to dissociation.
3. Dissociation is healed by association.
4. Association with self and others results in wholeness and thus integrity.

5. Association is fundamental in the shift from the individual to the relational paradigm.
6. Truth telling can be a potent catalyst in the relational paradigm.

The Epistemological Distinction Between Separate and Connected Knowing Is Important for Relational Theory

As indicated by theorist Sandra Harding, who referred to an "epistemological crisis of the West," the field of epistemology is in flux. As our culture grapples with postmodern concepts, we are struggling to understand how knowledge is gained.

A Harvard study on men's development (Perry, 1970) led to the concern that women's perspectives were missing from theories of psychological and ethical development. The book *Women's Ways of Knowing* (Belenky, Clinchy, Goldberger, & Tarule, 1986) was intended to describe not only the different ways that women know but also how women in the United States are socialized to know (Goldberger, 1996, p. 8). Belenky et al.'s conceptualization of the different ways that people know reflected what many theorists had already concluded: that the mind-body dualism of psychology, which artificially separates cognition, emotion, and behavior, has created a compartmentalized approach to understanding the human experience.

Belenky et al. (1986) introduced the concept of procedural knowing, which has two designations. The first is separate knowing, a distanced and impartial stance toward that which is to be known. This is the skeptical stance of the devil's advocate. Dating back to the Socratic method, separate knowing is the backbone of Western academia; it is the sort of inquiry that occurs in the classrooms of higher education. We can better understand separate objective knowing by looking at the etymology of the word *objective: ob,* "off"; *ject,* "throw." Separate knowing employs a "throwing off or away," which allows us to look at a thing critically. The second designation is connected knowing, an attempt to enter into the space of the thing to be known and to identify with it. This kind of knowing is conceived as a positive, effortful act that is more intuitive and less rational. Connected knowing requires not merely sympathetic understanding or the absence of negative evaluation but also affirmation of the other. It follows Martin Buber's recommendations to "image the real," to "make the other present," which requires "a bold swinging . . . into the life of the other" (cited in Clinchy, 1996, p. 218). *Women's Ways of Knowing* emphasized that connected knowing is not superior to separate knowing, but neither is it inferior. Although both are important, connected (that is, feminine) ways of knowing historically have been devalued (Golberger, 1996, p. 9). Blythe Clinchy (1996) observed that separate knowing requires a removal of the self, whereas connected knowing requires an investment of the self, which does not automatically accept the other but instead engages in self-reflection. The investigator "listens to the self in order to listen to the respondent. [The investigator uses] the self to understand the other" (Clinchy, 1996, p. 219).

Extreme Separate Knowing Can Lead to Dissociation

Our Western legacy of mind-body dualism and binary oppositions results in a tendency to split our experience. The culture's dualism is often mirrored in our personal experience: thoughts and feelings can suddenly split. On a conscious level, we are taught to isolate and then compartmentalize our experience. On an unconscious level, the psyche will split when traumatized or under stress. Dissociation takes place between oneself and the object of the trauma, between parts of our own experiencing, or both. We can become dissociated from our memory of an event or the feelings that surrounded it. This leads to a poignant dissociation of one aspect of our selves from another.

Carol Gilligan's explanation of emotional disconnection (1982) views psychological distress as a sign that inner connection is broken. Gilligan's perspective is congruent with Imago's notion of the Lost Self, those parts of the self that become fugitive and seem to be missing. The Lost Self emerges when we, as children, experience a parent devaluing our thoughts, leading us to lose confidence in our ability to think, or a teacher yelling at us, leaving us feeling no longer free to express ourselves. Certain aspects of our being go underground, perhaps so deeply that we lose our awareness of these parts. Once these parts are buried, they are not available to aid us in our quest for whole living.

On the macrocosmic level, public-private splits are encouraged when we are asked to honor espoused American truths instead of believing in our personal experience. When a cultural authority or image is supported over and against the actual truth of one's personal experience, the inner-outer, public-private split widens. Tragically, when people run from their own truth, they end up not knowing what they know.

For example, many of the civil liberties of gays and lesbians are denied, yet we are encouraged to overlook the inconsistencies, dissociate from these problems, and celebrate the glory of our political ideology. The problem of splitting also calls into question our cultural assumptions about how we are in relationship with each other and with our culture. For example, our society applauds the development of individuation and self-reliance, which undermines our sense of ontological connectivity and interdependency. Pushed into autonomy and thus separation, we dissociate parts of our selves from our selves and from broader connections with our culture as well (Gilligan, Rogers, & Tollman, 1991, pp. 10–31).[1]

Dissociation Is Healed by Association

The antidote to splitting is the practice of association, that is, connection or relationality. Connection between romantic partners is the primary objective of Imago Relationship Therapy (IRT) and is accomplished through the process of dialogue. When two people engage in authentic dialogue, connection becomes possible.

Thinkers from fields as diverse as contemporary physics and feminist psychology have focused on ideas similar to those proposed by Imago theory. For example, theorists from the Stone Center for Women derived a relational psychology based on a woman's perspective (although it is stated to be applicable to men as well). They charted the developmental process through which one gains the capacity to connect and be in relationship with one's context. These theorists maintain that a person achieves wholeness through relationship.

Feminist theorist Patrocinio Schweickart (1996) challenges the notion that dialogue consists of two people talking. In "Speech Is Silver, Silence Is Gold," she emphasized that dialogue is in fact about two people listening. She stated that often "the sound of speech masks the activity of the listener" (p. 318). We make the mistake of assigning voice the index of active assertion, because the listener appears to be just sitting there, passive and receptive.

Schweickart's drawing of an analogy between speaking and writing and listening and reading enables us to understand our misperception more easily. "The moment of assertion, writing, is detached from the moment of reception, reading, and both are reduced to silence, so that neither appears to be more nor less active than the other. . . . At the moment of reading, the reader, the only human agent present, is the producer of meaning. While it is easy to think of listening as doing nothing, everyone will agree that reading often takes considerable time and effort, and that comprehension does not happen mechanically" (1996, p. 318). This analogy clearly illustrates how listening is the meaning-making of speaking and that one completes and fulfills the other.

In describing listening, Schweickart refers to the concept of "negative capability," the ability not to be always full of oneself.[2] It is "the capacity to be susceptible, to allow one's thoughts, feelings, passions, and senses to be taken up, moved by, filled with, an other" (p. 316). Needed for true listening, negative capability often is overlooked in a society that promotes the expansion of the self and competitive achievement. About the "overvaluation of argumentation," Schweickart notes that "It is easy to be absorbed by the speaking role and to identify agency with having a voice. . . . The overestimation of the assertive agency of speaking goes hand in hand with the underestimation of the receptive agency (the paradoxical negative capability) of listening" (1996, p. 317).

Schweickart's ideas overturn common assumptions, inviting us to reevaluate our notions of what it means to be active and what it means to be receptive, and the value we place on these functions. Such ideas underscore our need to be more aware of the crucial role played by those who listen and who, therefore, are the holders of meaning.

Another key concept in relational theory is empathy, the capacity for attunement with another person. The oldest meaning of empathy is that one person's fullness comes to the psychological aid of another, creating authentic connection. Stone Center theorist Janet Surrey (1991) used the term "response/ability" to illuminate this type of connection (p. 63). She described moving from a relationship of caretaking to the capacity for a more conscious and fully responsible sense of relationship. This is the "pathway of development [that] includes both the outer, 'real' relationship and the inner sense of relationship" (p. 63).

Blythe Clinchy (1996) noted that the German word from which empathy was derived, *einfühlung*, literally means "feeling into" and implies "inference, judgment, and reasoned thought" (p. 224). Clinchy remarked that empathy has come to connote only "feeling" and that "the loss in translation of these cognitive aspects can be seen as an instance of the Western tendency to treat thinking and feeling as mutually exclusive" (p. 224).

Empathy has, in fact, two aspects. First, the empathic person learns to feel for the other, or as Kohut put it, experiences "the recognition of the self in the other" (1978, cited in Jordan, 1991, p. 68). Second, the empathic person grows to become self-empathic. One must learn to grow in relationship with others while staying attuned to one's self. When empathy is understood as total agreement, it suggests a kind of de-selfing, a merging in which there is no real individuated self to do the agreeing. With de-selfing, there can be no association between two distinct selves.

Stone Center theorist Judith Jordan (1991) proposed a solution for de-selfing. Distilling what such theorists as Buber and Kohut said about empathy, she reminds us of the necessity of self-empathy, a state of being attuned and in another: "Unlike empathy with another, where the self boundaries undergo more temporary alteration and the final accommodation may be slight, with intrapsychic empathy there is more opportunity for enduring change in both the representation of self taken as object and in the observing self" (1991, p. 77).

Psychological truth requires both an other and a true self. Without a strong capacity for self-empathy, one can't feel for another.

Association with Self and Others Results in Wholeness and Thus Integrity

For those committed to the relational paradigm, a key task is distinguishing between authentic and false relationships.

As stated earlier, distinguishing between separate and connected knowing allows us to discover the buried inner voice of connected knowing and to integrate it with the outer voice of logic and reason. When one relies on this kind of integrated knowing, the goal becomes not to align with an abstract truth but rather to move into a process by which knowing comes out of a felt experience—a unity between feeling and thought.

The etymology of *integrity* comes from *integer,* the Latin word for whole. Integrity is wholeness, something perfectly undivided. This kind of undividedness calls for the integration of the splits that are in our context and in our selves. It is living in right relationship with others within our context as well as being in right relationship with the many parts of our selves. Finding congruence between the inner and the outer is the path toward wholeness and integrity.

Imago theory uses the concept of the "four functions of the self" to illustrate how all the capacities of the self interconnect to form a whole, harmonious unit (Figure 2.1).

The theologian Kierkegaard said that we don't know truth, we become truth, suggesting that word and deed become one. The philosopher Kant said, "Autonomy and community can be realized only through one another" (quoted in Clohesy, 2000, p. 4). Such statements are consistent with the call for a radical symbiosis between our inner and outer worlds, between our cognitive, felt, and lived existence, which is now coming from studies of women's psychology.

Association Is Fundamental in the Shift from the Individual to the Relational Paradigm

The fifth theorem is that association helps us shift from the individual to the relational paradigm.

The energy born from association has meaning for a contemporary definition of the self that is consistent with the relational paradigm. In the early seventeenth century, Descartes's pure mental focus helped legitimize the idea of a private psychological self, which has been understood since then as the basis of human subjectivity. Given that this idea of the private psychological self is still accepted, some say that personality theory is not keeping pace with contemporary physics and philosophy. Imago theory is an exception. In addition to being a therapy for couples, Imago represents

Figure 2.1. The Four Human Functions and Their Manifestations.

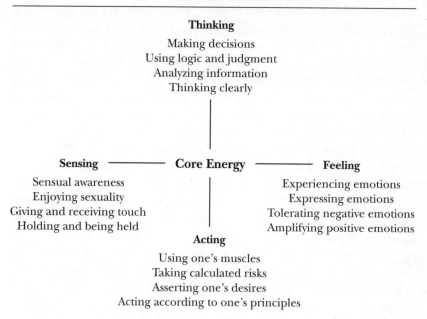

Thinking
Making decisions
Using logic and judgment
Analyzing information
Thinking clearly

Sensing ———— **Core Energy** ———— **Feeling**

Sensual awareness
Enjoying sexuality
Giving and receiving touch
Holding and being held

Experiencing emotions
Expressing emotions
Tolerating negative emotions
Amplifying positive emotions

Acting
Using one's muscles
Taking calculated risks
Asserting one's desires
Acting according to one's principles

a paradigm shift that is persuading our culture to think of the self in relational terms.

Hope Landrine (1995) explored two definitions of the self. The first follows the Cartesian model. Traditional Western culture conceptualizes the self as bound, singular, and existing within the mind, as the mind part of the mind-body duality. This model places the self in opposition to the body. The self is the thinking, conceiving part of the person. In the West, the self exists first, and all other things are seen in relation to it. In the West, whenever "I" is referenced, it is capitalized, even in the middle of a sentence. The "I" that Landrine called the Referential self is more significant than almost anything else. But Landrine also suggested another kind of self, the Indexical self. She noted that this view of the self is prominent in the more sociocentric as opposed to individualistic cultures. In the East, the self incorporates one's relationships, social interactions, and cultural context. The Indexical self has no traits, desires, or needs apart from its social context. It does not exist in isolation. Western culture construes persons as entities separate from community and family, and views these larger units as existing for the purposes of the individual. In sociocentric cultures, the family and the community take priority over the self, with relationships and community being primary and the self being derivative.

The Indexical self seeks to advance the group in society. Landrine (1995) described it this way: "One seeks to advance the family rather than the self, to assure the achievement and happiness of the relationship rather than the self" (p. 761).[3]

Overall, a sociocentric perspective is compatible with Imago and feminist theories and resonates with the relational paradigmatic shift. The distinctions between the relational paradigm, which Janet Surrey (1991) considered a "subject relations theory" as opposed to an "object relations theory" (p. 61), and the individual paradigm are outlined in Table 2.1.

To summarize, the delineations between things may be more porous than they appear. When Einstein proposed energy as the basic universal substance that is transformed into a variety of forms, not only did the universe become conceptually unified for the first time, but the firm categories that separated and classified things dissolved. A substance became understood as falling into multiple categories at the same time.

As we alternate between focusing on inner connection and on outer connection in our understanding of the self, I want to suggest the applicability of the concept of a "wavacle" (Zohar, 1991), which refers to elements that act like a particle one moment and a wave the next.[4] At times the self responds like an individual unit, and at other times as though it were in connection with its context. The self, therefore, is not one side of a duality but oscillates between both sides. It is both itself and its context. It is this broad and vibrant self that is compatible with the relational paradigm.

According to feminist psychology, context is not the environment that happens to be around the behavior; it is not something that exists outside the behavior, but rather is a part of the behavior.

Truth Telling Can Be a Potent Catalyst in the Relational Paradigm

Writing about organizational dynamics, systems theorist Peter Senge (1990) describes the "learning organization." Senge states that

**Table 2.1. Terms Used by the Traditional Individual
Paradigm and the Relational Paradigm.**

In Traditional Psychology	*In Relational Psychology*
Emphasis is on	
Independence	Interdependence
Detachment	Attachment
Autonomy	Connection
Self-sufficiency	Self-in-context
Self-actualization	Mutuality
Generating pulse	Resonance
Solo	Harmonics/harmony
Counter-dependent	Interdependent
Self psychology	Social psychology
Self-esteem	Contextual pride
Self-control	Self-enlargement
Self-development	Relationality
Self as expert	Group as expert
Self-reliance	Trust
Power over	Shared power
I-It	I-Thou
Subject-object	Subject-subject

when an organization is in crisis, "we may begin with a disarmingly simple yet profound strategy for dealing with structural conflict: telling the truth" (p. 159). Senge describes truth as "a relentless willingness to root out the ways we limit or deceive ourselves from seeing what is, and to continually challenge our theories of why things are the way they are" (p. 159).

Imago theory proposes that two people can move beyond their defenses, tell each other their truth, and be mutually held in such a way that both become transformed. According to Senge, "Structures of which we are unaware hold us prisoner. Once we can see them and name them, they no longer have the same hold on us. This is as much true for individuals as it is for organizations" (1990, p. 160).

A New Perspective

Now, at the beginning of the twenty-first century, we stand at the threshold of a new consciousness. Our Western legacy of individualism is evolving into a new way of looking at ourselves and the world. The paradigm that asserts one's right to declare oneself as warring against the forces of the universe no longer works. We are creating a new perspective on how to live, love, work, and tell each other the truth. Along with feminism, chaos theory, and other new movements, Imago is a fundamental partner in the creation of this new consciousness. Imago is building a bridge between the old and the new ways of seeing. Those who cross this bridge can gain a fuller understanding of how to create a world community that works toward justice and honor for every person.

Notes

1. As Gilligan (1982) describes it, this phenomenon is characteristic of boys early on and girls later in adolescence.
2. The poet John Keats (1795–1821) used this phrase to describe a central tenet of his philosophy, which focused on the importance of absolute receptivity to experience, allowing the mind to be a thoroughfare of all thought.
3. Landrine (1995) tells us that the individualistic culture may consider the Indexical construction as self-inhibiting, unhappy, and confining. The sociocentric view may see the Referential construction of the self as lonely, anxious, and isolating.
4. This original concept was developed by Danah Zohar (1991) in his book on the quantum self.

References

Belenky, M. F., Clinchy, B. M., Goldberger, N. R., & Tarule, J. M. (1986). *Women's ways of knowing: The development of self, voice, and mind.* New York: Basic Books.

Clinchy, B. M. (1996). Connected and separate knowing: Toward a marriage of two minds. In N. R. Goldberger, J. M. Tarule, B. M. Clinchy, & M. F. Belenky (Eds.), *Knowledge, difference, and power* (pp. 205–247). New York: Basic Books.

Clohesy, W. W. (2000). *Seeking altruism in Kant's practical philosophy.* Unpublished paper.

Gilligan, C. (1982). *In a different voice.* Cambridge, MA: Harvard University Press.

Gilligan, C., Rogers, A. G., & Tolman, D. L. (1991). *Women, girls, and psychotherapy: Reframing resistance.* Binghamton: New York Press.

Goldberger, N. R. (1996). Introduction: Looking backward, looking forward. In N. R. Goldberger, J. M. Tarule, B. M. Clinchy, & M. F. Belenky (Eds.), *Knowledge, difference, and power* (pp. 1–24). New York: Basic Books.

Jordan, J. (1991). Empathy and self boundaries. In J. V. Jordan, A. G. Kaplan, J. B. Miller, I. P. Stiver, & J. L. Surrey (Eds.), *Women's growth in connection: Writings from the Stone Center* (pp. 67–80). New York: Guilford Press.

Kohut, H. (1978). *The search for the self: Selected writings of Heinz Kohut: 1950–1978* (Vol. 1; P. H. Ornstein, Ed.). New York: International Universities Press.

Landrine, H. (1995). Clinical implications of cultural differences: The referential versus the indexical self. In N. R. Goldberger & J. B. Veroff (Eds.), *The culture and psychology reader* (pp. 744–766). New York: New York University Press.

Perry, W. G. (1970). *Forms of intellectual and ethical development in the college years.* Austin, Tex.: Holt, Rinehart and Winston.

Schweickart, P. (1996). Speech is silver, silence is gold: The asymmetrical intersubjectivity of communicative action. In N. R. Goldberger, J. M. Tarule, B. M. Clinchy, & M. F. Belenky (Eds.), *Knowledge, difference, and power* (pp. 305–333). New York: Basic Books.

Senge, P. M. (1990). *The fifth discipline: The art and practice of the learning organization.* New York: Currency Doubleday.

Surrey, J. L. (1991). The "self-in-relation": A theory of women's development. In J. V. Jordan, A. G. Kaplan, J. B. Miller, I. Stiver, & J. L. Surrey (Eds.), *Women's growth in connection: Writings from the Stone Center* (pp. 51–66). New York: Guilford Press.

Zohar, D. (1991). *Quantum self: Human nature and consciousness defined by the new physics.* New York: Morrow.

Chapter Three

Conscious Marriage as Covenant

Helen LaKelly Hunt, Ph.D.

The agreements made by partners in modern marriages are based on the concept of a civil contract. This has led to the experience of marriage as a balancing of the give and take of each partner in the relationship. From this contractual perspective, if either or both partners do not keep their agreements, there are sufficient grounds to break the contract and end the marriage.

Contract Versus Covenant

Whereas contractual theory is the basis of modern marriage, some ancient forms of marriage were based instead on the concept of covenant. A shift occurred, according to Paul F. Palmer (1972) of St. John's Provincial Seminary, when certain "theological villains" of the Scholastic Period, such as Albert the Great, Thomas Aquinas, and Duns Scotus, began to refer to marriage not as covenant but as contract. According to Palmer, this eventually led to a sense that marriages, which some church doctrine had graced as sacramental, could be severed by humans and could in fact be treated like other legal contracts. Palmer suggests that whereas contracts can be broken by mutual agreement, by failure to live up to the terms of the contract, or by civil intervention, "covenants are not broken; they are violated . . ." (p. 619). The indissolubility of two people in a covenantal relationship suggests a permanence of connection that endures through struggle. It suggests that no matter how either person in covenant behaves, their undying bond is "for better or for worse, until death do us part" (p. 622). The question then becomes, What is necessary for covenant to be present?

This chapter takes the position that the view of marriage as a covenant is more consistent with the Imago concept of the conscious marriage than is the contemporary view of contractual marriage. When marriage is considered sacramental, it takes on qualities that go beyond a rational understanding of the relationship. The achievement of a transrational view of marriage is possible when we explore the meaning of covenant by going to its roots and describing its historical evolution in the ancient Near East and in Old Testament history in particular.

Definition of Covenant

Covenant (Hebrew *berith* or *berît*) can be seen as "a solemn promise made binding by an oath, which may be either a verbal formula or a symbolic action. Such an action or formula is recognized by both parties as the formal act which binds the actor to fulfill his promise" (Buttrick, 1962, p. 714). Scholars indicate that our English word *covenant* does not capture the full meaning and nuance of the Hebrew word *berît* (Zimmerli, 1978). The most generally accepted derivation of the term is from the Akkadian word *birîtu,* meaning to fetter or "bond" (as in a binding contract), but scholars have failed to reach clear consensus on how this term grew to mean covenant (Buttrick, 1962). Old Testament scholar Walther Zimmerli suggests that this type of bonding has to do with both a cutting apart and a bringing back together so that "there is a sense in which the two parties are joined."[1]

Scholars suggest that an early use of covenant was to encourage two parties into a bilateral agreement of great significance and mutual obligation. Scholars also indicate that early connotations of covenant were both legal—that is, dealing with social obligations between two parties—as well as theological, offering the binding commitment of the relationship between YHWH and His people.[2]

Covenant in History and in Imago

Old Testament scholars postulate that Old Testament covenants such as the Sinaic Covenant were modeled after ancient Hittite treaties.

They see parallels in that they both emphasized relationship and were dialogic in nature. They posit that the sequence of steps in a binding agreement between Hittite rulers (suzerains) and their vassals is a precursor of Old Testament covenant. The steps of this formulary are as follows:

1. The first step of a Hittite treaty begins with the Preamble Particularies, in which the suzerain clarifies his identity and reality. This is clearly not an agreement between equals, and the hierarchy of the relationship is obvious.
2. The second step is referred to as the Historical Prologue or the Antecedent History. It summarizes the past relationship of the parties, particularly of the suzerain, who defines his great actions so as to legitimize the loyalty and submission he receives of his vassals.
3. In the third step, the Stipulations or Terms of the Treaty are clarified for the purpose of delineating what is needed for both the suzerain and the vassal to feel secure with one another. This was a very important part of the treaty, which was stated explicitly to ensure the mutual comfort, safety, and benefit of the two parties.
4. Next, the Deposition of the Treaty clarifies that the treaty be placed in the temple of the vassal's city, to be read periodically as a reminder to the people.
5. The List of Witnesses is articulated to specify who will oversee the pledging as well as the fulfillment of the covenant. Those named are usually the gods of the suzerain and the vassal.
6. In the last step, Curses and Blessings stipulate the ramifications of a breach of the treaty as well as the rewards for the faithful.

The suzerains had the power among their vassals to move in and conquer them at any time. They could simply expand by force and unilaterally enact new law and policies. At the same time, the Hittite treaties indicate a sensitivity of the suzerain toward the vassal and show a desire that the vassal retain some freedom within the relationship. Thus an inherent inequality remained despite the somewhat equalizing effect of the treaty. One of the Old Testament covenants that most closely resembles the Hittite treaty is the Sinaic

Covenant between God and the Israelites.[3] Old Testament theologians have been intrigued with the notion that the writer of the account of Sinai might have been directly or indirectly influenced by these ancient treaties as a model on which to establish YHWH's interaction with the Israelites.

The Covenant as a Dialogical Relationship

Though the treaty formula articulated here is one between unequals, its structure and the Old Testament covenants that followed can be useful models for couples to follow in making their own covenants. There is a dialogical component of these early agreements that mirrors the dialogic essence of Imago theory. A current model inspired by the covenant tradition and using Imago theory would have some of the following features:

1. Partners declare their identities to one another.
2. Partners articulate the history of their relationship, how it evolved, and the current context.
3. Partners stipulate how they will relate to each other. This is the most important part of the treaty, and, as is true of the Imago system, there must be specificity as to guidelines. For example, using the conditions of a conscious marriage, both partners pledge that they will protect each other by making the relationship safe at all times. They make a commitment to heal each other's childhood wounds. They pledge to inject into all their interactions the spirit of dialogue. They agree to use dialogue whenever they are in conflict. They promise to replace all emotional attacks with specific behavior change requests. They make a "no-exit" decision to remain in the relationship. They commit to learning each other's love language and to speaking it through daily caring behaviors.
4. Partners then decide on a physical location where their covenant will be placed, and they agree to review the covenant regularly. They may decide to place it in a manual or notebook and to review it every weekend. Or they may choose to attach it to a mirror or some other prominent place where they can see it at the beginning of each day.

5. The couple then agrees to select witnesses, so that what is private can be made public. Witnesses could include a close friend or their therapist. In keeping with tradition, couples may prefer their witness to be the God they honor and worship.
6. In the presence of the witnesses, partners cite the blessings of keeping their covenant. These may include being healed of their specific childhood wounds or, more generally, enlarging their awareness of the depth of their connection. They also cite the curses of abandoning this covenant, which could include marital misery, unhappiness, and, possibly, divorce.

Hosea and Gomer, a Relationship Symbolizing Covenant

Whereas the covenant in the Old Testament was between YHWH and the people of Israel, it is personified in the book of Hosea by an allegory of the relationship between Hosea, an eighth-century BCE prophet, and his wife, Gomer. This story provides us with a case study of the dynamics and transforming power of a covenantal relationship.

The book of Hosea[4] illustrates YHWH's desire for covenant with His people. In his prophecy, Hosea warns the Israelites that their behavior is not faithful to YHWH; they act as though the "spirit of prostitution is in their hearts" (5:4), and their love is like the "morning mist / like the early dew that disappears" (6:4). Following the command of YHWH, Hosea marries a prostitute named Gomer, a woman who represents the faithlessness of Israel.[5] Parallel to YHWH's relationship with His wayward people, Hosea is bound to a woman whose devotion is weak. In spite of Hosea's love, loyalty, and protection, Gomer is unfaithful to him. He chastises her yet stays connected, representing the enduring love of YHWH in covenant.[6] Although both relationships are strained and despairing at times, they endure. Hosea and Gomer's relationship reflects the content and spirit of a covenantal relationship and represents the potential for a covenantal relationship to endure and be transformative.

Features of the Covenant

Five features define the convenant: relationality, connection, differentiation, forgiveness, and paradoxicality. We will explore each in detail in the sections that follow.

Relationality Is Our Essence

Given the relational nature of a covenant exchange, we can extrapolate that YHWH must be relational at His essence. Further, the Hittite treaties invite a kind of intimacy or informality that legal documents of the same time do not evoke (Hillers, 1969). As Old Testament scholar Jon Levenson notes, "The ancient Near Eastern covenant was not an *impersonal code*, but *an instrument of diplomacy* founded upon the *personal relationship* of the heads of state" (emphasis added) (1985, p. 28). If scholarship is correct, and there was some sort of transfer of the sentiment of these treaties into the covenantal attitude underlying Old Testament history, then a radical concept was being birthed: that of a deity significantly engaged with His creation. It was out of a relational matrix that the God of Israel emerged on the historical world stage. The depiction of YHWH's relationship with His people is not like one of a suzerain to a vassal. Rather, the idea of God and Israel as man and wife is a metaphor with personal and intimate connotations. The beloved and the lover have pledged themselves to one another for better or for worse, until the end of time. Similarly, when couples engage in the daily practice of Imago's dialogical tools, the relationship serves as a matrix that brings the couple into a divine union, into a commitment far surpassing the modern civil contract. It is this relational matrix that enables the couple to remain connected throughout the very real difficulties of forging a relationship.

The Role of Wounding in Connection

YHWH is a God of feelings, a God who exhibits the full range of human emotions. In Hosea, we find a deity that experiences brokenness and yearning at the unfaithfulness of His people. Israel's wandering from her divine husband, giving her loyalty to foreign gods like Baal, led YHWH to declare of Israel, "She is not my wife, neither am I her husband" (2:2). These words convey a profound sense of betrayal and brokenness. Verse after verse of YHWH's outpouring reveals a sorrowfully wounded God who is vulnerable enough to admit a yearning for connection with a wayward people. Such a deity is a God in process, evolving from a God of wrath to one of yearning and compassion.

In his parallel story, Hosea realizes that the children Gomer has given birth to are not his. This brutal realization of Gomer's betrayal evokes an almost unbearable agony and brokenness in Hosea. Nevertheless, Hosea struggles to stay in covenantal union with Gomer.

Imago theory has a great deal to say about this phenomenon, in which an acknowledgment of wounding begins the process of reconnection. Imago practice is based on the belief that by opening to the awareness of our woundedness, we can heal. By recognizing and embracing our own and our partner's wounds, we become enabled to experience true intimacy.

Differentiation

The covenantal relationship gave greater coherence to the roles of both YHWH and His covenant people. As Old Testament scholar Andy Dearman notes, "The concept of both YHWH and Israel has suffered fragmentation, and the Deuteronomistic formulation of the covenant sought to reinstate a coherent identity for the covenant giver (YHWH) and the recipient" (1992, p. 135). The point of covenant negotiation was to evolve an instrument by which the connection between the two partners was regulated and brought into union. Once delineation and differentiation were clarified, relationship became possible. Within the relationship of YHWH with His people, the people remain free to choose their own responses. The covenant between YHWH and His people illustrates that domination or oppression does not play a role in covenantal spirit. A covenant is not a mercenary bargain. The blessings of covenant are to be a consequence of faithfulness, not the motivating cause. The primary motive of keeping the covenant is being in relationship.

The usefulness of a covenant for clarifying and delineating the roles of each partner provides another parallel between the covenantal relationship and committed romantic partnership, as viewed by Imago theory: in a romantic partnership, freedom and choice must be maintained for differentiation to be sustained. Covenantal agreements within a relationship can help both partners honor their differences as a source of strength.

The Centrality of Forgiveness

Forgiveness transforms the story of Hosea from a near disaster into one of eternal hope. This is illustrated in Hosea's statement, "I will make the Valley of Achor a door of hope" (2:15). *Achor* is a technical term meaning the "breaking of a taboo," or "troubling" (Knight, 1960). Hosea's suggestion is that Israel, at the very point when it is most wayward and troubled, even as it breaks all taboos, is nevertheless profoundly loved by YHWH. In Hosea's shift of awareness, the valley of trouble is made into the door of hope; and there is no wider door that could be opened, especially in times of great pain. YHWH stays faithful to Hosea and says He will restore the lost years: "I will show my love to the one I called not my loved one" (2:23).

Hosea uses the word *hesed* (2:19) to suggest the faithfulness and forgiveness YHWH brings to His people. Old Testament scholar James Luther Mays (1969, p. 51) defines *hesed* as "the attitude and activity which founds and maintains a relation." This attitude is expressed by YHWH when He instructs Hosea to "Go show your love to your wife again, though she is loved by another and is an adulteress" (3:1). Forgiveness is accompanied by the promise of reconciling action and the end of anger in YHWH's ultimate word: "I will heal their waywardness and love them freely, for my anger has turned away from them" (14:4). Out of the pain of betrayal, through forgiveness, love has the potential to be born.

In "Law and Love in Jewish Theology," Byron Sherwin notes that "divine anger is an expression of frustrated love" (1982, p. 476). God's anger toward Israel was not meant to destroy her. Faithfulness to the covenantal structure itself may be seen as transforming YHWH's explosive rage into forgiveness and a prevailing love. Likewise, Hosea's admonitions were not meant to destroy Gomer. Hosea was reacting to his sense of isolation and rejection; he was attempting to evoke Gomer's recognition of her role in the covenant, so that the two could be in relationship. Gomer hopes for her redemption. Her goal is similar to the goal of Imago therapy, to heal childhood wounds and create wholeness.

The Paradoxical Quality of Covenant

We see in the concept of covenant both a sense of mutual obligation and a sense of grace and forgiveness. Both aspects of covenant, although seemingly contradictory, are needed for the alchemy of covenant to occur.

Let's look for a minute at one end of this spectrum. Covenant evolves out of mutual obligation. It is not a gift given freely, with nothing being asked in return. Both parties have stipulations that they have to fulfill. Covenant requires responsibility and reciprocity. YHWH was not in covenant with all people. Rather, He was in covenant with a people on whom He imposed firm criteria.

At the same time, a covenant by its very nature endures even when one party fails. This aspect of covenant is embodied less at Sinai than in the covenant between YHWH and David. It is the Davidic Covenant which suggests that the love and faithfulness of YHWH is permanent. Thus, covenantal relationships cannot be broken, even when they become neglected or strained. In the words of Jon Levenson, "The covenant is not contingent upon the vassal's fulfillment of stipulations. If he errs, he will be punished but not dethroned" (1983, p. 50).

These two concepts, conditionality (Sinaic law) and indissolubility (Davidic grace), might seem antithetical and thus paradoxical, but within the Old Testament concept of covenant, both exist simultaneously. Jon Levenson (1979) explores the polarized scholarly thinking regarding these two understandings of covenant, and ultimately notes that "in short, there is no tension between the two covenants, but rather an organic continuity" (p. 209).

The richness of the Bible is that its truths are often beyond our comprehension, and it asks us to understand its teachings in a larger framework of knowing beyond our usual categories of logic. Therefore, to stay with and embrace the fullness of the concept of covenant, we need an exploration of paradox and a transrational understanding. Embracing the concept of paradox will invite us into the greater depths and power of the concept of marriage.

A Relational Covenant

A brief survey of the concept of covenant in the Hebrew scriptures suggests that each covenant was initiated by YHWH for the purpose of manifesting His eternal union with His people. Out of this history of interaction between YHWH and humankind emerges the thesis of this chapter: that YHWH Himself is deeply relational. According to Mays (1969), YHWH "takes the redemption of Israel wholly upon Himself. In the final tragic days of Israel's existence, Hosea gave Israel a prayer as a way to return to their God (14:1–3), who never gave up His desire to be their Savior" (p. 15). The fact that YHWH Himself is depicted as having such a strong impulse toward connection suggests that being in relationship has a divine impetus and reflects a process that is sacred in its origin. Furthermore, if scriptural accounts of our interaction with the divine suggest a paradigm of universal order, the emphasis on relationship might suggest the important ontological status of relationality and interconnectivity. Martin Buber expressed this essential connectedness in this way: "The purpose of relation is the relation itself—touching the You. For as soon as we touch a You, we are touched by a breath of eternal life" (1970, p. 112).

Covenant appears to be a combination of law-obligation and forgiveness-grace that results in a profound union of these opposites. Such a union enlarges our understanding of the powerful dynamics within marriage. The legal aspect describes the work needed for consciousness to emerge. Imago theory offers a detailed map of dialogue and communication. Yet superceding the legal is the spiritual dimension of relationship. Imago illuminates the concept of sacred space that can emerge when two people move into true mutual regard. Thus the Imago process can help delineate the rules of the relationship and also make room for the divine. The union becomes a covenantal love, which is then unseverable.

Covenantal relationship is universally attainable. It is a reflection of our innate relationship with the divine, through which we recognize the indissolubility of our relationship to one another as members of the human family. The relational skills we learn to develop within a conscious marriage extend beyond the marital relationship, and open us to the fullness of life itself. As Abraham Heschel says, "God is not hiding in a temple. The Torah came to tell inattentive man: 'You are not alone, you live constantly in a holy neighborhood; remember: Love thy neighbor—God—as thyself'" (1993, p. 12).

Notes

1. As the text of an Aramaic treaty from the eighth century BCE reads, "Just as this calf is cut up, so may Matiel be cut up." Among the Israelites, a common way of identifying the parties to a covenant with the victim was to cut up the animal and pass it between the parties (Hillers, 1969, cited in Zimmerli, 1978, p. 49).

2. Although I prefer to use a gender-neutral pronoun to refer to God, I use the masculine here to remain congruent with the presentation of YHWH in the Hebrew scriptures.

"In the world of the ancient East, however, 'covenant' was at first not a theological concept at all. On the contrary, *berît* was a common legal institution. When we speak in the ecumenical movement today about 'covenanting,' about covenants between human beings, the biblical basis for doing so seems to lie precisely in legal alliance of this kind" (Falcke, 1986, p. 258).

3. Zimmerli (1978) points out that nowhere in Hebrew scripture is a structuring of a covenant synonymous with these six points, so the association between the Hittite formulary and the evolution of Old Testament covenant is in many cases only suggestive. What is significant, however, is that many of the Old Testament covenants do take several of these six points and evolve them into an agreement between YHWH and Israel.

4. The book of Hosea is the only record of prophetic writings preserved from the northern kingdom of Israel. It is believed that Hosea probably lived his life in Ephraim or in Manasseh in the eighth century BCE, toward the end of the reign of Jeroboam II. As to the preservation of his manuscript, an unknown disciple may have escaped the Assyrian invasion and gone south with Hosea's writing. It is believed that this disciple reproduced and edited the material to preserve it for the future. We know as fact that a century later, Jeremiah drew heavily from and quoted Hosea's work. Though his is a simple story, there is evidence that Hosea was one of the great personalities in Israel's history. It is through his suffering that we gain increased revelation of the nature of YHWH and of the transforming effect of covenantal love.

5. Whether Gomer is an actual woman Hosea married, whether there are two unfaithful women, or whether it is simply an allegory is debated by scholars. The distinction is not relevant to this chapter.

6. The evoking of universal meanings out of such parables—described by H. Wheeler Robinson (cited in Knight, 1960) as "prophetic symbolism"—points the way to a unified world where thought and action are connected. Within such symbolism, Hosea saw himself as a divinely chosen catalyst for acting out and speaking the yearnings and will of YHWH.

References

Buber, M. (1970). *I and thou* (W. Kaufmann, Trans.). New York: Scribner.

Buttrick, G. A. (1962). *The interpreter's dictionary of the Bible.* New York: Abington Press.

Campbell, J. (1988). *The power of myth.* New York: Doubleday.

Dearman, A. J. (1992). *Religion and culture in ancient Israel.* Peabody, MA: Hindrickson.

Falcke, H. (1986). Biblical aspects of the process of mutual commitment. *Ecumenical Review, 38,* 257–264.

Heschel, A. J. (1993). *I asked for wonder* (S. H. Dresner, Trans.). New York: Crossroads.

Hillers, D. R. (1969). *Covenant: The history of a biblical idea.* Baltimore: Johns Hopkins University Press.

Knight, G.A.F. (1960). *Hosea: Introduction and commentary.* London: SCM Press.

Levenson, J. D. (1979). The Davidic covenant and its modern interpreters. *Catholic Biblical Quarterly, 41,* 205–219.

Levenson, J. D. (1983). Covenant and commandment. *Tradition, 21,* 42–51.

Levenson, J. D. (1985). *Sinai and Zion: An entry into the Jewish Bible.* San Francisco: HarperSanFrancisco.

Mays, J. L. (1969). *Hosea: A commentary.* Philadelphia: Westminster Press.

Palmer, P. F. (1972). Christian marriage: Contract or covenant? *Theological Studies, 33,* 617–665.

Sherwin, B. L. (1982). Law and love in Jewish theology. *Anglican Theological Review, 64,* 467–480.

Zimmerli, W. (1978). *Old Testament theology in outline.* Edinburgh: Clark.

Part Two

Perspectives on Comparisons with Other Models

Family Systems Theory and Imago Therapy
A Theoretical Interpretation
Randy Gerson, Ph.D.

Having spent most of my professional life studying family systems theory, particularly multigenerational family patterns, I have in recent years attempted to integrate the extremely useful approach of Imago Relationship Therapy (IRT) as developed by Harville Hendrix into my thinking and practice. I believe that the two very different approaches have much to teach each other. This chapter has a dual purpose: (1) to expose Imago therapists to some useful systemic concepts, and (2) to explore commonalities and differences in the two approaches and begin a constructive integration.

Due to the difficulties of defining these two approaches, this chapter is necessarily my individual interpretation, and one that neither side is likely to endorse. Murray Bowen often decried efforts to simplify or explain his theory. Harville Hendrix is continually evolving in his thinking and, to my knowledge, has never formally presented his ideas in a scholarly format.

I recognize that many readers are well versed in systems theory. Please forgive my somewhat simplified account of a very complex set of ideas. You may also disagree with my interpretations.

Systemic Theory

Over the last forty years, systemic thinking has revolutionized the theory and practice of psychotherapy. Although the mental health field was once almost the exclusive bastion of individual psycho-analytic or behavioral concepts, the importance of taking a larger systemic interactive perspective has permeated almost all new theoretical thinking in the field. Hendrix's focus (1988) on the couple's relationship and how that relationship has been influenced by each partner's larger family context is a good example of involving a systemic context larger than just the individual.

In this chapter, I will focus on some general systems concepts and then the family systems theory of Murray Bowen (1978). Bowen, who died in 1990, developed over a period of thirty years a comprehensive theory of systemic family functioning. Although many theorists have contributed to systemic theory, I believe Bowen's work is the best application of systems thinking to family and relational functioning to date. It is not possible to cover such a comprehensive theory thoroughly in a chapter of this scope. Rather, I have chosen to emphasize those concepts that are most immediately relevant to working with couples.

Although this term can easily be overused and sometimes takes on almost mysterious qualities, the concept of "the system" is at the core of all systemic thinking. Put simply, a system is an organized group of interrelated and interdependent parts. In the human domain, this means that when people become organized in a group, they become part of a system with emerging rules and norms that govern the functioning of that group.

A couple's relationship is a good example of a system.[1] As the relationship develops, interactive patterns emerge that seem to govern the relationship. The relationship system becomes larger than the individuals involved. The couple is in a dance that neither may intend but both feel helpless to discontinue. Systemic interactions take on a life of their own.

The Importance of Context

One of the implications of a systemic perspective is the humbling realization that our behavior is not as self-determined as we would like to believe. Much of what we do is governed by the organization of the system to which we belong. Who we are is to a large degree determined by our relational context. The recognition of the critical importance of context, particularly social context, is a hallmark of systemic thinking.[2] No longer does one look primarily inside the individual to understand behavior. Rather, one must look at the individual in his or her context in order to understand, predict, or change behavior. Decades of psychological research have confirmed that we are quite variable in our behavior, and few characterological traits persist across various contexts. If you want to change a person, change that person's context. This has been the rationale of many systemic psychotherapeutic approaches.

The systems perspective has provided an expanded view of what we mean by context. The most important contexts are ones involving intimacy, particularly relationships with spouses, significant others, and other family members. These are the people we care about. From a systemic perspective, marriage and the family are the most intense and tightly organized systems to which we belong. A family or marital system has a set of norms or rules that govern the people in that system. Members of the family or couple may not be aware of these norms or even realize they are operating, but people outside the system can often deduce a system's operating principles simply by observing how family members interact. Context involves not just the ways in which we are affected or stressed by our environment or other people, or how we experience our lives or perceive others, but also the organization of the relationships that regulate the roles and patterns of the individuals involved in the system.

The Multigenerational Context

Bowen has argued that investigating the current context is not enough and that a systemic understanding would need to include the temporal, multigenerational context as well. He tracked patterns in some families back as many as nine generations, using the family diagram or "genogram" (McGoldrick & Gerson, 1985), which he developed as a tool to explore the multigenerational context of a family.

Theorists going back to Freud have recognized the importance of family history in understanding the individual, particularly the formative early years of a person's life. Hendrix has especially focused on the emotional "wounds" that often occur in childhood. Bowen, however, has expanded the meaning of one's historical context in a dramatic way. Not only does our experience in our own lifetime influence our relationships, but systemic events and patterns going back many generations can reverberate throughout a family's history. Patterns and ways of coping and interacting get passed down from one generation to another in what Bowen called a "multi-generational transmission process." One can think of a family system as a superorganism that spans many generations. Different family members are born and die, but the family's organization and patterns continue on.

Marriage takes on an added significance when seen from this broader multigenerational perspective. Although Hendrix sees marriage as nature's way of *healing* itself, Bowen viewed marriage as the family system's way of *continuing* itself and as the joining of two family systems to become part of a larger multigenerational system. Although we don't usually realize it, we are like ambassadors or delegates for the family systems from which we come, and will automatically continue many of our family's patterns in the families that we create. Even when we consciously try to reverse what we experienced in our own families growing up, we often find ourselves repeating many of the behaviors of our parents despite ourselves, or end up perpetuating subtle family patterns we do not even recognize. Such is the power of the family system.

Differentiation and Reactivity

Bowen has posited two major forces at play in all family systems: togetherness and individuality. Togetherness "propels an organism to follow the directives of others, to be a dependent, connected, and indistinct entity" (Kerr & Bowen, 1988, p. 65). Individuality "propels an organism to follow its own directives, to be an independent and distinct entity" (p. 64). Both are seen as "biologically rooted life forces (more basic than being just a function of the brain)" (p. 65). These forces can cause family systems to become imbalanced in one of two ways. There may be too much togetherness at the expense of individuality. Bowen calls this "fusion" because family members act as if they are fused together without distinct identities. Or there may be too much individuality at the expense of togetherness. This can lead to what Bowen called "cut-offs"—that is, family members are disconnected or estranged from each other. Either extreme is a sign of immaturity or of a low level of differentiation in the family. Although the balance of these two basic forces may differ between cultures, Bowen sees the struggle between them as universal.

Differentiation is the underlying goal of all Bowenian therapy. Differentiation is the mature balancing of togetherness and individuality in one's family. One is differentiated to the degree that one can maintain intense emotional togetherness with family members while still maintaining one's own individuality. It is important to note that the concept of differentiation is not the same as those of separation, individuation, or autonomy as described in most developmental theories. The goal is not to grow up and disconnect from one's parents. Rather, the goal is to be able to maintain an emotional connection with significant others, including one's parents, while maintaining one's own sense of self. Disconnecting from others is just as immature as losing oneself in others, and these two are thus opposite sides of the same coin.

Bowen argued that each family has its own level of differentiation. Individuals within a family may vary in their maturity within a limited range, but for the most part we inherit our level of reactivity from our families. Reactivity is the tendency to react automatically to the emotional forces of the family. According to Bowen, more differentiated family members can better differentiate between their intellectual and emotional functioning. The less differentiated that family members are, the more reactive they are—that is, the more they are controlled by their emotional functioning and the patterns of the family system. The more reactive and less differentiated a family system, the more emotional and relational problems that system is likely to have. Fortunately, through therapy, we can gain more control over our reactivity in order to reach a more functional level of differentiation.

The implication for couples is clear. We bring our reactivity from our families of origin into all our relationships, particularly the intimate ones. For Bowen, as for Hendrix, the goal is to prevent reactivity from taking control, by helping partners contain reactivity and thus become more conscious and intentional in the relationship.

Anxiety and Family Patterns

When we are under stress, our functioning becomes less differentiated, and we are more reactive. For Bowen, when a family system experiences stress and uncertainty, anxiety in the system begins to rise. Systemic anxiety is different from individual anxiety; it is a measure of the degree of tension and reactivity in the system. When the anxiety in the family system is high, family patterns become more rigid and automatic, and family members more reactive. Besieged family systems, like individuals, seem to cling rigidly to old behavior patterns. Not surprisingly, the couples we see in crisis are often at their worst.

Much of Bowen's extensive description of family functioning details the multitude of ways a family system can handle anxiety. Interestingly, not all family members are affected by systemic anxiety. But the less differentiated a family, the more it is vulnerable to systemic anxiety. When stress goes up, more people will become reactive, and functioning will be more impaired. In families with a low level of differentiation, just a little anxiety may create extensive problems, but in fact almost any family enduring enough stressors and losses may become more reactive and dysfunctional. According to Bowen, systemic anxiety that is not adequately dealt with in one generation will be passed down to the next generation. It is unfortunately a case of the "sins" of the parents being visited on the children. A major motivation for many in Bowenian therapy is to short-circuit this multigenerational process.

Another major focus of Bowenian therapy is the analysis of family patterns. These are the behavior and relationship patterns that describe how a family system operates. For example, there is a strong tendency in many families, whenever tension develops between two people, to involve a third party in the interaction and to shift the focus toward that person. This process is called triangulation. It is predictable that whenever the tension or anxiety in a system reaches a high enough level, triangles will begin to form. This is common in couples who, rather than dealing with problems between them, are always focusing on something external to the relationship, be it the in-laws, an ex-spouse, a problem child, television, or the bottle. Thus, the problems in the relationship are not faced and often become worse. A Bowenian would predict that a similar pattern of triangulation would also be found in previous generations.

A catalogue of different family patterns is beyond the scope of this chapter. Suffice it to say, Bowenians spend much time in therapy uncovering these family patterns both in present and past generations, believing that the more awareness one has of one's unhealthy family patterns, the more ability one has to change them.

For therapists working with couples, some of the most useful family patterns to understand are those involving negative feedback loops or vicious cycles. The feedback loop—the tendency for a sequence of interactions in a system to repeat itself and intensify whatever is happening in the system—is a characteristic of all systems. A classic vicious cycle for couples is the pursuer-distancer relationship. One partner seeks intimacy and emotional closeness while the other partner wants distance and more emotional space. The more the pursuer pursues, the more the distancer distances, setting up a vicious cycle of pursuit and distance. It is as if each person's overreaction to the other brings out the worst in the other. (Hendrix describes a similar maximizer-minimizer cycle in which each person does exactly what most "wounds" the other, but his explanation is characterological rather than systemic.)

From a systemic perspective, such interactional cycles are a natural part of how systems work. They help keep a system stable. As problematic as pursuer-distancer relationships might be, they can persist for years. Partners become used to their role in the relationship and become interdependent on one another to continue the cycle. Although family patterns may predispose someone of a particular sex or sibling position to take one role or another, the systems perspective focuses more on the dynamics of the repeating cycle than on the characteristics of any one individual. In fact, partners in a relationship may begin with one person being slightly a pursuer and the other slightly a distancer, but the polarizing effect of a vicious cycle can create intense pursuers and distancers in a short period of time. It is even possible for partners to switch roles, as we often see when the pursuer begins to create distance or decides to leave the relationship.

Fortunately, not all cycles are vicious. There are also virtuous cycles, as we have all seen in the dialogical process, in which understanding leads to more understanding, and giving leads to more giving.

Therapist as Coach

Bowen saw his role in therapy as that of a coach. Rather than encouraging an artificial transference relationship in the therapy room, Bowen focused on coaching people in understanding and changing the most important relationships in their lives. Bowen de-emphasized the role of technique in therapy. He believed that if the therapist-coach had a good grasp of systemic thinking and could communicate this understanding to the system while remaining nonreactive, then the system would be more likely to change.

Therapy proceeds from grasping an understanding of one's family system to changing one's role in that system. The goal is to develop a more differentiated position in one's family, where one can stay emotionally connected to family members while expressing one's own individuality. The Bowenian coach strategically plans the client's visits to the client's family of origin, exploring and suggesting ways the client can change how he or she interacts in reactive family patterns. This is not as easy as it may sound. In most families, the established reactive patterns are very strong. It may take numerous phone calls, letters, or visits home before the client can become less reactive and more differentiated.

In Bowenian therapy, it is not one's goal to change other family members. This is seen as a sure-fire way of becoming part of a reactive system. Most family systems are used to reformers and are quite capable of neutralizing them. Only by taking personal responsibility for one's own behavior and ideas, and forging nonreactive, noncoercive, emotionally involved relationships with other family members can one raise one's functional level of differentiation.

Bowenians who work with couples usually see personal differentiation as the *sine qua non* of a healthy relationship. Partners are encouraged to look at the family-of-origin issues and patterns that they bring into the relationship and to work to become less reactive with each other. Both partners are asked to take personal responsibility for their own growth and needs in the relationship.

Commonalities

It is hoped that the description in this chapter, though abbreviated, provides some sense of Bowen's family systems approach to working with couples. Some readers may be wondering what any of this has to do with IRT. So let us now explore some of the commonalities between the two approaches.

The Role of Nature

Both Bowen and Hendrix are "big" thinkers. That is, neither is content to simply see himself as trying to help people in distress; rather, both strive to understand the meaning of the relational process in the greater scheme of things. Interestingly, both are philosophical naturalists. Both see relationships as a crucial aspect of nature and evolution. Bowen sees the relational process as part of a larger evolutionary trend that interconnects the different parts of a system into a functioning, stable organism (Kerr & Bowen, 1988, p. 253). Hendrix sees marriage as nature's way of healing itself (Hendrix, 1992b, p. 45). Admittedly, Hendrix is more teleological ("nature healing itself") and metaphorical ("the tapestry of being") in his description of nature.

Both theorists use similar biological explanations to understand why relationship and individual change is so difficult. Bowen sees much of our automatic tendencies to react in social situations as biologically programmed into us by our evolutionary history. Our automatic reactions come from our limbic system, whereas our ability to deliberate and make intentional decisions comes from our neocortex (Kerr & Bowen, 1988, p. 35). Bowen, in fact, sees our "emotional" functioning as being the part of who we are that we hold in common with all the other species. Hendrix also sees the Imago process as automatic and as rooted in the unconscious functioning of the "old" brain, rather than as being part of the intentional abilities of the "new" brain (Hendrix, 1992b, p. 40). For both theorists, a therapeutic goal is to become less automatic in our biologically based reactions. Bowen is less optimistic than Hendrix in how fully humans can accomplish this.

Unresolved Issues

Both Bowen and Hendrix are also developmental theorists who see many of today's difficulties as being rooted in the developmental snags or unresolved issues of the past. Hendrix, like Freud, focuses on the events of early childhood. The most critical events are what Hendrix calls the "wounds" of childhood. Although such wounds can occur at any time during childhood, the most painful and damaging ones are usually inflicted in the first few years of life. Wounds are the ways in which parents either intentionally or inadvertently did not meet the needs of the child. Such needs that are not met continue to exert themselves into adulthood. For Hendrix, this is the basis of the imago match: partners who embody the qualities of the other partner's parents, who did not meet their child's needs. They couple in the attempt to finally get those needs met. For Bowen, the developmental focus is not on the individual but on the family system. Unresolved family issues span the generations, not just the lifetimes of the family members involved. How the family dealt with systemic anxiety generations ago can still be having an impact on the family today. Although their scope is different, both theorists use the unresolved issues of the past to understand the present.

Complementarity

Both family systems theory and IRT use complementarity as an important concept for understanding relationship dynamics. Complementarity involves the fitting together of differences in a relationship to create an interdependent whole.[3] For Bowen, relationships become unbalanced, and partners take complementary roles as a way of coping with systemic anxiety and of stabilizing the system. For example, when one partner becomes the pursuer while the other partner becomes the distancer, a typical systemic feedback process (the vicious cycle) may take over and polarize and exacerbate the differences. For Hendrix, complementarity comes from the imago selection process. A basic premise of IRT is that in order to be healed we search for a mate who has characteristics similar to the parents who wounded us. Our imago match often has many of the most distressing qualities of our caretakers—usually, those that we have worked hardest to suppress in ourselves. The result is that the partner we choose is often the complement of ourselves. Thus, a maximizer chooses a minimizer, and vice versa. From this perspective, complementarity leads to the "power struggle" but is also part of the healing process.

Mate Selection

Bowen and Hendrix are quite similar in their theories of mate selection. Even though the partners might be very different in a number of ways, both theorists would agree that people unconsciously choose partners who are near the same level of emotional development as themselves. For Bowen, this means that partners select those who are near the same level of differentiation (Kerr & Bowen, 1988, p. 225). For Hendrix, this means that partners select mates who have become stuck at similar levels of child and adolescent development (Hendrix, 1992b, p. 60). The critical point for both theorists is that despite apparent differences in personality or behavior, it is more likely than not that both partners in a relationship are very similar in their basic maturity and emotional functioning.

Therapist as Coach

There is also a convergence in the two approaches as regards the role of the therapist. Both Bowen and Hendrix view the therapist as more of a coach than a significant emotional figure in the therapy. Bowen realized many years ago that if his goal was to assist people in working with their emotionally significant others (that is, family members), then his role as a transferential object was not only unnecessary but could be disruptive to the therapeutic process. Bowenians have even developed ways to minimize transference in the therapeutic relationship. Hendrix has come to similar conclusions in describing his therapeutic stance. For the Imago therapist, the therapeutic focus should be on the couple's relationship, not the relationship between the couple and the therapist. Hendrix has also described therapy as "coaching" the couple in healing each other through the use of Couples Dialogue and other processes.

Critical Issues

Despite the aforementioned commonalities, there are some important differences in the two approaches that I will now review.

Emotionality

Probably the most misunderstood concept in Bowen's theory is that of emotionality. Many have criticized Bowen for favoring the rational and cognitive over the emotional side of life. Bowen has written that in more differentiated people the "intellect recognizes that a bit of discipline is needed to overrule the emotional system" (Kerr & Bowen, 1988, p. 35). In Bowenian therapy, much effort is expended to cognitively understand one's family system and control one's emotional reactivity in dealing with one's family. There is often little focus on what the client is feeling during the session.

It is important to recognize that Bowen used the term "emotional system" in his own peculiar way. For Bowen, the emotional system does not refer to feelings or the affective life. It is a much broader concept, "defined to include all of an organism's mechanisms for driving and guiding it through life" (Kerr & Bowen, 1988, p. 28). The emotional system is the automatic behavioral wiring that we all have inherited through evolution. Feelings and affect are the natural product of our biological heritage that automatically go into operation within the family system.

This brings us to the real reason why I believe Bowenians do not feel they need to encourage affect. Emotionality and reactivity are among the most common phenomena in family relationships. Bowen believed that at best we can function on a conscious, nonreactive level maybe only 10 percent of the time. In many therapies, emotional exploration is encouraged in the therapy room, where it is easy for individuals to stay calm or guard their feelings. A major focus of many therapies is to work to uncover repressed or guarded feelings. Bowenians, however, believe that once people begin to intervene in their own families, feelings and affect will be everywhere. The Bowenian therapist usually does not have to worry that emotions will be repressed. The more likely concern is that the feelings that do come out will be explosive and destructive and will not lead to real change in the system. The goal of Bowenian therapy is to help people choose the when and how of the expression of their strongest feelings, and not be overwhelmed by their own reactivity or the systemic anxiety and automatic reactions of the family.

The contrast with IRT is dramatic. Although there is a strong educational and cognitive component in IRT, there is also a great emphasis on emotional expression. Through creating a safe environment with the Couples Dialogue, partners are encouraged to let down their defenses and reveal their wounded vulnerable selves to each other. They may even be encouraged to regress in their feelings to a time in childhood when they were wounded, allowing the child within to be heard and validated by a soothing, comforting partner. When partners' anger is interfering with their reimaging, the therapist may use a Container exercise to both intensify and contain the anger. Clearly, IRT does not avoid the expression of strong emotions in the session.

What is less clear in IRT is what is seen as the main healing process when couples are encouraged to share their intense emotions. Is the emotional catharsis in itself healing? Is it the hope that the adult wounded child will finally get his or her basic childhood needs met by an understanding partner? Is it that the adult wounded child is finally allowed to express the pain and then be mirrored, validated, and responded to empathically by someone with characteristics of the person who inflicted the wound? Or is it the increasing ability of the receiving partner to contain his or her reactions (facilitated by the dialogical process) while listening to the partner's accusations and pain, which leads to emotional growth and maturity? Or could it be the sending partner's strengthened ability to contain his or her anger long enough to send a message that can be heard? If it is the last two, then the two approaches are not that far apart after all. Both are concerned with learning to contain one's reactivity.

Nevertheless, there is a difference in the loci of emotional action in the two therapies. The Bowenian therapist plans how the individual will interact with the family, often hoping to keep the emotionality down long enough to allow something new to happen in the system. Actually, Bowenian therapists will sometimes plan ways to generate feelings and anxiety in the family system in order to get the family unstuck, but the emotionality occurs outside the session. The Imago therapist brings what he or she considers the most important relationship in the system—the couple—into the session and uses intense emotional sharing to promote mutual healing.

Shame and Blame

All therapies must address the issue of shame. Many (if not most) people go into therapy already feeling inadequate, believing that there is something seriously wrong with them or that they should be able to handle their problems on their own. This sense of shame often undermines their morale and makes it difficult to take the steps necessary to solve their problems.

A challenge for any therapeutic approach is to explain the source of the therapeutic problem in a way that does not promote even more shame. Part of the brilliance of the psychoanalytic approach was that it provided a rationale for irrational or maladaptive behavior (the unconscious) that did not blame or impugn the intentions of the individual. In fact, the individuals undergoing psychoanalytic therapy often would feel relief when they realized that they were not to blame for their problems and that there was still something they could do to overcome the forces of the unconscious.

Family systems theory has had to deal with a comparable problem in interpersonal relationships: the tendency for everyone in a system to blame others for what goes wrong. Such blame often leads to defensiveness and paralyzing shame, and is more likely to perpetuate family problems than to solve them. Even more difficult for the therapist is recognizing that joining in the judgmental process will invariably alienate some part of the system. Only by seeing the family system in its totality can one avoid the problem of judging one part of the system in favor of another. In other words, therapists who work with families need a way to look at the individuals involved that allows them not to blame anyone. Systems theory is just such a way; it views everyone as interdependent and subject to the dysfunctional patterns of a larger system. All are seen as contributing toward the problem, yet also as well intentioned and doing the best they can, given their role and experiences within the system.

IRT has had to deal with the same issue with couples. Almost all partners come into therapy feeling that the other is to blame and is the one who needs to change. This blaming process is an essential part of the power struggle. IRT's solution to the blame problem is an ingenious one. First, it normalizes this control battle as a necessary prelude to the Imago healing process and the development of a conscious relationship. Next, it provides a rationale for problems in the relationship by focusing on the wounds of childhood. By helping each spouse see the other as a wounded child, IRT replaces blame and control with compassion and understanding. Finally, IRT reframes the differences between the spouses not as something to be blamed or changed but as disowned parts of the spouses that are waiting to be discovered and that offer an opportunity for healing.

From a systemic point of view, I believe that there is one unfortunate consequence of the Imago displacement of blame: the parents are often blamed instead. Hendrix clearly asserts that parents should not be blamed for wounding their children. After all, they too were wounded as children. But I believe that this point is all too easily forgotten in the process of therapy. Part of the powerful emotional Imago therapeutic process involves the wounded children getting in touch with their anger and disappointment in their parents. This blaming of parents often displaces their blaming their spouse.

An important difference exists in the way the two approaches address the issue of blame. Family systems theory says no one is to blame, whereas IRT says, in a sense, that everyone is to blame: the parents for wounding their children, their parents who did the same to them, and so on. Even the term *wound* is a powerful metaphor for one person harming another. The family systems view of family dysfunction is both more benign and more pessimistic. For the most part, family systems theory prefers to see people not so much as harming each other as being caught in the same unfortunate family patterns. The view is pessimistic because such patterns are seen as part of the human condition and not changeable by way of parents becoming "perfect."

Individual Responsibility

In trying to avoid blame, the therapist must also confront the opposite side of the ledger: the problem of individual responsibility. On the one hand, we do not want to blame our clients, but on the other hand, we do want them to take individual responsibility. In this area as well, Bowenian and Imago therapists take different approaches.

The problem of individual responsibility brings us to one of the major critiques of systems theory. Many advocates who seek to protect the rights of victims have seen systems theory as providing excuses for those who perpetrate injustices. One of the most obvious examples is that of spousal abuse. If both spouses are caught in the system, reacting to one another and following old family scripts, family systems theorists often assert that everyone in the system is contributing to the problem. Feminist theorists have accused family systems theorists of ignoring the true power differential often present in abusive relationships. However, there is nothing in systems theory that says power is not an important factor in understanding family process. Just because everyone is contributing to the continuance of the system does not mean that everyone is contributing equally. In fact, a number of family therapy approaches have particularly focused on power and hierarchy in the system (Haley, 1976; Minuchin, 1974). Nevertheless, in their effort to avoid blame and in the rush to see each person's contribution to the problem, family systems therapists may too easily forget that sometimes particular individuals need to be held accountable for their behavior.

The issue of individual responsibility is a major focus in Bowenian therapy. Bowen insists that each family member work individually on his or her own contribution and role in the family system. Part of becoming less reactive is taking individual responsibility for one's reactions to others. In couples therapy, each partner is encouraged to make "I" statements and take a "self-focus"—that is, to look at his or her own contribution to the problem. This usually involves looking at the family-of-origin issues that one has brought to the relationship and learning to work through those issues within the appropriate relationships—that is, within one's family of origin. Each partner is responsible for limiting as much as possible the spillover of unresolved multigenerational issues into their relationship and future generations. Many Bowenians are hesitant to assign concrete tasks or exercises to couples because they believe that differentiation and personal responsibility require that clients come up with their own solutions. Bowen was very much against technique for this reason. Imago therapists, in contrast, view techniques or processes (for example, the Couples Dialogue or developing a Relationship Vision) as giving couples the tools for developing a more conscious relationship.

On the surface, in IRT, it might appear that individual responsibility is replaced by mutual responsibility. Partners are encouraged to see one another as wounded children and to agree to provide a safe environment for healing. When IRT really works, each partner becomes a sort of therapist for the other. Each partner "stretches" to give what the other partner really wants. But what of individual responsibility? Paradoxically, IRT has been very careful to include personal responsibility in its general framework for mutual caretaking. In the No Exit process, each partner is encouraged to make a personal commitment to the relationship. Through the Couples Dialogue, partners are taught how to make their own needs heard. Each partner is responsible for initiating Couples Dialogue when he or she needs it, expressing frustrations, and making Behavior Change Requests. Each partner is also personally responsible for mirroring, validating, and empathizing, and for making it safe for the other to communicate. In the end, the Couples Dialogue allows both partners the opportunity to take individual responsibility for giving one another what is really wanted, rather than what they *think* is wanted.

IRT also encourages individual responsibility by emphasizing the "conscious" relationship, one in which partners are making conscious, deliberate choices in working toward their relationship vision and no longer reacting almost solely to their imago projections and childhood wounds. As one's wounds begin to be healed with the help of one's partner, one becomes more responsible in maintaining a more conscious relationship. More subtly, the whole process is framed as a voluntary one. It is each partner's choice to help the other. In requesting a dialogue, one respects the other person's needs and space by asking for an appointment. An agreement to make behavioral changes is seen as a "gift" rather than an obligation. Again, the focus is on each person's responsibility for providing a mutually healing and safe environment, rather than each person's right to depend on and demand from the other.

Interdependence involves individual responsibility in the context of mutual cooperation. I believe both theories strive for this ideal but come at it from different directions. Bowenians tend to focus on what gets in the way of individual responsibility, believing that healthier relationships and better cooperation come with less reactivity. From the beginning, Bowenians try to break the spell of fusion—that is, the immature need for the other to meet all of one's needs. In contrast, IRT starts at the level of most people at the early stages of therapy—that is, needing and desiring fusion. Then, within the promise of a mutually need-satisfying relationship, the Imago therapist nudges each partner toward taking individual responsibility for giving and receiving in his or her relationship.

Focus of Intervention

The considerations discussed here lead Bowenian and Imago therapists to have very different foci of intervention. For the Bowenian therapist, the focus is on the individual's relationship to his or her family of origin. Family members are coached to take individual responsibility for their reactivity and change their position or role in their family relationships. Because multigenerational family patterns are so influential, the most potentially liberating relationships to change are those with the preceding generation, particularly one's parents. If one can be more differentiated and less reactive with one's parents, one may be able to change in small ways the multigenerational transmission process. This is recognized by Bowenians to be a very difficult process, requiring a great of deal of analysis, strategizing, planning, and courage. Even when Bowenian therapists are working with couples, they are still likely to focus at times on each partner's family-of-origin relationships.

In contrast, the focus of intervention for Imago therapists is the intimate couple. Imago therapists feel they are able to bring into the therapy all the important unresolved childhood issues without directly involving the family of origin. After all, we continue our childhood issues with our imago match partner, who has many of the most difficult and problematic characteristics of our parents. Both partners recreate the core scenes from their childhoods in their relationship with each other. This is the source of the power struggle and why intimate relationships invariably seem so frustrating. However, Imago therapists also see the Imago process as a tremendous opportunity for growth, and through IRT, partners resolve to meet one another's unmet childhood needs. Theoretically, the setup is perfect, because each partner should now be able to get from the other (who is like his or her frustrating parent in many ways) what the partner was more than likely unable to get from that parent: mirroring, validation, and empathy. The healing potential of a validating, fully conscious, intimate relationship is seen as capable of undoing the wounds of childhood. When partners are able to provide safe, nurturing, healing environments for each other and can learn to contain their reactivity to one another, it may not be necessary to confront the original source of the wounding. Even when the Imago therapist is working with singles, his or her focus is on helping individuals clear the roadblocks to, and prepare for, a transformational intimate relationship.

Deprivation and Adaptation

There is a metatheoretical difference between family systems theory and IRT that pervades all the discussion here, which has to do with the role of deprivation and deficits in understanding human problems. Freud and the psychoanalytic tradition, following the medical model, have tended to see human problems as diagnosable neuroses resulting from childhood deprivations. Theirs is a developmental deficit model; that is, certain childhood needs were not met, and adult problems are the result. Alternatively, family systems theory has adopted an adaptive or functional model of human problems. Problems, rather than being seen as resulting from an illness or disorder, are usually viewed as "problems in living," or functional adaptations to living in ever-changing systems. Family patterns develop because they work to maintain the system. They become problematic for the family when conditions change and the family doesn't. Family patterns become problematic for the individual when a family member's functioning is sacrificed in service of the family system.

Hendrix, following the psychoanalytic tradition, views relationship problems in terms of childhood deprivation. "Wounding" and "healing" are strong emotional metaphors for describing the deprivation and restoration experience. In contrast, Bowen sees human functioning as adaptation to ongoing changes in an evolving system. Problems may be both a reaction to organizational stress and change, and a functional adaptation in the service of the system. To highlight these differences, let us consider which child would be most at risk in a family, according to these two theoretical approaches. From the IRT perspective, it would be the child who received the least positive attention from the parents during the most critical developmental period. Having been ignored and unnurtured, and possibly criticized and shamed, that child would be "wounded" and go through life seeking the essential validation and empathy from which he or she was deprived. Maturity would require a "healing" of those wounds. In contrast, from the Bowenian perspective, the child perceived to be most at risk would be the one who received most of the parents' attention, either positive or negative. This would be the child who would be most likely to be inducted into the system and to sacrifice his or her functioning for the stability of the system. Ignored or forgotten children, although they may complain of a lonely, deprived childhood, may actually function better than their more attended to or recognized siblings.

Toward Integration

Can two such different approaches with their unique focuses and biases be somehow integrated? First, we must distinguish three types of integration: theoretical, empirical, and therapeutic. A theoretical integration would involve developing a common terminology and overarching constructs that would incorporate the basic concepts from both approaches. Ideally, an integrative framework would resolve all the inconsistencies and incompatibilities between the two theories without losing the richness of either. In reality, most efforts at theoretical integration have involved assimilating one theory into another. I do not believe a theoretical integration would be acceptable to either approach at this time.

A less comprehensive effort would be what I call an empirical integration. This involves letting research determine under what circumstances and conditions each approach is applicable or not. For example, when is it more useful to focus on the couple rather than on the family of origin? Without even trying to resolve philo-

sophical differences, let empirical research settle testable differences. Of course, theoretical differences will eventually come into
play. Do we measure therapeutic outcome by degrees of "healing"
or "reactivity"? Nevertheless, we could develop empirical constructs
that apply across both approaches. The necessary research has not
yet been done.

Finally, we come to what I call a therapeutic integration. One difference between doing therapy and science is that as therapists we
do not have the luxury of waiting until social scientists have resolved
the important theoretical and empirical questions before we make
therapeutic decisions in our efforts to be helpful. Every day we have
to make critical decisions that affect other people's lives, often based
on insufficient information and unproven theoretical assumptions.
We do this, I believe, by weighing what is scientifically "known" and
combining the different theoretical approaches we have learned into
a therapeutic integration that works for us based on our experiences
and biases. No, we are not able as therapists to resolve all the conceptual and empirical problems and inconsistencies posed to us by
the different theories we embrace. So we learn to live with inconsistencies and develop heuristic rules for when to use what and for
what reason. At worst, such therapy is an eclectic hodgepodge of inconsistent concepts and techniques. At best, it is a well thought out
integration with relatively clear rationales for when to do which type
of therapy. What follows are some of my thoughts for integrating the
family systems and IRT approaches.

Different Stories

I see the two approaches as evoking two very different stories or
dramas of the human condition. Family systems theory, as developed by Bowen and his followers, focuses on the multigenerational
family saga, a chronicle that shows the individual as caught up in
an historical web of intrigue and drama that flows down through
the generations. Not surprisingly, in this tale individual behavior
and adaptation are often explained in terms of the person's historical and interpersonal context, which is the theoretical contribution of family systems theory. IRT focuses on the personal quest
to get one's childhood needs met and the resulting marital melodrama. Here we have the story of the wounded adult child seeking

to connect with another in order to be healed and the sometimes tragic, often farcical, relationships that develop in this quest. Again, not surprisingly, in this tale individual behavior is usually explained in terms of the imago psychodrama—events occurring in the minds of the actors involved. The genius of IRT is the development of language and experiential exercises that bring into awareness this psychodrama in a powerfully emotional way.

The different therapies are a response to these two very different stories. In a sense, Bowenians try to add the individual hero to a story that seems overwhelmed by family emotional forces. Alternatively, Imago therapists add the transformational potential of the relationship to a story of individual needs and narrow self-interest. For both, therapy can be seen to add what is missing in each story: the individual hero is added to the family saga (Bowenian), and the transformational relationship is added to the personal quest (Imago).

For therapists who believe that both tales are shaping dramas of the human condition, the challenge lies in determining when to focus on which story. Perhaps in an ideal world we would have the time to develop both stories to their fullest potential. But in a world of limited resources, managed care, and people wanting timely relief, we often have to make hard choices. We focus on one approach or another in order to get the job done.

For me, the crucial decision is over which story is most likely to lead to change at each point in the therapy. Often, a couple comes into my office ripe for beginning the process of understanding and healing each other. Perhaps they have taken an Imago workshop[4] or have not been struggling so long that they have completely lost their loving feelings. They seem ready and eager to find a concrete way out of their impasse, and the Couples Dialogue and other Imago processes prove very helpful. Interestingly, as the relationship improves, family-of-origin issues sometimes arise, leading to a focus on the family saga.

All too often, however, a very different type of couple will come into my office. This is what I call the "high anxiety" couple. The conflict and anger may be overt, with the couple screaming at each other in my office. Or the tension may be below the surface, but so intense that one can cut it with a knife. The couple may be glaring at each other or seem totally indifferent to one another. In either case, the power struggle and mutual wounding have been going on for so long, and the anxiety in the system is so high, that the relationship is not yet a safe place for mutual growth and healing. This is when I find the family saga very useful.

Clinical Example

The wife called, saying she wanted to set up an appointment for marital counseling, and quickly proceeded to let me know that her husband had a problem with irresponsibility. There was a tinge of contempt and righteousness in her voice that made me uncomfortable. We set up the appointment.

EARLY TREATMENT

The Thorns[5] walked into my office in obvious distress. Mr. Thorn had a hangdog look, as if he felt he couldn't do anything right. Mrs. Thorn looked angry and disapproving, as if she agreed. They were handsome-looking people, dressed immaculately, and both clearly cared about their appearance. He was a lawyer, and she owned a small company. I asked them how I could be helpful. Mrs. Thorn immediately answered that her husband had, over the last two years, become withdrawn and unable to get his work done. She feared that there would be serious economic consequences unless he soon began to fulfill his responsibilities. Mr. Thorn said in a subdued, emotionless voice that he believed there were marital problems that they needed help to work out.

I asked both of them to write down what they thought the other would say were their biggest frustrations in the marriage. Mr. Thorn came up with a list of fifteen complaints, all having to do with his failing to perform one of his responsibilities as a husband or father. These ranged from his not cutting the grass to his not being an exciting sexual partner. His wife added a few more. Mrs. Thorn could think of only one complaint that her husband might have of her: that she was always on his case. He agreed and could think of nothing else to add to her list. I asked them to tell me how the problem began. Things began to change in the marriage when their daughter, now four years old, was born. Both agreed that they took their parenting responsibilities very seriously and that much of their focus had been on the daughter and their work, rather than their relationship. However, about two years earlier the husband became withdrawn and depressed. His work suffered, and although he still spent much time with his daughter, he could never get his household duties done. His family physician gave him some antidepressant medication, which made him feel better but did not solve his motivational problem. The wife felt unsupported and overwhelmed, would plead, complain, and eventually badger her husband, all to no avail. When she asked him what was wrong, he would simply say that he felt there was something missing in the marriage, but didn't know what it was. That was why they were here.

I decided to coach them through the Couples Dialogue. Neither of them did very well. He either could not remember what she said so he could mirror it back or said he just did not understand what she was saying. This obviously very intelligent man could not understand the simple complaints his wife was making. She could not let him speak without interrupting to correct or disagree with him. Despite my coaching, she had difficulty containing her reactions so that she could hear her husband. Neither was able to validate or empathize at all. As the session was ending, I reassured them that dialogue would become easier with practice. I gave them an article on IRT to read, and told them that for the next few sessions I would be gathering more information on their backgrounds.

I see my first session with a couple as primarily an assessment as to how I can be most helpful. I want to know how each partner sees the problems, grasp the major relationship frustrations, and hear their stories about how the problems began. If I have time, I also want to see how well they engage in the Couples Dialogue. One early therapeutic decision I must make involves how much background information on each partner's family history I should gather. Putting together a good family genogram and history can take up to two sessions. There is often a trade-off. On the one hand, delaying the couple's work for a few sessions to gather background information may seem to the couple as either irrelevant or unresponsive to their immediate distress. On the other hand, family information is usually easier to gather at the beginning and will often give me an invaluable overview of the family and personal issues contributing to the couple's problems. I know that theoretically important family information should come out in the dialogical exploration of childhood wounds, but a broader systemic understanding demands a more comprehensive exploration. Nevertheless, when the couple is in distress and eager to begin talking to each other, I may forego extensive family histories, sometimes to my later regret. In the case of the Thorns, the decision was easy: I did not think they were ready yet for Couples Dialogue, and I hoped that a focus on individual backgrounds might calm down the system.

LATER TREATMENT

I did in fact apply an individual focus over the next two sessions. Mr. Thorn won the coin toss and told his story first. I did a four-generation genogram.

Mr. Thorn came from a family in which successful sons were heroes and were adored by their mothers. His father was an only son with three sisters and had been the first person in his family to go to college. He was very successful. The father had an especially close relationship with his mother, who was very proud of her accomplished son, but he did not feel very close to his father. Mr. Thorn was the oldest son among his siblings, and great things were expected of him from his parents. He said he had always tried to live up to his parents' ambitions for him, and he was the first person in his family to go to graduate school. He, too, had a very close relationship with his overprotective mother, who felt he could do no wrong. The story was very different with his father. Theirs was a tense, competitive relationship in which the son never felt he received his father's approval. His father went to his grave two-and-a-half years ago without ever once telling his son he was proud of him. Mr. Thorn was determined to be a more nurturing father than his father had been. He also wanted a woman more independent than his mother.

Mr. Thorn went through a dramatic change as he told his family story. In contrast to the lifeless, unanimated character in the first session, he beamed with pride and enthusiasm as he talked about his family's accomplishments. He was almost in tears as he described his disappointment in never receiving his father's validation. The wife remarked that she had not seen him so emotional in years. And for the first time in therapy, she was able to show some empathy toward him, particularly regarding his disappointment in his relationship with his father.

Mrs. Thorn had a very different story to tell. I could get information for only three generations on her genogram. Because her parents had died when she was young (her mother when Mrs. Thorn was five and her father when she was nine), she knew very little about her grandparents, who died before she was born. After her mother died, she was raised by her mother's sister and her husband, who already had five children. Mrs. Thorn felt that she was left alone to raise herself and that she never fit well into her adoptive family. She learned very early to be independent, self-sufficient, and in control. From stories she had heard, she was just like her mother, who had been a strong, outspoken woman. She also was told that her father had been a weak, ineffectual man. As a teenager, she would fantasize about a "knight in shining armor" who would take her away and care for her. As she talked, she made the connection between her dreams and her disappointment in her husband.

Talking about her early childhood was very painful for Mrs. Thorn. At times, she was in tears. Her husband, hearing many of the details for the first time, appeared very concerned and even tried to soothe her at times. The family histories, in addition to providing valuable information, had begun the Imago process, each partner reimaging the other in a more sympathetic light as wounded children.

In the session following the history taking, I felt they were ready to try the Couples Dialogue again. It went much better this time around. Much of the edge had disappeared. Even though the couple still needed coaching on how to validate even when they disagreed, they were beginning to hear each other. Over a number of sessions, they practiced the Couples Dialogue by talking about their frustrations, and they also made Behavior Change Requests. Mr. Thorn was even able to expand his list of frustrations with his wife, mostly around his desire to feel more appreciated by her.

We went over Imago theory, particularly regarding the unconscious process of mate selection, and they completed the Profiles of Childhood Caretakers and Partners from the *Couples Therapy Manual* (Hendrix, 1992b). Upon learning the results of these profiles and their family stories, the Thorns were able to see why they had selected each other. Mr. Thorn had wanted someone more independent than his mother but had ended up with someone whom he perceived as judgmental and demanding like his father. Mrs. Thorn wanted someone who would take care of her, but had ended up with someone she experienced as weak and ineffectual like her father. They could see that he had been stronger and she more appreciative earlier in the marriage. Somehow they were bringing out the worst in each other.

The greatest emotional intensity came out in the Parent-Child Dialogues. Mrs. Thorn was able to talk to her mother about her pain at being abandoned and having to grow up so fast. She asked her father why he had not cared for her when her mother died. Mr. Thorn was able to talk to his father about never being good enough for him. He was also able to talk to his mother about her overprotectiveness and overdependency on him. Even though both spouses recognized that the other was talking to them as well as to the imagined parent, they were able to understand the other's pain, maintain the role play, and offer reparation both as parent and spouse.

CLOSING STAGES OF TREATMENT

The relationship improved. There were many setbacks, and therapy did not always go as well as this condensed, highlighted account might suggest, but slowly and surely both partners began to hear each other's pain. Mr. Thorn struggled to become reinvolved with his wife and family, and Mrs. Thorn struggled to be less critical and more appreciative of what her husband *did* do. In addition, they began to structure nurturing time into their relationship.

Although Mr. Thorn became more involved with his family, things were not improving in his work life. He just could not get himself motivated to tackle the huge backlog of work that he had let pile up. He felt hopeless. Almost guiltily, he asked if he could focus on his work rather than relationship issues. His wife readily agreed, as this was why she had wanted to come to therapy in the first place. His work had begun to suffer when his father was ailing and died, and I was convinced that he had gone on strike psychologically at that time. Focusing on Mr. Thorn's relationship with his father, I coached him on how to gather more information on his father's family, both from his mother and his father's sisters. We were able to reconstruct in more detail why his father had been so competitive and withholding and why he was so threatened by a son who might be even more successful than he had been. I had Mr. Thorn write letters to his father and present them at his grave site. Mr. Thorn finally began to grieve the loss of his father and to understand why he had given up when he realized he would never be able to please him. We even role-played what he would have liked his father to have said to him. He was eventually able to find a friend of his father who had told him that his father was secretly proud of his son. Although he said he didn't believe it, all this work on his relationship with his father seemed to lead to a more relaxed, more energetic individual. Slowly he began to tackle his workload. Following her husband's improvement, Mrs. Thorn decided to work on some issues with the living aunt who had cared for her when her mother died.

Not all my cases are so successful. And it is possible that a more experienced Imago therapist could have accomplished the same thing without gathering all the family history. Or a better family systems therapist could have done just as well working directly with each partner on his or her family-of-origin issues. However, because I find the personal quest and marital melodrama of IRT and Bowen's family saga such fascinating and meaningful tales, I choose to use these stories in my therapy when it seems appropriate to do so.

Notes

1. Actually, a couple can also be seen as a subsystem in the larger family context. This is true of most systems; that is, they are subsystems when viewed in a larger context.

2. In fact, Bowen tended to de-emphasize social context in favor of the biological and multigenerational context. The importance of contextual variables such as gender and ethnicity as compared to universal family system processes has been a source of major debate among Bowenians.

3. Therapists should be aware of a number of specific complementary patterns common in distressed couples. See Gerson, Hoffman, Sauls, and Ulricit (1993) for details.

4. Some people come to me asking for IRT, and we immediately begin with the Couples Dialogue. This makes my decision very easy.

5. All the facts in this composite case have been changed to protect confidentiality.

References

Bowen, M. (1978). *Family therapy in clinical practice.* Northvale, NJ: Aronson.

Gerson, R., Hoffman, S., Sauls, M., & Ulricit, D. (1993). Family of origin frames in couples therapy. *Journal of Marital and Family Therapy, 19*(4), 341–354.

Haley, J. (1976). *Problem-solving therapy: New strategies for effective family therapy.* San Francisco: Jossey-Bass.

Hendrix, R. (1988). *Getting the love you want: A guide for couples.* New York: Henry Holt.

Hendrix, H. (1992a). *Keeping the love you find: A guide for singles.* New York: Simon & Schuster.

Hendrix, H. (1992b). *A couples therapy manual.* New York: Institute for Imago Relationship Therapy.

Kerr, M., & Bowen, M. (1988). *Family evaluation.* New York: Norton.

McGoldrick, M., & Gerson, R. (1985). *Genograms.* New York: Norton.

Minuchin, S. (1974). *Families and family therapy.* Cambridge, MA: Harvard University Press.

Chapter Five

An Exploration of Imago Relationship Therapy and Affect Theory

Joseph Zielinski, Ph.D.

The purpose of this chapter is twofold: first, to introduce the reader to the combination of affect theory and script theory as a system of understanding the biology and socialization of facial affective display and its resultant dynamics; and second, to demonstrate the exquisite interplay between Imago Relationship Therapy (IRT) and affect theory. Both IRT and affect theory have attracted a coterie of professional followers in different though not opposing camps, and the psychotherapeutic community stands to benefit from exposure to both approaches.

IRT in Brief

The uniqueness of IRT rests in its premises of romantic partner selection, the purpose of the stage of romantic love, and the polarity of the power struggle, along with the application of these principles to

Special thanks to Patricia R. Zielinski, Dorothy C. Saynisch, and Stephen Carroll for their personal contributions to the thoughts developed in this chapter, to Sunny and Mark Shulkin and the Philadelphia Imago Relationship Therapy training group from fall 1995, to Vic Kelly for his helpful comments on an earlier draft of this chapter, and to Nordic Track, upon which many of these ideas were born and nurtured.

the therapeutic endeavor. Thus IRT encompasses etiology, dysfunctional process, and therapeutic cure.

IRT (Hendrix, 1988) has been challenged to mature theoretically as other clinical approaches have countered its theory, techniques, and philosophical underpinnings (Bader & Pearson, 1988; Bader, Schnarch, & Hendrix, 1995; Bailey, 1996; Schnarch, 1991). However, an essential ingredient missing from these discussions is the role of affect, its origins, and its salience in couples therapy as well as in all human relationships.

According to Imago theory, romantic partners use complementary defensive styles to deal with overriding anxiety resulting from fears of either abandonment or engulfment. Hendrix (1994) applies the terms *minimizer* and *maximizer* for opposing adaptive styles that develop in response to deficient parenting across childhood developmental stages. Hendrix provides a list of descriptors for how minimizers and maximizers operate in intimate relationships. For the purposes of this chapter, important characteristics include the tendency of the minimizer to internalize and diminish affect and of the maximizer to externalize and expand affect. Given the complementarity hypothesis of mate selection, maximizers tend to marry minimizers, which results in a misfit of affective display and reception.

The importance of safety in relationships is critical, as research suggests that negative experiences color marital satisfaction and have more impact than positive experiences, as though negative qualities command more attention than positive qualities (National Advisory Mental Health Council, 1995). Thus the importance of affect and its modulation in intimate relationships, as well as in IRT, are paramount.

Affect theory, developed over decades by Tomkins (1962, 1963, 1991), offers a compelling view of the processes by which IRT helps couples change.

Basic Tenets of Affect and Script Theory

Affect theory is an interdisciplinary theory of emotion based on the innate biological quality of affects as hard-wired centrally in the brain, neuromuscularly and neurocutaneously displayed on the face, experienced physiologically, and subjected to lifelong shaping by parental and social forces on affect expression (Nathanson, 1992). For Tomkins (1962), affect is a biological event triggered by a stimulus, with each affect being experienced according to its own unique facial neural firing in response to stimulus gradient and density, independent of space and time contexts. Feeling is an indication that an individual has become aware of an affect; emotion is a complex combination of an affect with memories and the affects that the memories themselves trigger (Basch, 1976).

Nathanson (1992) suggests that every emotion consists of a four-part experience initiated by some stimulus, which then triggers an affect. Afterwards, the individual recalls previous experiences of this affect and then reacts to this stimulus in a manner influenced by that affective history. An example would be the jilted lover who responds with distress-anguish to the rejection, who quickly remembers every other significant romantic rejection, and whose affective response now becomes powered by the collection of past rejections. An emotion can give way to mood, a persistent state of emotion in which an individual can remain for hours, even days (Nathanson, 1992). Thus, although affects are building blocks for the experiences of feeling, emotion, and mood, they are not seen in pure form, due to socialization and affect combinations and sequences.

Affect Theory

In affect theory, most of the innate affects are given two-word names that indicate the continuum on which these feelings may be experienced, from the mildest to most extreme version. The positive affects are interest-excitement (opening a wrapped gift) and enjoyment-joy (watching one's children play). These feel wonderful. The neutral affect is surprise-startle (such as when a car backfires), which is so brief that it has no distinctive flavor and functions as a reset mechanism. The negative affects are fear-terror (being robbed at gunpoint), distress-anguish (an unexpected pink slip at work), anger-rage (seeing a grave injustice), disgust (seeing a sloppy drunk behaving badly), and shame-humiliation (a social gaffe), which feel awful. Affect theory notions have no direct relationship to mood disorders or affect disorders as diagnostic entities.

Tomkins (1962) describes each affect as having inherent urgency, an abstract quality, and generality. Each affect is an analogue of its triggering stimulus and interacts with its receptors both to stimulate more affect and to provide the information from which an individual realizes that an affect has been triggered. Finally, affect theory posits that affect can be assembled with any drive, voluntary action, function of the mind, and other affects.

According to Tomkins (1962), affect has the capacity to cause internal contagion, in which each affect may trigger more of the same affect, as well as contagion from the outside—that is, from other people. This contagious quality of affect has such power that adults typically learn how to build a shield of protection from the affective experience of the other person; Nathanson (1992) calls this the empathic wall, a learned mechanism by which an individual can more or less monitor the affect display of another without unwillingly being overwhelmed by the other's affect.

It is not surprising that innate affects can interact with child-rearing and socialization practices. For example, a parental affective excess of anger can create terror of this high-density affect (density being the product of intensity and duration), whereas parental suppression of the display of particular affects can lead to the relative absence of these affects being displayed by children. Difficulties in parental affect modulation are commonplace. They lead to similar difficulties in offspring and are likely to appear yet again in later intimate relationships. Thus, affect theory holds that styles and deficiencies in affect display, regulation, modulation, and inhibition can pass on intergenerationally.

According to Nathanson (1992), the pain of love comes from shame affect, as any impediment to either of the positive affects will be amplified by shame and experienced as hurt feelings. Tomkins (1963) argues that shame is wounding in direct proportion to the degree of preexisting positive affect that it restrains. Thus, the more one is excited by the person who has become the object of love, or the more one anticipates the contentment to be achieved from the relationship, so much more is one susceptible to the misery of shame. Furthermore, Nathanson (1992) argues that love is the sequence that occurs when an infantile need has triggered negative affect and the caregiver responds by providing solace, determining the source of the affect, relieving the underlying need, and accepting the resulting positive affect. According to Nathanson, love implies not only positive affects but also a series of negative and positive affects linked together sequentially to form a scene. From an individual's accumulated scenes of urgent need and solacing, a script develops, one we commonly called love. Finally, Nathanson uses the affect term *disgust* to build a model of the phenomenology of divorce, epitomizing the force and tenacity of marital hate.

Nathanson's masterpiece on shame (1992) offers an affect theory understanding of shame that few have considered. According to Nathanson, defensive scripts around shame fall into four major patterns, which he has named the compass of shame: withdrawal, avoidance, attack-self, and attack-other. Nathanson argues that withdrawal is likely to be accompanied by distress and fear; attack-self by self-disgust; avoidance by excitement, fear, and enjoyment; and attack-other by anger. Nathanson recognizes that in psychotherapy as well as life, shame affect is experienced as a reaction pattern that is determined by the point on the compass of shame where the person has learned to function most comfortably to defend against shame. For Nathanson, what is often seen is shame bundled with the affect of disgust, along with shame embedded in anger, distress, and fear.

Script Theory

In Tomkins's script theory, the basic unit is a scene—that is, any sequence of events linked by the affects triggered during those events. According to Tomkins (1991), all people experience stimulus-affect-response sequences that they assemble into groups, clusters, or families of scenes. At some point in each individual's history, these groups of scenes become capable of triggering new affect. People respond to the patterns into which their affective sequences fall, and these patterns can be assembled into whole groups of scenes that resemble each other on the basis of similar sequences of events and affects. The affective reaction to the group or family of scenes forms a new psychological entity called a script. The affects triggered in response to a family of scenes act on all the affects contained within those scenes; that is, the affect magnifies the contents of a script.

Each individual has relatively few nuclear scripts and scenes, but they are composed of very large numbers of families of such scenes (Tomkins, 1991). Scripts owe their power to the way they accrete analogues and metaphors (Nathanson, 1996). They are cognitive-affective-behavioral templates with which an individual is prepared, by past learning, to interpret, feel, and behave, in a self-fulfilling prophecy fashion, in new situations.

Nuclear scenes are about good events turning bad in the formative years and how the individual reacts to them as a means of regaining the good scene. Nuclear scripts that reward people with deep positive affect leave them forever greedy for more; if punished with deep negative affect, people can never entirely avoid, escape, or renounce the attempt to revenge themselves, despite much punishment (Tomkins, 1991).

A ready example of a positive affect greed nuclear script would be the entrepreneur who repeatedly begins and develops new and successful ventures only to sell them and begin anew, despite the costs to his personal life. This individual is driven by the excitement of novelty but cannot savor the enjoyment of success, tasting instead the distress of boredom. An example of a person using an inescapable negative affect nuclear script is the individual who espouses a strong work ethic toward success but who repeatedly interprets results as less than optimal by focusing on the inevitable disappointments in even positive results. This individual is repeatedly distressed and angered by the unfairness of what is perceived as inadequate rewards for hard work, yet continues to work hard and to be disappointed. Both individuals just described are prone to find themselves, in the future, in similar circumstances (analogues). Such analogues are created both by the individual and by life's circumstances, and the affective responses of each individual are governed by the affective history of the related scripts.

Scripts are not about events per se, but rather about the ideo-affective responses the individual develops in reaction to those events. Nuclear scripts limit flexible responding, and analogues of these scripts continuously evolve within the individual in response to internal and external events. There are no gradations in nuclear script space, which radically diminishes the possibilities of graded responses that might be more effective with good scenes turned bad (Tomkins, 1995, p. 381).

Thus, script theory is one model for understanding marital conflict, the change from romantic love to the power struggle, and the resulting unmodulated intensity of affects and unmet emotional needs. Many nuclear scripts become autonomous of their origins in evolving analogues, which allows individuals to be unwittingly seized by the effects of those scripts. Successful psychotherapy requires the formation of counteractive scripts containing intense affect. Therapists interrupt maladaptive scripts, teach alternative healthy scripts, and set up environments so that corrective scripts can occur. Patients can then begin to build their own new and more functional scripts, which allows them increasing freedom from the constraints of scripts that earlier ran their emotional life (Nathanson, 1996).

Assessment of Intimacy

Kelly (1993) has used affect theory and script theory for the assessment of intimacy. He convincingly argues that there are three interaffective failures of intimacy: failure to maximize positive interpersonal affect, failure to minimize negative interpersonal affect, and failure to minimize the inhibitions of interpersonal affect. Kelly also posits two lack-of-capacity failures in intimacy: first, those resulting from a lack of developmental acquisition, and second, those resulting from a biological interference.

Kelly (1996) defines intimacy as an interaffective process through which the inmost parts of the self are communicated to the other by tangible displays of affect. When successful, the direct, open, and vulnerable verbalization of feelings triggers some of the warmest moments in a loving relationship. According to Kelly, couples must be specifically taught to express their feelings with clarity and precision in the here and now.

Affect Theory as Process

The Imago therapist's role makes considerable demands on the personhood of the therapist: it includes educational, philosophical, and psychological requirements as well as therapeutic holding, persuasion, role modeling, and the maintenance of hope for the couple during their periods of despair. The role also demands the therapist's own continuous evolution in living in a conscious marriage or committed partnership or, alternatively, in effectively coping with the absence or loss of such a relationship. Although effective treatment of a particular diagnostic category does not hinge on the therapist's having suffered from the same disorder, having successfully negotiated a significant portion of the power struggle in his or her own committed relationship would seem to be a core feature of a successful Imago therapist. Traversing the power struggle successfully also exposes the therapist to the full range of affects experienced in a long-term committed partnership. Conversely, the therapist's own partnership can experience a vicarious positive effect as the therapist works with couples whose functioning is improved through the therapy. The therapist may experience shame in the face of couples' success, particularly when their success surpasses that of the therapist's own relationship or, alternatively, distress at couples' failure to fulfill their own potential.

In affect theory terms, the effective Imago therapist will experience interest-excitement and enjoyment-joy in doing therapy and will thus be subject to feeling shame. Management of this shame is necessary to minimize the possibility that the therapist, however inadvertently, will shame the couple. The Imago therapist must develop a flexible and porous empathic wall to become capable of affectively resonating with clients without becoming overwhelmed by couples' positive and negative affects.

Safety and Danger in the Couples Dialogue and Other Techniques

The Couples Dialogue was developed by Hendrix (1988) to create and maintain a sense of safety in couples' communications regarding conflictual issues. Couples introduced to the Couples Dialogue will often experience initial relief (distress reduction) that they will not have to replicate their painful daily interactions in therapy. The Couples Dialogue provides safety through its predictability, ritual, invitation to disclose, and corrective feedback, and the resulting feeling of being heard and understood.

For the sender, there is the potential therapeutic benefit of deepening affect in the process of intimate communication, because if the process goes well, issues from a wounded childhood are often resurrected. Such experiences can be illuminating as well as frightening. In affect theory language, a number of potential affect sequences could result from the practice of the Couples Dialogue. For the sender, shame or fear about self-disclosure and the partner's reaction to it could be salient; so too could shame be experienced if there is interruption of affective resonance anger over a conflictual issue. Fear abatement upon being heard could follow, as well as interest-excitement about what one is sharing and enjoyment-joy at being heard.

With deepening of content, especially in the Parent-Child Dialogue, fear-terror could be awakened by trauma from childhood, but so too could anger-rage, distress-anguish, shame-humiliation, and disgust. For the receiver, there is the responsibility of containment and the temporary suspension of subjective thought, opinion, and affect, with the ever-present possibility of breakthrough under affective volume and pressure from the sender. The receiver must affectively resonate without complete affective contagion and must avoid erecting an impermeable empathic wall. The receiver might feel mild surprise and interest-excitement at what he or she is hearing and mirroring. More likely, however, would be shame induction, no matter how carefully the sender has been sending the message. Given the cognitive and affective disorganization inherent to the physiology of the innate shame affect, this could cause breakdown in the mirroring process, precipitating further shame at the receiver's felt inability to mirror effectively. With conflictual information, anger, fear, and even disgust could be aroused within the receiving partner. Therapist support, coaching, and education about shame dynamics are therapeutic necessities at these interludes.

Although Hendrix (1988) does not specifically address the issue, the affective experiences of the Couples Dialogue can continue for minutes, hours, and days after the therapeutic encounter with or without a therapist, as the cognitive-affective sequences unfold and interact with lifelong affective scripts. When a couple has effectively and consistently used the Couples Dialogue and its variants in place of their customary style, it can be convincingly argued that they have replaced the affective scripts of their past interactions with affective scripts that are more likely to induce positive rather than negative moods (persistent states of emotion [Nathanson, 1992]) in their partner.

Behavior Change Requests

Behavior Change Requests, perhaps more so than the Couples Dialogue, have the potential for generating negative affects in the receiver, as they are most likely to result from negative affects in the sender. Because a Behavior Change Request is a specific request for altered behavior, by definition it directly touches on the inadequacies, imperfections, and lack of wholeness of the partner. They hearken the receiving partner to grow in a manner that is virtually always within a behavioral deficit area that is difficult to change. Generally, the use of the Parent-Child Dialogue before introducing Behavior Change Requests enables both partners to re-vision the other as wounded, which potentially creates mutual empathy and a general lessening of shame-based defenses. Clearly Nathanson's compass of shame conceptualization (1992) makes sense in the use of the Couples Dialogue and Behavior Change Request processes, among other techniques, in that they require the ability to tolerate varying degrees of shame affect without avoiding, withdrawing, attacking the self, or attacking the other to any appreciable degree. The success of these techniques depends on containing shame affect without rupturing the interpersonal bridge (Kaufman, 1985), while the individual makes appropriate behavioral changes for the benefit of his or her partner. Because Behavior Change Requests also require the receiver to stretch into new behaviors that are probably difficult, fear, distress, and anger are commonly elicited in the power struggle couple. Effective teaching of the Behavior Change Request by the therapist ensures only the development of doable requests, which will often create relief (reduction of distress and fear) in the receiver. Long-term, successfully consequated Behavior Change Requests have the potential for eliciting interest-excitement and enjoyment-joy in both partners as the Behavior Change Request receiver consistently gifts his or her partner with the new behavior desired by the sender. Persistent induction of the positive affects will likely endure as positive moods, for the giver will be gifting the Behavior Change Request sender with precisely those things that the sender most desired and that the Behavior Change Request receiver was previously least able to give.

Container Exercises

Container exercises potentially generate the most fear, distress, shame, and disgust in the receiver due to the intensity of anger-rage, disgust, and shame that may be directed at the receiver. It is imperative that Imago therapists guide couples strongly in this area, although couples frequently can force therapists into teaching this technique earlier than therapists might prefer. The Container exercises may superficially resemble maladaptive scripts that the couple has been living out for years, so dense negative affect is likely to be induced in each partner. For the sender, obvious anger-rage, and probably underlying fear, distress, and shame, power the interaction with the ultimate goal of fully experiencing dense distress-anguish, fear-terror, and shame-humiliation. Nonetheless, appropriate modulation of anger over time in the sender, and fear reduction via graded exposure and rehearsal in the receiver decreases the intensity of both negative affects. This allows for the lowering of inhibition in the appropriate expression of negative affect (anger) in the sender and a healthful minimization of negative affect (fear, disgust) in the receiver. At the end of Container exercises, the sender deliberately initiates interest-excitement and enjoyment-joy.

Safety and Danger in Positive Flooding, Caring Behaviors, and Surprises

Interest-excitement and enjoyment-joy are the intended affects of Positive Flooding, and the process does indeed generate these positive affects when properly used. Partners are able to experience an entire continuum of affect ranging from neutral surprise to interest-excitement and enjoyment-joy. Less obvious is the potential for shame, described by Nathanson (1992) as an inborn attenuator system that can be called into operation whenever there is an impediment to the expression of either of the positive affects, enjoyment-joy or interest-excitement. During Positive Flooding, this potential affect can occur in both sender and receiver. Positive Flooding strongly activates entire social learning histories around the giving and receiving of compliments and the giving, showing, and sharing of intense positive affect. Attenuation of positive affect, shame, can occur in the receiver who does not completely believe all or some of the accolades bestowed by the sender. Means of decreasing shame include tuning out (withdrawal on the compass of shame) or internally disputing the positive statements (attack-self, attack-other on the compass of shame).

The sender, too, can experience surprise at his or her own reactions, particularly when initiating the exercise for the first time. The sender must be genuine, and any diminution of positive affect can generate shame in both sender and receiver. Remnants of anger, fear, and disgust can interfere with the generation and maintenance of positive affect required by the sender in Positive Flooding. Caring Behaviors and Surprises may activate similar dynamics, but probably of lesser intensity. Because the ideas for Caring Behaviors and Surprises are most often supplied by the potential receiver from previous Couples Dialogues, there is less chance of a mismatch with a receiver's needs. Nonetheless, an empathic breach can occur for the giver (sender) if the receiver does not maximize positive affect in accord with the level expected by the giver. The meaning of the gift for the giver is as important as its meaning for the receiver.

I would like to offer the following case illustration as an example of the exquisite interplay between the use of IRT and the explanatory process of affect theory in working with a highly motivated couple.

Case Example

The case of Mr. and Mrs. A is a good example of the use of IRT with affect theory helping to identify the processes of IRT and impediments to intimacy. I knew Mr. A from approximately five years earlier when he had presented with severe job dissatisfaction and clinically significant depression. He elected to switch jobs within his company at that time and began taking fluoxetine (Prozac) prescribed by a consulting psychiatrist, and eventually increased his dose to 60 mg with good results. Mr. and Mrs. A had consulted with me together approximately three years ago for distress, anger, and shame around secondary infertility issues. Later, the birth of their second son alleviated this concern. The present episode of treatment involved couples treatment, as they had seriously considered separation for approximately six months due to their perceived chronic lack of intimacy. At the time of this writing, they had completed twenty sessions of conjoint IRT, were doing much better, but planned to continue in treatment.

Both Mr. and Mrs. A were shame prone, as predicted by affect theory when couples are in crisis, yet desirous of improving their relationship. Their continued return to me as their therapist highlights a good therapeutic script that could easily be termed a damage-remediation script, as well as a more enduring life-long extant script that another person can be a reliever of distress. The IRT premise is to teach each individual partner in a couple to reduce the other's distress and thereby elicit enjoyment-joy and become once again mutual sources of interest-excitement and enjoyment-joy.

Both Mr. and Mrs. A were taught the Couples Dialogue; Mrs. A was far superior in her ability to articulate her thoughts and feelings, to send effective sound bites of information, and to invite collaboration from her husband. It is important to note that Mrs. A was the maximizer-pursuer in Imago terms, and Mr. A was the minimizer-distancer. Both were able to recognize their respective woundedness with their own parents. Mr. A was more halting and fumbling despite the fact that he was a corporate executive, much more obviously shame prone than his wife despite the Prozac, and much less able to identify either cognitive or emotional concerns. This required much therapist empathy around his difficulty, resulting in didactic and psychoeducational approaches to teach him about shame as an affect and about affect theory more comprehensively. These psychoeducational strategies first included bibliotherapy using Nathanson's text (1992), which is only feasible for those who learn well through reading. This was supplemented by direct discussion using everyday-life examples of shame's link to attenuated interest-excitement and enjoyment-joy, as well as teaching the compass of shame with both general and couple-specific examples.

After preliminary teaching, both Mr. and Mrs. A were coached as receivers during empathy portions of the dialogue. Time-out supportive prompts for the overwhelmed Mr. A were also provided to help both partners identify their respective affective states during Imago processes. Periodically, Mr. A had to be rebriefed in affect theory dynamics. His angry outbursts, which elicited much shame, warranted instruction about the anger-rage dynamics that led to Mr. A's attack-self, attack-other shame pattern. Mrs. A would nod knowingly during these educational discussions. With therapeutic direction, Mr. A was able to learn how to express his shame and embarrassment in the Couples Dialogue while actually discussing his difficulty in doing the Couples Dialogue, a definite shamolytic process.

The couple was then taught the Parent-Child Dialogue, which was an easy therapeutic step for each of them, although it is by no means easy for all couples. Both were clearly able to identify the fact that they had selected an imago match. The couple was then taught the Behavior Change Request, and Mr. A had much more difficulty both in articulating his own requests and in acceding to his wife's requests. Nonetheless, a surprising shift occurred. Mrs. A was able to see her husband's difficulty as an inability rather than a deliberate withholding, quickly lowering her distress level. Despite struggling with his Behavior Change Requests, which included requests from him for more shared time, shared spirituality, and more sex, Mr. A was able to initiate Caring Behaviors, and the couple started to date and to attend some of his business trips together. Not surprisingly, Mr. and Mrs. A expressed much shame and even distress around learning the Positive Flooding exercise. Although each was able to complete it, their embarrassment and the resulting relief when they were finished were obvious.

It became evident that Mrs. A was becoming able to see her husband's absorption in his work as less of a rejection of her and more of her husband's own temporary incapacity for interest-excitement and enjoyment-joy. She was able to reduce some of her pursuit behaviors and demands, which freed up her husband to initiate more efforts toward her, rather than fending her off and exiting from emotional contact. Mrs. A's shame level decreased when her positive affect was less frequently rejected, and Mr. A's shame level decreased when he less frequently had to try to match his wife's positive affect.

In summary, Mr. A represents an individual in whom there is a biological impediment to intimacy given his both biological and reactive depression, as well as a very evident struggle with shame-based dynamics around interest-excitement and enjoyment-joy. It is likely that this also represents a developmentally acquired impediment to intimacy a la Kelly (1993), as his feelings were consistently ignored in his family of origin despite apparently otherwise adequate parenting in terms of financial security, housing, appropriate limit setting, and expectations for achievement. Mrs. A was able to see her felt rejection as being shame based, and she was able to look at the frequency and intensity of her demands so as to decrease her pursuer dynamics, resulting in less felt shame by her and less felt shame by her husband in not being able to fulfill her requests. Mrs. A was also able to see how her own father's emotional distance toward her led her to again experience feelings of rejection in her marriage.

This couple is not considering separating at this time, both are committed to their marriage and the ensuing therapeutic work, and we are all optimistic about their future together. In fact, during a recent weekend business trip to Paris, the couple reported that they had mutually dialogued using the Couples Dialogue about Mr. A's job distress, culminating in his decision to leave the company where he had worked for twenty years. During this extended weekend, the couple expressed much genuine pleasure in each other, obviously using the novelty of Paris to experience much interest-excitement and enjoyment-joy with each other. Both beamed when discussing this wonderful weekend and were able to effectively handle the ensuing letdown in the first few days back home. In a collaborative effort at understanding themselves and their relationship, they used the Couples Dialogue to compare their interactions in Paris with their relating at home.

Creating Commitment Scripts

IRT capitalizes on the dialectic nature of committed relationships in terms of the safety-danger, love-hate polarities. Peck's memorable classic, *The Road Less Traveled* (1978), speaks directly to the myth of romantic love and the associated risks of loss, independence, commitment, and confrontation. He urges discipline in love and faith in the process that unfolds within a committed relationship as a means to the emotional and spiritual growth of each partner. IRT holds at its core the development and maintenance of such a commitment script (Tomkins, 1991), a script that is unambivalent and evocative of courage and that encompasses the ability to absorb negative affect.

In affect theory terms, successful IRT will create new scripts, which supersede maladaptive ones. Such scripts will be uniquely each couple's own creation in a spiraling positive-negative-positive affective interaction, as there must be a safe place for expressing and resolving conflict, and an acceptance of some conflicts that may never be resolved. In fact, Tomkins (1995) defines one such nuclear script, a damage-reparation script, in which good scenes of affluence are damaged, but repaired. Such scripts are optimistic in that the individual comes to believe and behave according to a script in which, having lost something of value, can recover it, in damaging something of value, can have it repaired. These new scripts will make use of dense affect, and they will continuously evolve as the couple works through their own individual developmental lifespan challenges.

With a knowledge of affect theory and script theory, the Imago clinician can more quickly recognize interactional patterns by expecting certain common sequences, acknowledging the ubiquitousness of shame and defenses against it in all intimate relationships, and providing a specific direction to therapy in what needs to be accomplished. In other words, the techniques and premises of IRT will guide the therapist and couple to allow specific changes in their affective responses. Certainly, the affect sequences previously discussed in the development of safety and passion represent a simplification of permutations of stimulus-affect-response triads that could occur between partners in any couple. Over time, the successful use of IRT will change behavioral patterns, attitudinal preferences and expectations, affect sequencing, and the induction of positive mood states, while minimizing negative mood states. New scripts and ideoaffective assemblies can then develop and be rewarded. IRT has the structure to harness the power of affect in the service of healing.

One final conclusion is that we are first and foremost biological creatures, but in a fuller sense than psychoanalytic drive theorists ever considered. One example is the stimulation of anger on exposure to a steady-state negative stimulus of sufficient density. Another is the experience of shame as a given during the attenuation of interest-excitement and enjoyment-joy. The importance of the face, the display and experience of affects on the face and in the body, and the existence of substrates in the brain, place specific potentials and limitations on all human beings. Affect theory is biological, intrapsychic, interpersonal, relational, psychodynamic, and, most of all, human. Thus it has a natural place in IRT.

References

Bader, E., & Pearson, P. T. (1988). *In quest of the mythical mate: A developmental approach to diagnosis and treatment in couples therapy.* New York: Brunner/Mazel.

Bader, E., Schnarch, D., & Hendrix, H. (1995). *The role of empathy and differentiation in couples therapy.* [Two audiotapes.] San Francisco: Milton Erickson Foundation.

Bailey, D. (1996). Bader, Schnarch, and Hendrix. *Journal of Imago Relationship Therapy, 1,* 35–51.

Basch, M. F. (1976). The concept of affect: A re-examination. *Journal of the American Psychoanalytic Association, 24,* 759–767.

Hendrix, H. (1988). *Getting the love you want: A guide for couples.* New York: Henry Holt.

Hendrix, H. (1994). *Getting the love you want: A couples workshop manual.* New York: Institute for Imago Relationship Therapy.

Kaufman, G. (1985). *Shame: The power of caring* (2nd ed.). Cambridge, MA: Schenkman Books.

Kelly, V. C., Jr. (1993). Affect and intimacy. *Psychiatric Annals, 23,* 556–566.

Kelly, V. C., Jr. (1996). Affect, by any other name. *Bulletin of the Tomkins Institute, 4,* 33–34.

Nathanson, D. L. (1992). *Shame and pride: Affect, sex, and the birth of the self.* New York: Norton.

Nathanson, D. L. (1996). The Philadelphia system. *Bulletin of the Tomkins Institute, 4,* 21–26.

National Advisory Mental Health Council. (1995). Basic behavioral science research for mental health: A national investment emotion and motivation. *American Psychologist, 50,* 838–845.

Peck, M. S. (1978). *The road less traveled.* New York: Simon & Schuster.

Schnarch, D. M. (1991). *Constructing the sexual crucible.* New York: Norton.

Tomkins, S. S. (1962). *Affect/imagery/consciousness: Vol. 1. The positive affects.* New York: Springer.

Tomkins, S. S. (1963). *Affect/imagery/consciousness: Vol. 2. The negative affects.* New York: Springer.

Tomkins, S. S. (1991). *Affect/imagery/consciousness: Vol. 3. The negative affects: Anger and fear.* New York: Springer.

Tomkins, S. S. (1995). Script theory. In E. V. Demos (Ed.), *Exploring affect: The selected writings of Silvan S. Tomkins* (pp. 312–388). New York: Cambridge University Press.

Chapter Six

Relationship Knowing
Imago and Object Relations
Stephen R. Plumlee, M.Div., Ph.D.

What is the relationship of knowing to the human personality, as it might be understood in Imago theory? Are there types of knowing? Is connected knowing truly in contrast to separate knowing, or is it instead opposed to disconnectedness and therefore to unknowing? Is the contrast with separate knowing not, in fact, symbiosis, merger, in which there is no distinct knower? Is knowing developed in the process of establishing the imago, or does it occur as part of the neurological given of the human person?

Theories About Knowing

Theory of knowing, epistemology, is most often thought of as a branch of philosophy. When psychologists comment on this activity of the mind they tend to emphasize that all knowing is actually apperception. It soon becomes clear, as one reflects on these questions, that the issue is larger than a definition of knowing and the description of types of knowing. Indeed, the matter of knowing is directly seated in that of being, for how a person experiences what he is and who he is, is the very source of his knowing. Thus the matter is a core one for Imago theory, for the Imago perspective is that the who-ness and the what-ness of personal experience are both the products of relationship and the shapers of relationships.

Transformational Stage

There are indeed different types of knowing, but what are they? It is helpful to approach this question from a developmental perspective. In some formulations of infant life, it has been said that the baby lives in a state of symbiosis with his[1] mother. That concept indicates that the neonate experiences life as if he and the mother were one, or rather as though the universe consists only of himself, with the mother a merged part of his being. In this view the baby has no perception of himself as a self[2] or as a subject.[3]

Although it is undoubtedly true that the infant does not yet have the neurological development to be self- or other-conscious, he does in fact experience the mother figure as the one from whom comes gratification of needs and desires, as well as frustration of them. When baby's needs for nurturance, warmth, and safety are met, he is satisfied, although he is not conscious of the presence of a satisfying person. Likewise when his wishes or needs are not fulfilled by the mothering presence, the child is forced to accommodate. Perhaps he cries until the message is received and the need granted; perhaps he has to endure his discomfort or displeasure; perhaps he learns to soothe himself with sucking fingers or toes and falling asleep.

Whatever the response to gratification and frustration, the infant is by necessity in the way of being transformed, or rather transforming himself, adapting his demands to what can be expected, inventing new skills to communicate his wants, perhaps giving up in despair. When this relationship between maternal caregiver and infant goes well, it has the quality of what Winnicott (1965) calls a "facilitating environment," with the right balance of care and withholding to allow the infant to unfold his capacities to meet changing expectations. Thus she who is the major component of the infant's environment relates to him to accommodate and assimilate the rest of the environment on her behalf in such a way that the baby continues his self-transformation.

The key concept here is that of relationship, a notion that is dear to every Imago therapist. We say that the first task the infant has is that of attachment, to experience being wanted, to be able consistently to expect warmth and requisite nurture, but not to be lost in a sea of undifferentiated availability. When this format goes well, the infant continues his transformational development. The maternal figure might thus be called a "transformational object," who is experientially identified by the infant with the processes that alter his experience of himself. And although the infant cannot yet think consciously of her as a distinct relational object, he is nonetheless having a subject-object relationship with her. His capacities for thought have not yet matured, but he is already knowing. He is beginning to carry knowledge that is the unthought known, and he develops this knowledge as a result of the peculiar relationship he has with his mother. From her responses to him he is learning the rules of life within the context of the universe he shares with her, although he is not yet able to know that he knows. His native physical and mental capacities, his unique combination of energies, strengths, and characteristic temperament gradually shape themselves to the environment mediated by his caregivers, while he simultaneously shapes their behavior toward him. He knows increasingly, but only through the dialectic of his relationship. Who the baby is, is what he knows conceptually, and what he knows derives from the constant ebb and flow of physical and psychic energy between him and his caregiver. His knowing cannot be said to be solely though the identification and oneness, as he already "knows" that his facilitating environment is not identical with himself. However, he also cannot be said to know in a thoroughly analytical and separated way, for he has not yet developed a consciousness of his own separateness.

This is a state of prelanguage, and the languaged discourse that one has with oneself and others is often thought of as essential for the process of knowing. That is, the use of symbolic encapsulators for one's thoughts and experiences is the way in which knowledge is formulated. Indeed, the acquisition of language is the most significant transformation that takes place in the infant's alteration of the experience of himself. Thus the preverbal and predifferentiated child continues to use bodily movements, cries, silences, and even miming others to penetrate the other and make that other experience what he himself experiences. This can be seen, for example, in the behaviors of autistic children.

Transitional Stage

But as the child enters well into his second year, he starts to differentiate himself from his mothering caregiver. As he becomes increasingly aware of her as more than a transformational process and as a discrete object in herself, his way of knowing changes also. Heretofore, his knowing has been principally in the form of bodily memories, outside his conscious mental operations. Through them he has a knowing of which he is not aware. As the child continues his development he begins to engage in more individuated activity, distinct from that which he has with his mother. He separates from her, to explore in a wider circle of activity, both mental and physical; he becomes increasingly aware that he has experiences that she does not. His distinctiveness as a person becomes more apparent to himself and to mother.

This shift of focus from total involvement with the maternal (and to some extent the paternal) figure does not mean total separateness, however. Even as the child is coming to know consciously and distinctly, he continues to need the reassurance of that provider of needs, to return for brief periods of visual, vocal, and physical reintegration with her. To a very large degree she is still the source of safety, particularly as the child experiences moments of pain and finds healing and solace, and of meaning, as he returns to recount his unique experiences in the unconscious belief that she understands what he recounts and the significance of the content.

This is the stage of development at which relationship with father and other objects becomes important. Father provides him with another source of derivation of knowledge, both of himself as he relates to his parent in identification with his values, beliefs, and foci of attention, but also as a separate person with whom he is related not as the undifferentiated source of his process of transformation, but as one with whom he interacts conscious of their differences. This shift in the principles of relationship apply also to a widening circle of other persons: other adults, age mates, and play companions, for example.

During this period, as in all other developmental stages, the infant continues to assign meaning to the behavior of those with whom he is related. Earlier these psychic contents were known in a precognitive way but were held with an absoluteness of which he was not aware. The process was not one of primary repression of knowledge that cannot be held in the consciousness because of the threat of its meaning; rather, the infant had not been developmentally ready for conscious thought. Now, in the stage of separation and individuation, he can assimilate information borne by stimuli, consciously interpret it, and either retain it in forms that are recognizable to him or repress it because its content floods him with more knowledge than he can sustain, or threatens his being. The infant gradually alters his relationships with objects. He no longer has a sole object, transformational of his being through his knowing in a symbiotic way and through which relationship he is transforming his environment through his emerging ego capacities of integration, perception, and spontaneous action. Now the child shifts from the process of experiencing the transformation to that of articulating it. He can symbolically enact the illusion of his own omnipotence and his own creativity to replace the disappearing transformational object. His new idiom expresses his differentiation symbolically, and he can even play with the grandiose idea that he can eliminate the maternal object and that she will nonetheless survive. The transition is an era of playing with ideas, of fantasies that brilliantly portray the infant's outgrowing of the maternal matrix, his relief and rage at that loss, his illusory belief in the might of his own power as he discovers his prowess in his individuated ego strengths.

In this phase, knowing takes on quite a different meaning from the transformational process. The infant now has multiple objects with which to interact. He still performs the operation of internalizing his perceptions of them, the meaning of their behaviors, especially toward him, and the laws of life he assimilates from them. This is a period of socialization, when the young child makes the transition from knowing what will help him shape his own being and that of the transformation-self; he now works at knowing what form he must take to be acceptable to the larger community. No longer is it enough to be aware of how to sustain life-giving communion with one object, for now there are an increasing number of objects, each with its own peculiar expectations and beliefs. Knowing becomes a more self-conscious act, an awareness of an experience that is different from oneself, that is distally observable. This separate object is of course known truly to the extent that it is incorporated internally, with definition and value bestowed upon it by the subject, who then symbolizes his knowledge not usually in a conscious process, but through fantasy and language. He gives word to what he has made a part of himself mentally; he assigns relational value to it and develops a set of beliefs pertinent to that relationship.

Knowing and the Imago

The fertility of meaning attributed to the relationship adds still another layer to the deposit of memories and unconscious expectations that make up the imago. In fact, the imago itself is constructed of at least three relationships that the person has observed and experienced; knowledge of all three, preconceptual and repressed alike, makes up the content of it. Most powerful, of course, is the relationship of the parental caregivers to the child. The experiences on which that knowledge has been built begin very early in the prenatal period of the infant's life, and extend into the later years of childhood. The elements of that knowing which is unknown are therefore a compound of the unthought and that which was thought but repressed. Second, but profoundly influential in the development of the imago, is the relationship between (or among) the caregivers themselves, for it has a strong impact on the infant who is perforce within their field of interaction. The effects of this relationship are also quite powerful for the intrauterine infant through direct physical impact on the child who is contained within the mother's body, but also through her neural, muscular, and hormonal responses to the events of the relationship. Of course the child is within the range of the parents' interactions with each other throughout childhood, and from it he develops an enormous treasury of expectations and beliefs about the nature of intimate relationship. Finally, but also intensely important, is the relationship each caregiver has with herself or himself. Whether that behavior is respectful or disrespectful of the self, sustaining or destructive, energized or defeated, has a lasting effect on the unthought known of the appropriate relationship to have with oneself. This knowing can also be repressed because of fear associated with shame, sadness, or contempt, but it can also be dreadfully conscious for the adult child.

This amalgam that is the imago is, therefore, a complicated component of the mental apparatus. Partially conscious, but to a large degree preconscious and unconscious, it contains innumerable bytes of knowledge. Some of them are known as certainties but have never been differentiated thoughts; others are the residue of direct bodily experiences recorded permanently like a dent made in the earth by a falling meteor; still others have resulted from distal observations and have been filed away and are referred to constantly with unconscious automaticity.

Knowing Is Holistic

Whatever the source of the individual element in the imago, it is always the result of knowing that has been derived from preconceptual experience, when the transformational object is the intimate influence in one's development (and this process continues throughout life, although it is superseded in importance in successively later stages of development), and from separate knowing, when the relational objects are clearly known as other. Every piece of knowing is related to every other, and there is finally no knowing that is not both connected and separate. Without a sense of oneness, shared reality, and corporate meaning there is no relationship from which to derive knowing; without differentiation there is not an apperceived other to know. W.R.D. Fairbairn (1952) demonstrates clearly that libidinal yearnings impel one to fulfill them, but satisfying them is not the end in itself; they are tools to attain the ultimate goal, relationship with the other. Fairbairn's dictum applies: "The ultimate goal of libido is the object" (p. 4). The lifelong process of attaining this goal of relationship with the other, starting with the earliest moments of conception, causes the person to know what will facilitate that relationship, what will destroy it, and indeed how the relationship can destroy the self. From the beginning, the newly conceived infant has some awareness of the otherness of the other, even when it is the transformational object, essential for life itself; for the person there is never a point of absolute psychic symbiosis. At the same time, total differentiation is impossible, for then there is no knowing of the other to relate with. Knowing, essential for sustaining the life of the self, is always, at every stage of life, an imago experience: connected and separate, differentiated and undifferentiated, held in a holistic tension. Without that *tension vitale* the personal organism would disappear, either by undifferentiated absorption or total isolation. In either case, there is no imago, the treasury of knowing; without the imago there can be no knowing, and without knowing there can be no relationship, the source of the self.

Case Illustration

Karen and Gregory entered couples therapy about four years ago; they have been in treatment weekly since then. When they began, Greg was a forty-two-year-old white male in his second marriage of some four years. He has a daughter from his first marriage who was then thirteen years old. He has no education beyond high school, but is a brilliant inventor and craftsman. Karen was thirty-nine years old at the time. This is her first marriage, and she has no children. She is an emergency room physician.

Personal Backgrounds

Greg is a fraternal twin; he and his twin sister have one sibling, who is older. The twins were premature; his sister was strong from birth, but Greg was sickly, and his life hung in the balance many times during his infancy. When he was three years old his father committed suicide. Greg's view of his upbringing is that he was expected to be the replacement for his father to take care of his mother and sisters and simultaneously viewed as insufficient and unreliable because he was a male.

Karen is the oldest of three siblings; she has two younger brothers. Her mother was a paranoid schizophrenic who critically attacked her, sometimes physically, and withheld from her. Karen's father was a successful professional man who dealt with his psychotic wife by working many long hours and weekends. He left Karen with the responsibility to mollify and later to take care of the mother; the brothers were left largely to bring up themselves. She became a doctor because her father, her savior, directed her to that profession.

Presenting Problems

When Karen and Greg presented themselves for therapy, they were in a state of constant bickering, mutual criticism and sarcastic attacks, and defensive counterattacks. Greg *knew* that his wife despised him, that no matter what he tried to do it would be found insufficient, and that it was only a matter of time before she would discard him as useless. Karen *knew* that she was intellectually inferior and valuable primarily as a source of steady income that allowed Greg to do his creative work. She was resentful, bitter, and outraged at his long, exhausting hours in his workshop. She was aware that her suspicious outlook and contempt for her patients and other workers at the hospital made her husband want to avoid her, especially as it appeared that she had more love for her dogs than for him. Greg was convinced that because he was a male his wife expected him to make all problems go well for her, including that of making a living. In fact, however, he produced almost no income, and what he did bring in was destined to go for child support. Karen found herself essentially supporting the two of them.

Their sexual relationship was a shambles. Each partner claimed to find the other attractive, but they had sex only very occasionally. Greg was convinced that Karen found his lovemaking insufficient and that she would devour him if he did not keep a distance. In reality she lived a life of such emotional exhaustion and hostility that she seldom responded to his infrequent overtures, and then only for physical gratification. They had no spiritual practice; Greg had been brought up without one and seemed incurious on the subject; Karen reacted to the strictures of her childhood religion, which she resented because her father had cited it as his reason for keeping his children and himself chained to the psychotic mother.

Ostensibly a successful couple with a pleasant home, brilliantly creative husband, and high-achieving wife, they were psychological neonates whose mothers were preoccupied with themselves, the one in psychotic incompetence and vicious competition with her own same-sex infant, the other identified with her daughters and resentful of the caretaker who had abandoned her in a catastrophic exit (suicide) and of the child who was made in his image.

EARLY TREATMENT

The early treatment of this couple can be seen as an articulation of their respective knowing. Karen experienced constant frustration of her every desire for affiliation with a responsive object, in this case Greg. It was the task of the therapy to allow her to verbalize her preverbal anxiety. Her communications were attacks on Gregory for his failure to provide her with a matrix in which she could experience herself in a relaxed, nonvigilant way. Gregory was sure, in ways he could never have conceptualized, that his undifferentiated self would be consumed by Karen's demands, that he could not relate to her as an object that would help him define himself. His solution was to admit abjectly all his failures, which proved that it was hopeless for him to become a functional interactor in the relationship; simultaneously he presented criticisms of Karen's failures, which were provocative but so highly intellectualized as to be incomprehensible. My countertransference was rage, exhausted futility, and arcane intellectual interpretations. As I learned to hear their remarks as wails of despair rather than as cognitive declaration, the therapy began to take direction.

In dealing with narcissistic couples, I mirrored each partner directly. This helped me ascertain that I had understood, soothed each in turn as they realized that I had actually attended to their experience, and calmed the other as well. Gradually they were able to question what they had *known*. As they, working through me, slowly differentiated from each other and the imago expectations they had held, a subtle relationship started to develop. As I reflected to Greg, for example, the terror of being destroyed by the anticipated overwhelming demands of Karen, who represented in a precognitive way his dependent and demanding mother, he started to recognize to himself that Karen indeed required little in the way of life care from him. This did not, of course, spontaneously eliminate his *knowledge* that he was viewed as a non-person to be used as an instrument for the reduction of her anxiety.

Nevertheless, slowly and gradually these two partners started precognitively to *know* the other as a person with his or her own perspective, although they each remained basically the process-object for the other as they struggled against ancient and unthought *knowledge* that now had to be reexamined. A decisive moment in their therapy came when they attended an Imago couples workshop about four months into their treatment. In that setting, where they could remain for hours and interact with each other in the safety of my functioning as interlocutor, they were able to see more clearly the entire frame of the Imago perception of relationships and the nature of the power struggle. This new cognitive *knowing* became a component of their preverbal *knowledge;* I as presenter and the other couples took on the role of supplementary ego.

LATER TREATMENT

Slowly Karen and Gregory began to *know* each other distally, as other than themselves, persons who had a self that was not totally defined by their participation in each other's self. This became a self-defining process as they added their newfound perceptions to their imagos. This internalization both of the continuing, dependable presence of the other and of new representations to whom they related helped them continue the process of differentiation and simultaneously achieve a degree of secure attachment that neither of them had before; the anxious-ambivalent attachment of Greg and the depressive-schizoid attachment of Karen declined perceptibly.

Several developmental moments occurred over a period of months. Gregory had a history of anxiously attaching himself to male figures, oftentimes as employers. He began to recognize that these men had served as internal objects for him, shaky stand-ins for his absent father. Through these affiliate objects he had attempted to confirm his *knowing* of his own existence through their confirmation of his competence and accomplishments and through their presence as a libidinal pole to help him protect himself from disappearing into the allur-ing abyss of the dependent, ungratifying maternal figure. Also through his adu-lation of these men he was able to attain some temporary degree of validation for his own worth as a male. However, this *knowledge* was laid on a base of a poor self-object relationship and an unstable perception of himself as a person, and the relationships always ended in bitter disappointment and grievous loss for him. Now, as his internalized images of Karen provided for more attach-ment based on self rather than accomplishment, his relations with other males became less of a life-and-death issue for him.

Karen, the more schizoid and depressed of the two, has not succeeded in mak-ing the same degree of attachment to Greg as a process-object, so that her self-differentiation is still some degrees behind his. Nevertheless, she has ex-perienced me as a male figure who attends to her as an actual being, and through her work with both me and her female individual therapist is develop-ing a clearer self-awareness.

About eighteen months ago Karen began to press that they have a baby. She reasoned that before long she would be too old to have a child safely, that she felt more capable of being a mother without behaving ragefully or psychoti-cally at the child, and that her marriage was secure. Greg was more hesitant; he had one daughter already and saw many deficits in his capacities as a father; his doubts about his parental skills were a cognitively delineated way to symbolize his still insubstantial sense of self. Furthermore, he had experienced Karen's retreats to cold, withdrawn, rejecting ways when she was under stress. He suggested that with the continuous strain of parenthood she might regress. This *knowing* declaration from Greg infuriated her; she felt deeply hurt and counterattacked frequently during sessions.

Nevertheless, Greg eventually began to see that his *known* doubts about Karen were to a large extent projection; he began to incorporate a differentiated *knowledge* of himself and to understand the gains he had made as a father, consequent to more caring, graceful attitudes toward himself. Eventually both partners entered the "Let's have a baby" mode energetically. The process, how-ever, was disappointing. They resorted to *in vitro* fertilization; Karen eventu-ally became pregnant, but lost the baby in her fourth month. For a considerable time I made the couples therapy a container environment in which they could express their intense grief and anger: at Karen for not having taken good enough care of herself, at Greg because he had postponed his acquiescence until Karen was too old for a viable pregnancy, at me for not having cured them fast enough to begin the pregnancy earlier. For perhaps the first time, these two people understood that they were quite separate persons for whom the experience had its own meaning, that they could share an empathic support for each other, and that, through my example, it is possible to receive the other's anger without being annihilated, rejected, or abandoned by it. Indeed, for perhaps the first time Karen and Greg were clearly in a transitional stage of personal development. Their *knowing* seems increasingly to belong to each of them individually, but because of their growing differentiation they can share their *knowledge* with each other as never before.

Two other major shifts have taken place because of these partners' journey through becoming transformational objects for each other into differentiation and more secure attachment and growing individuation. About two years ago, Greg gave up his studio, where he had worked exhaustively to prove the reality of his self; he sold the rights for a major invention to a small company and became an employee, responsible for creative innovations. For the first time in his life he is making a real living; he pays his share of the couple's expenses, and Karen does not have to be responsible for a portion of his child support payments.

This change has provoked a developmental crisis. Previously, Karen kept her income and assets separate from Gregory's; in fact she has been somewhat secretive about her holdings. As he has become more consistently contributory to their joint life and there have been more financial decisions to make together, their system has come under question. I have continued to hold them therapeutically in the *knowledge* that they can live with the tension, anger, distrust, and yearning for trusting affiliation with each other. The choice of financial system is theirs, and they move closer to commingled assets and expenses. However, there are occasional steps away from that position when one of them (usually Karen) is unhappy with a joint decision and feels a sudden urgency to regain veto control.

CLOSING STAGES OF TREATMENT

At this stage of treatment Karen and Gregory still struggle with the preconscious *knowing* that they will be used, consumed, and discarded (Greg) or attacked and rejected (Karen). She still recedes to a terrified belief that she is a nonperson to her current self-object; in those moments she can become cold, contemptuous, and attacking. Greg is increasingly sure, however, that these declarations are in fact the wounded cries of a desperate infant. Recently Karen has made the pained and painful charges that Greg will never take care of her as she wants to be, while simultaneously enumerating the attention and care she does receive from him. Of course, she is correct that no one will ever be able to carry her as an infant. Nevertheless, Greg, through my careful support and insistence, is able to reflect to Karen his understanding of her *knowing* experience and solicit from her the healing behavior changes that will help transform her internalized representations and object relations.

Gregory's anxiety still overtakes him at times, and he reverts to the abstract and convoluted intellectualization that represents not so much his deepest *knowing* but an effort to distance himself from the terror of his own inadequacy. Karen is usually surprised at Greg's fear and lack of security. In our sessions I can often help her convey to him her own perceptions of his strength. In earlier times this process would have been useless, and he could not have accepted it. Now, with a much more consistent experience of many internal relationships, both with Karen and others, and a stronger *knowledge* of himself as a self, he is individuated enough to hear her view of him as her own, receive it as a reflection from her as a self-object, and reconfirm a clearer *knowing* of himself.

CURRENT PROGRESS

Karen and Gregory are at a working-through phase of their therapy. The crises they encounter are no longer insurmountable. Their *knowing* of themselves as selves and of each other as differentiated persons who can when necessary continue to act as both transformational objects when necessary and as transitional objects allows them gradually to create new imagos. Will these new sets of *knowing* expectations ever replace their old ones that were so damaging to them? Probably not. What we can expect, however, is that as their *knowledge* continues to be built on differentiated experience, and indeed to inform still other *knowing* behaviors and beliefs, the multiple internal relations that make up their respective imagos will continue to grow in healthy, realistic expectations. Their *knowing* becomes both individuated and undifferentiated, a holistic activity.

Notes
1. Throughout this chapter, the pronoun *he* is used for the infant because it helps to maintain clarity of reference in the frequent juxtaposition to mother *(she)*.

2. In this view, self is an historically consistent experience of many internal relationships, which are mentally objectified, related to, and known.
3. Subject is a meaningful understanding of one's own and others' existence, with a capacity to relate with them and oneself.

References

Fairbairn, W.R.D. (1952). *Psychoanalytic studies of the personality*. London: Routledge.

Winnicott, D. W. (1965). Psychiatric disorder in terms of infantile maturational processes. In *The maturational processes and the facilitating environment* (pp. 230–241). London: Hogarth.

Chapter Seven

Contemporary Psychoanalytic Relational Theories and Imago

Concepts for Relational Healing

Mona R. Barbera, Ph.D.

There has been a sea change in analytic theory in the last two decades. The older Freudian-based theories focusing solely on the inner life and conflicted drives of the individual, isolated from his or her environment, are no longer in the forefront. Even self psychology and object relations theories are being partially eclipsed by more vital and relevant theories that focus on relatedness as central, not peripheral, to development and healing. Contemporary psychoanalytic offices are humming as analysts forego a remote, uninvolved stance and emphasize healing through relationship.

These contemporary analytic theories provide rich concepts that can help us, as Imago therapists, understand and expand the richness of our theory and practice. Also, making links between Imago theory and contemporary analytic theory gives us the option to use language that could be more accessible to our colleagues who read and practice analytic psychotherapy, thus allowing us to communicate with and learn from each other.

There Is No Being Outside Relationship

Unlike traditional psychoanalytic theories, contemporary relational theories view development in radical relational terms. Children not only need but actually come to exist within relationship

(Mitchell, 1988). These theories do not see development or pathology in terms of processes located solely within the person but rather as occurring in the "evolving psychological field" between the child and parent (Stolorow, Brandschaft, & Atwood, 1987, p. 2). There is actually no person, no sense of being outside of relationship (Mitchell, 1988). This sounds similar to Hendrix's statement, "There are no entities as such except as distinguishable points, or nodes, in the tapestry of being. Relationship is not only the primary reality, but the nodes are essentially constructed by their interaction with their context, which is essentially comprised of other energetic nodes" (1996, p. 10).

If there is no being outside relationship, then we all come to be within the context of association with people. And because the people we associate with are by nature imperfect in some way, the relatedness they provide will always have a shape—more of some things and less of other things. As Mitchell (1988) says, we are bent into shape by the inherent emotional and relational conditions of early life. "One cannot become a human being in the abstract; one does so only by adopting a highly specific, delimiting shape, and that shape is forged in interaction between the temperamental givens of the baby and the contours of parental character and fantasies. . . . That self-organization becomes my 'nature'; those attachments become my sense of the possibilities within the community of others" (pp. 275–277).

Because children have a basic need for relationship in order to form themselves, they will do anything that is needed to maintain relationship with the primary people in their environment. The child learns and performs whatever relational behavior the parent wants (Mitchell, 1988). In healthy families, parents will be flexible about how children can interact, allowing a greater range of connective styles. Healthy parents will be more integrated within themselves and have fewer disowned parts and thus more parts available for interchange. In unhealthy situations, parents will communicate great anxiety, distress, or anger if the child steps out of certain boundaries of behavior and relatedness, and they will have fewer parts within themselves available for interaction, thus giving the child a skewed idea of what people can do, feel, and think in relationship. Thus the child is left with a narrow repertoire of relational styles, unable to adapt to changing circumstances later in life.

Enactment: Adults Actively Create These Shapes

Having grown up embedded in a particular relational matrix, people continue to perform the activities that in childhood provided connection with their parents. They actively and intentionally create interpersonal environments, prodding, compelling, coercing, and manipulating people in a determined and "unconsciously accomplished" way to play the positive and negative roles their parents played (Bollas, 1989; Sandler, 1976). There is deep loyalty (Fairbairn, 1946) to the familiar attachments of childhood, including both the negative and positive experiences. This loyalty endures into adulthood, despite ensuing pain or limitation, because such familiar experiences are equated with having a self and being in connection with others (Mitchell, 1988). Relational theories refer to this phenomenon as "enactment."

Hendrix echoes this view when he says, "What appears to be dysfunctional behavior at the conscious, interpersonal level in committed partnerships is actually, at the unconscious level, functional; it serves the survival directive which is to remain connected to context" (1996, p. 14). These relational matrices, no matter how dysfunctional, are the mode of connecting with others, and no matter how healthy or fragile we are, we must connect with others (Mason, 1997). Relational theorists propose that the form and substance of connection mirrors that of childhood, and we actively enact the relational scenarios to which we are accustomed (Mitchell, 1988).

Adults Enact in Therapy

Adults enact their familiar patterns with those in their environment, including their therapists if they are in individual psychotherapy. From the relational point of view, psychotherapy patients are not just passively deficient and in need of missing developmental ingredients but are also actively re-creating their familiar bad situations, prodding the therapist into a "concealed repetition of earlier experiences and relationships," through a "complicated system of unconscious cues" (Sandler, 1976, p. 47). As Stark (1999) says, patients are not simply deficient, needing more "good" things in their lives; they are actively creating the old "bad" to which they are accustomed.

From this point of view, when therapists find themselves deeply caught in countertransference, thinking they have made an error or failed the patient, they could actually have a major opportunity to enter into the patient's relational world and help in a profound way. Perhaps there has been an empathic failure because of some blind spot in the therapist's personality, but it is also possible that the patient actively (albeit unconsciously) cued the therapist to respond in a way that re-created a familiar disappointment from the past. The therapist who understands this can avoid unnecessary self-judgment and use these moments of failure to help the patient become aware of embedded relational patterns. Relational theories propose that we, as therapists, cannot be all good all the time to our patients. We will fail them, partly because they make us fail them. In the beginning of therapy, as I sit with someone and experience our relational worlds intersecting, I often say to myself, "How will I fail this patient? How will they make me into the person who disappoints them in the old familiar way? What part will be mine, and what part will be theirs?"

This view of people as active re-creators of their childhood scenarios is similar to that found in Imago therapy. For example, Shulkin (1996) describes a couple's dynamics this way: "She saw that when she became critical of Jim, she recreated the painful loneliness she had tried at all costs to avoid. . . . [Jim realized] it was often his distancing which evoked her anger" (p. 78). This is a description of people who are actively re-creating the bad scenarios they learned in childhood, not of people who are passively experiencing loss.

Enactments Provide Opportunities for Healing in Psychotherapy

Although they may cause repetitive problems, enactments also provide opportunities for healing. When patients in individual relational therapy create their familiar scenarios in the therapy relationship, drawing the therapist in to fail them in the way to which they are accustomed, they then have a powerful opportunity to heal through a new relational experience (Casement, 1986; Stark, 1999). Sometimes, as Casement (1986) says, patients provoke therapists to fail them in ways that are amazingly accurate recreations of original traumatic experiences; the specificity makes the ensuing healing all the more powerful.

Relationally oriented individual therapists allow themselves to be drawn into the patient's relational world and then use that experience to help the patient. They seek the "intimate edge" (Ehrenberg, 1974) between them and their patients, and use their own feelings (partly induced by the patient) to help patients know and experience relatedness in new ways and to think and speak what they previously only knew to be familiar but without words (Bollas, 1989).

Rather than striving to remain consistently neutral and attempting to metabolize countertransference so that it does not interfere with empathy, relational therapists are skilled at using inner experiences and responses and, at the opportune moment, sharing them with the patient. The relational therapist's feelings are not trimmed and self-analyzed to keep them out of the way, nor are they defended against, but rather they are valued as the royal road to understanding the patient's relational world as a participant. "The analyst welcomes news from within himself that is reported through his own intuitions, feelings, passing images, phantasies and imagined interpretive interventions" (Bollas, 1989, p. 201).

In summary, healing in relational therapy happens through this re-creation of familiar old pain in the current relationship with the therapist, and the ensuing new, corrective relational experience. There is a "broadening of the relational matrix to allow new experiences of self in relation to others" (Mitchell, 1988, p. 301), in which past bad experiences become new good experiences, and what was the bad object, hurting us in familiar ways, becomes the good object, offering the experiences we yearn for. No longer are analytic therapists looking only for the patient to have a sense of mastery or control solely within himself or herself; they are looking for new relational experiences between themselves and the patient.

Partners Enact in Marriage

Most relevant to Imago therapists, people enact in their marriages, and, as couples therapists know, they do it with considerable affect and intensity. As Mason (1998) says, the transference is already there in couples therapy, in the relationship between the partners; we don't have to wait for it to become clear and available between patient and therapist, as is true of individual psychotherapy. So, unlike many therapists who may take a long time to experience, understand, and speak about relational patterns with their individual patients (Bollas, 1989), the couples therapist finds it accessible very quickly.

Three Ways We Suffer in Relationship

Analytic relational theories provide language and theoretical context that can elucidate the depth and richness of Imago Relationship Therapy (IRT). Combined with Imago theory, they can help us understand three different ways we can suffer in the relationship nightmare.

1. Enactment—provoking the partner to hurt us in the familiar ways. The pain of enactment arises when we train our partners, through various cues, to do the things that have hurt us in the past. We have become accustomed to certain pain, and we re-create it in our lives by acting in ways that provoke it.

2. Imago match—choosing our imago match provides an experience of hurt. Pain from our imago match comes about when our partners actually have the negative qualities we are complaining about. Hendrix (1988) has done an excellent job of explaining that we choose our partners because they give us familiar experiences: our imago match is someone who resembles our parents, in both positive and negative ways. The negative characteristics enable them to wound us as when we were in childhood, giving us an experience of familiar pain. This concept is not found in relational theories, which focus more on how we, in enactment, provoke the hurtful behavior of others. Hendrix's idea of the imago match shows how we don't have to provoke the hurtful behavior at all—it can just happen because it is already there, coming from the person we chose, and in fact that's partly why we chose him or her.

3. Projection—perceiving that our partners are hurting us in the old bad ways when actually they aren't doing this. This concept is identical to the object relations concept of projection. Projection doesn't include the other person's active participation—it is a story about one person only. This is not enactment, because the receiver of projection hasn't taken the cues to become hurtful and is not actually doing anything. However,

it still leaves us feeling pain because we believe our partners are hurting us.

We Heal Through New Corrective Relational Experiences

In addition to explaining different ways we suffer in relationships, contemporary analytic relational theories, in combination with Imago theory, also help explain how we heal. IRT says that we heal best in relationship with our imago match, by experiencing the old familiar hurts that we had in childhood, but this time with consciousness and in the context of safety. This Imago concept is similar to the relational theory concept that we create enactments in psychotherapy because we need them in order to heal; the healing comes when we have a new, corrective relational experience that specifically replaces the repetitive and hurtful earlier experience.

This type of healing often happens in an Imago session through the Couples Dialogue and the Parent-Child Dialogue (PCD) and by guiding listeners to be empathic where previously they had been reactive. Following are three ways healing can occur in IRT:

1. We understand our own role in enactment. This type of healing occurs when we are enacting, and come to realize that our actions have led to the pain we are experiencing. For example, Laura complains that Paul does not help enough with the children, leaving her feeling overly responsible and trapped. Through dialogue, she realizes that she is helping create this situation by doing too much, thinking she is only lovable if she takes all the stress upon herself. Effectively, she is teaching Paul through subtle cues that he doesn't have to participate. Through the PCD, she realizes that she has learned this pattern in childhood, and she decides to make changes in her behavior. In this case, the healing comes from Laura becoming aware of her enactment (her part in actively creating the pain) and experiencing expanded possibilities.

2. We understand that our partner's frustrations point out our (imago match) negative characteristics and areas for growth. Using the example of Laura and Paul, this type of healing would arise when Paul realized through listening to Laura's frustration that he was in fact self-absorbed and unaware of the

needs of the family. Through listening to his partner's pain, Paul could come to know something about himself. A PCD could follow in which both partners learn how Paul came to be this way. The focus would be on Paul embracing some new behaviors to replace his self-absorbed ways.

3. We heal by sustaining hurt and pain while staying connected. The partner who is enacting, projecting, or demonstrating negative imago match characteristics has opportunities to grow, often as the speaker in dialogue or PCD. But what about the listeners? Listeners also have opportunities to heal when they stay present and connected, avoiding fighting or flight, while their partners express pain and frustration. Schnarch (1997) aptly describes this as the capacity to maintain our own course when we feel most triggered, deprived, or angered by our intimate others, while remaining connected in the relational field, modulating emotions and resisting infection by the other's anxiety. Listeners can grow in differentiation and self-esteem when they stay present without reacting.

Listeners need to be nonreactive in order for safe, new relational experiences to arise. But how is this nonreactivity achieved? Do listeners achieve it by denying any emotional responses they have while listening? Or is there another way? Reviewing the differences between object relations individual therapists and analytic relational individual therapists in terms of the listening stance can clarify two different ways listeners can achieve nonreactivity.

The classic empathic stance of object relations emphasizes the need for the therapist to become aware of and remove countertransferential responses as soon as possible, in order to stay close and "experience near" to patients, and to help them develop disavowed or stunted aspects of themselves (Schwaber, 1981). In contrast, analytic relational therapists value and use their emotional responses to their patients (Bollas, 1989). Relational therapists could be feeling, for example, angry, bored, or guilty and could use these responses to understand what it is like to live in patients' relational worlds. Then, having this present-time relational experience with patients, they can, through carefully chosen authentic responses, help them experience healing through a new relational experience. In the object relations stance, the goal is to help the patient grow as an individual by facing conflicts and frustrations, so the therapist stays out of it as much as possible. In the contemporary analytic relational stance, the goal is for the patient to grow through a new relational experience, not merely as a separate individual, so the therapist uses his or her emotional responses to enter into relationship.

These differences in therapeutic stance indicate that there are two ways that listeners can deal with their emotional responses as they listen and that there are different implications for each. One way is for listeners to put aside or ignore their emotional responses and focus on providing empathy for the speaker. This is comparable to the object relations stance. Another way is for listeners to be aware of their emotional responses as they are inducted into their partner's world but still sustain their connection and nonreactivity. This is comparable to the analytic relational stance.

I believe that the second stance is more helpful and realistic, because our partners do, in fact, engender negative responses in us through enactment. I also think the second stance is more helpful for couples when they leave the therapy office and return home, because they will be better prepared for negative experiences when they listen in dialogue. Instead of thinking to themselves as they listen, "I should be neutral; I shouldn't have any negative feelings," they could be thinking, "Of course I am having negative feelings. Some of them are mine and some of them are being engendered by my partner. It's best for our relationship if I feel them but don't react right now."

In summary, I believe that it is important for listeners to experience negative emotional reactions and to survive them while remaining in connection, rather than trying to suppress them or filter them out.

Healing Through Dialogue

The concepts of enactment, imago match, and projection as ways of suffering and healing in relationship help us see the breakdowns in a couple's dialogue as great opportunities for change. I suggest that we view a couple's progress not as predicated on good dialogue but as generated by frustration and breakdown. As Hannah and Marrone (1997) stated, partners are always connecting in some way, regardless of their level of success with dialogue. Difficulties with dialogue can be seen as enactments, imago match scenarios, or projections, all of which can provide a direct route to healing. When the old nightmare is living right in front of us, we can become aware of it, and we have an opportunity for profound and specific relational healing. I suggest that more lasting healing occurs when we allow the old pain to arise in dialogue, rather than when we create an artificially sanitized interchange by, for example, coaching couples to use "I" messages. Of course, safety must be created for healing to occur, but couples must at some time experience the nightmare rather than bypass it. In Imago Relationship Therapy, the PCD is a brilliant way to guide a couple safely from nightmare to a new relational experience.

The Parent-Child Dialogue Heals Through Specificity and Corrective Relational Experiences

The PCD is potent partly because it addresses specific hurts and thus can provide specific healing. As Casement (1986) says, we must create the specific situation that hurt us in order to heal the resulting wounds in a specific and therefore powerful way. We do not heal generic pain; we heal specific pain. The PCD arises out of specific, immediate, emotionally charged frustrations in the relationship, transporting the speaker-child back to the original specific pain in the past. Then healing can occur in a very specific way and in the most hurt place.

There are several ways that new, corrective relational experiences can arise in the PCD. First, the speaker-child in the PCD can experience a corrective relational experience with the partner, who is listening in the role of the parent. As the listener-parent offers mirroring, understanding, and validation, the speaker-child has experiences of connection with the partner where previously there was repetitive hurt and disconnection. The new corrective relational experience occurs between the partners, as the listening one offers compassion for past hurts.

Second, the speaker-child can also experience a new, good relationship with the parents, as if they were actually there. The juxtaposition of present and past pain through enactment and imago match potentiates the experiences in the PCD, towing the speaker-child directly back to childhood. As Hendrix (1979, 1992) and Scharff and Scharff (1991) say, it is only the physical-emotional intimacy of the marriage relationship that can recapitulate the intensity of childhood experience (of course, many therapists would say that such healing relationships occur over time in individual therapy). The listener-parent actually plays the good object, which the parent could have been if he or she had been able to listen to the child's hurt or to not have hurt the child in the first place.

Third, as already mentioned, the listener-parents can also have corrective relational experiences. These occur when they understand how their partners were hurt as children, and they experience compassion instead of reactivity. This is not only healing to the partner but also to themselves as the listener-parents. When listeners have experiences of compassion and connection, where previously they were angry or distancing, they experience more self-esteem and pride (S. Shulkin & M. Kollman, personal communication, 1997).

Enactment or Imago Match

The first two kinds of suffering listed earlier, enactment and imago match, share a characteristic that is not present in the third kind, projection. In both enactment and imago match situations, one partner is actually doing something that is hurting the other. In the third pain-generating scenario, projection, there is no actual hurtful behavior going on: it is only in the mind of the projecting partner.

Because there is hurtful behavior going on in both enactment and imago match situations, they can appear similar. One partner complains about the other, and the other really is doing the hurtful thing. The difference is that in enactment, we have provoked our partners to do the hurtful thing, whereas in imago match they do it just because that is who they are. Enactment and imago match situations give couples different opportunities for growth. Depending on whether it is enactment or imago match, therapists can make different decisions about who should play the child in the PCD and who has a Lost Self that needs to be activated through responding to a Behavior Change Request (BCR).

Of course, romantic partners in any couple have intertwined psyches, and both are enacting, projecting, or just naturally being their imago choice match, with the negative qualities for which they were chosen. However, in order to unravel the relationship nightmare, we must focus primarily on one person at a time. For example, at any given moment, only one partner can explore childhood pain in the PCD and only one can use BCRs to fill in his Lost Self. Over the course of IRT, both partners have the opportunity to use the conflicts and frustrations of the relationship to explore their childhood wounds, heal themselves, and change their interactions. But in the short run, therapists have to choose whose childhood pain will be explored in the PCD and who will have the opportunity to change their relational repertoire with a BCR.

How do we choose? One way is to discriminate between enactment and imago match. When one partner is expressing frustration about the other, we can determine whether the pain comes from enacting by the complainer or because the other partner actually has negative imago match characteristics that are creating the pain. In the example that follows, when Edward expresses frustration about Rochelle, we can determine whether the conflict arises, at the moment, more from enactment by Edward or from negative imago match characteristics that Rochelle actually has. If it is enactment, then Edward is orchestrating his own frustration through subtle cues and behaviors. He can best grow by understanding how and why he is doing this and by having a new relational experience with Rochelle. If it is imago match, then Edward is suffering not because he is provoking Rochelle but because Rochelle actually has the negative characteristics that are causing the pain. In this case, healing is best achieved by focusing on Rochelle's behavior and how she learned it.

Following are a description of this couple and examples of how to work with the enactment concept at one point and the imago match concept at another point.

Vignette: Edward Feels Left Out Because He Is Enacting

Edward and Rochelle came to couples therapy in extreme breakdown: Rochelle was having severe anxiety attacks, and Edward was depressed, locked in stony silence, and unable to move forward in his artistic career. At one point, Edward complained in the Couples Dialogue that he felt left out because Rochelle did not include him in family decision making. I thought that Edward was acting in a way that provoked Rochelle to leave him out, so I thought of this situation as an enactment. I led them into the PCD, with Edward as the child, in which he told Rochelle, who was playing his mother, that she listened to all her six older children but ignored his input and sometimes laughed at him, leaving him feeling outcast, devalued, and shamed. Rochelle-Mom asked, "How did you try to protect yourself?" Edward answered that he learned to pretend that he did not want to add anything, to deny that he wanted anything before they told him he could not have it, and to look forbidding so no one would even ask for his input. When she asked what he needed that she, as mother, failed to give him, he answered, "To be told I counted, listened to, to be asked for my input." Through this PCD, Edward realized how his actions led his present-day family to leave him out. Because I saw Edward as enacting the situation that led to his pain, I used the time after the PCD to help him see how he acted remote and uninterested in present-day family decisions, just as he did in childhood, and how this behavior influenced Rochelle to leave him out. With this new knowledge, connection with the emotional antecedents, and a new relational experience with Rochelle in the PCD, he was freed to try new ways of being with Rochelle and the family.

Vignette: Rochelle, as the Imago Match, Leaves Edward Out

At another point in Edward and Rochelle's therapy, Edward was again complaining that Rochelle left him out, saying that she opposed his input about how to handle their eldest son. This time it seemed as if Rochelle were actually doing something that made Edward feel left out, so I conceptualized this as an imago match problem, not an enactment. The pain did not come from Edward's enacting his rejection, but rather because Rochelle, chosen for her (partly negative) imago characteristics, was actually being rejecting. Because I thought it was better for Rochelle to have the opportunity to grow, I led her to speak as the child in the PCD. She said that her father either didn't pay attention to her point of view or told her she was wrong, to the point that she felt "X'd out." She tried to escape this pain by arguing and fighting with her father, trying to get him to see her point of view. After the PCD, I focused on how Rochelle, given her childhood environment, had failed to develop the ability to accept feedback in a positive way, but rather had learned to become defensive. She came to realize how she resisted Edward's input about the children because it brought up old painful childhood feelings. In order to grow, she needed to develop her ability to take feedback from Edward without automatically becoming defensive. We completed this segment of therapy with Rochelle making some BCRs of herself so that she could practice new ways of responding to Edward's input.

When It Is Projection

In my experience, simple projection, without the complication of enactment, is rare in couples therapy. Most of the time, people have had enough exposure to each other to have intertwined psyches. They will usually give in to the pushes and pulls of enactments and respond in the expected negative ways. In healthier people or in those further along the road of healing, projection may occur.

Vignette: George Doesn't Love Me

Marilyn complains that George doesn't really love her. In fact, he has expressed his love in many ways, though possibly not in the exact way she is currently wanting. Her perception that he doesn't love her is, in this case, a projection, deriving from childhood experiences of loneliness and rejection. Because Marilyn is projecting, her growth could come in the Couples Dialogue, from sharing how she felt unloved in childhood. She could learn, through BCRs from either her partner or herself, to avoid these assumptions and to focus on the love she is actually getting.

Forward Thinking

We have seen how contemporary psychoanalytic relational theories are vastly different from traditional psychoanalytic theory, and how they conceptualize development and healing through relationship. We have seen how these theories can be combined with Imago theory in describing three ways of suffering in the relationship nightmare and in clarifying the kinds of healing that can happen when there is enactment, imago match, or projection.

References

Bollas, C. (1989). *The shadow of the object: Psychoanalysis of the unthought known.* New York: Columbia University Press.

Casement, P. (1986). Some pressures on the analyst for physical contact during the reliving of early trauma. In G. Kohon (Ed.), *The British school of psychoanalysis: The independent tradition.* New Haven, CT: Yale University Press.

Ehrenberg, D. (1974). The intimate edge in therapeutic relatedness. *Contemporary Psychoanalysis, 10,* 423–437.

Fairbairn, W. R. (1946). Endopsychic relationships and dynamic structure. *International Journal of Psychoanalysis, 27,* 30–37.

Hannah, M. T., & Marrone, J. G. (1997). The predialogical couple: Theories and strategies. *Journal of Imago Relationship Therapy, 2*(1), 63–70.

Hendrix, H. (1979). *Getting the love you want: Therapist's instructions to a couple's therapy manual.* Winter Park, FL: Institute for Imago Relationship Therapy.

Hendrix, H. (1988). *Getting the love you want: A guide for couples.* New York: Henry Holt.

Hendrix, H. (1992). *Keeping the love you find: A guide for singles.* New York: Pocket Books.

Hendrix, H. (1996). The evolution of Imago Relationship Therapy: A personal and theoretical journey. *Journal of Imago Relationship Therapy, 1*(1), 1–18.

Mason, R. C. (1997). Imago: A theory of connectivity. *Journal of Imago Relationship Therapy, 2*(1), 33–45.

Mason, R. C. (1998). My view of Imago. *Journal of Imago Relationship Therapy, 3*(1), 5–10.

Mitchell, S. (1988). *Relational concepts in psychoanalysis: An integration.* Cambridge, MA: Harvard University Press.

Sandler, J. (1976). Countertransference and role-responsiveness. *International Review of Psychoanalysis, 3,* 43–47.

Scharff, D. E., & Scharff, J. S. (1991). *Object relations couple therapy.* Northvale, NJ: Aronson.

Schnarch, D. (1997). *Passionate marriage: Love, sex and intimacy in emotionally committed relationships.* New York: Norton.

Schwaber, E. (1981). Narcissism, self psychology, and the listening perspective. *Annual of Psychoanalysis, 9,* 115–132.

Shulkin, S. (1996). Case study: Treating an exploratory wounded couple. *Journal of Imago Relationship Therapy, 1*(1), 77–80.

Stark, M. (1999). *Modes of therapeutic action: Enhancement of knowledge, provision of experience and engagement in relationship.* Northvale, NJ: Rowman and Littlefield.

Stolorow, R., Brandschaft, B., & Atwood, G. (1987). *Psychoanalytic treatment: An integrative approach.* Hillsdale, NJ: Analytic Press.

Part Three

Perspectives on Clinical Theory

Chapter Eight

Imago, Relationships, and Empathy

Randall C. Mason, Ph.D.

A relationship can be described simply as two or more people coming together to relate: the individuals "have a relationship." The perspective taken by Imago Relationship Therapy (IRT) is much more complex: in a committed adult relationship, the relationship takes on a life of its own—but only to the extent that the relationship has at least as much power over the individuals as the individuals have over the relationship. IRT suggests that rather than there being individuals *having a relationship,* the *relationship has individuals.* When that relationship is good, it undergirds and enhances the functioning of individuals. When it is conflictual, it can destroy their well-being.

Empathy is the major condition of and means toward a connected relationship, and empathic breaks are the primary source of disconnection in relationships. Defining empathy as "standing in the place of the other," the Imago process facilitates the experiencing of empathy by couples in a committed relationship. Through empathy, partners move from disconnection to connection. As this movement occurs, the relationship becomes a source of healing for the individuals in it.

Some might wonder why, in a chapter on Imago therapy, there are references to self psychology and to the Stone Center at Wellesley[1] (Jordan, 1991). These traditions are included because they, like

Hendrix (1992) but in contrast to others, have focused specifically on empathy in relationships and have thus enhanced my understanding of the Imago model.

The references to the analytic tradition and analytic treatment might also be puzzling, because Imago focuses on romantic partners and analysis works with individuals. However, Imago and analysis are similar in their concentration on "intense" relationships. The powerful bonding of the couple's relationship is also found in the relationship between the analyst and the analysand, whose connection is built by their meeting several times per week over a period of years. Before my work in Imago, I saw the intensity of the couple's relationship as being most like the analytic relationship, but now I see the analytic relationship as being most like the couple's relationship.

The intensity of the analyst and analysand's contact and the use of their relationship for healing serve as a bridge between analytic therapy and Imago couples therapy. Although in some ways the analytic relationship is unique, it shares some similarities with couples work. Present in both therapeutic situations is the transference-countertransference cauldron—the interaction of two different subjectivities in the intersubjective arena or space. The role of the Imago therapist could be compared to that of the analytic therapy supervisor: in analysis, the crucial interchange occurs between analyst and client, with the supervisor playing a peripheral role. In IRT, the therapist's activity is secondary in importance to the "real" action, which occurs between the partners in the relationship.

Both meanings of empathy used in this chapter constitute the core of Imago. Both are about "feeling with or into the other" and connote an activity of coming to know the other. The Rogerian meaning of the term *empathy* is similar to that of the third step of the "mirroring, validation, and empathy" sequence of the Couples Dialogue, where empathy is the capacity to reflect the feelings of the other. Kohut (1991) provides a broader definition of empathy with his notion of *vicarious introspection,* which requires us to step into the shoes of the other and see reality from the other's perspective. Within the Imago framework, vicarious introspection is the outcome of the three-step dialogical process of mirroring, validating, and empathizing.

Relationships

Neither the general public nor the therapeutic community has expressed, as of yet, much more than a faint recognition of the power of the committed relationship over the individuals who compose it. Relationships might be thought of as "good" or "bad" to varying degrees, but they are not usually considered, in and of themselves, to be a major source of personal difficulty. "Bad" relationships are usually handled either by treating each individual's problems or by terminating the relationship—not by treating the relationship.

Impact on the Individual

As long as there is intact connection within their relationship, people do not realize the impact that the relationship has on their personal functioning. But once they experience the pain of a breakup, they begin to realize how profoundly the relationship affects their own well-being. Even then, they might not understand why they experience the breakup as so disturbing. Often they attribute their pain to something negative about their own personality makeup or to their immaturity, and many therapists would agree with their assessment. Likewise, during marriage, people might develop problematic symptoms or behaviors that stem from the relationship but that they attribute to their own intrapersonal issues. And when undesirable traits or symptoms appear in their partner, they often fail to consider that the relationship might be the basis of their partner's difficulties. Some people, in fact, live their entire lifetime convinced of their individuality and separateness from others. Unless they encounter the pain of an empathic break or loss, their convictions remain unchallenged. Even when people do experience such a loss, they might fail to appreciate the profound impact that that loss has on their personal as well as relationship functioning.

View of Behavioral and Physical Sciences

Robert Stolerow challenges the pervasive myth that selves are immune to happenings outside themselves. In a chapter titled "The Myth of the Isolated Mind" (Stolerow & Atwood, 1992), he describes this mythical self as a computer that somehow thinks and feels independently of its biological and social milieu.

Both psychology and the physical sciences have tended to view the world as a set of separate and discrete objects, human and non-human, that relate to one other. Implicit in this perspective is the assumption that the newborn infant is separated from its mother, and so the task of early infancy is to attach. It is equally plausible, however, to infer that the infant experiences the self as one with the mother and that the task of differentiation begins at birth and is completed over time within the context of connection. Because the former assumption has seemed so self-evident, theorists simply have not, until recently, considered the latter.

Consistent with the views of the behavioral and physical sciences, self-sufficiency and autonomy have represented the pinnacle of maturity. One's expression of the need for another person does not necessarily imply immaturity, as long as the absence of the other does not impair one's functioning in any way. In our culture, for example, one is permitted and even expected to mourn the loss of a mate. But allowing grief to interfere with one's work for more than a few weeks might elicit shame. A full appreciation of the primacy of relationships and of the impact of losing them, however, would lead to an acknowledgment that the grieving process should take a long time.

The Power of Relationships

The emphasis of the new paradigm, then, is on the understanding of discrete objects within the context of relationship. Without abandoning any understanding of the self that we gained from more atomistic investigations, we now view the relationship as the central unit of analysis. Jordan (1988) succinctly contrasts the scientific worldview: "Moving from Aristotelian logic and Newtonian physics to quantum physics, we begin to see reality defined by relationships, continuities, and probabilities rather than by discrete objects and dualities" (p. 1).

The potential power of the committed relationship is dramatically and qualitatively different from that of other relationships. Especially when the interaction between two individuals generates romance, individual functioning becomes as much a function of the relationship as the relationship becomes a function of the individuals who are in it.

Imago theory has described the destructive power as well as the healing potential of relationships. The relationship's potent effects are demonstrated when couples enter a therapy session discouraged and exhausted but, after they have worked on their relationship, leave with high energy. This is particularly evident after their use of the Couples Dialogue. Such demonstrations reveal as a narcissistic fantasy the notion of an isolated and contained self that remains the same regardless of circumstances. Equally fictitious is the belief that a person can become fully healed outside of a committed relationship.

Influence on the Self

The Stone Center group at Wellesley has effectively articulated the influence of the connected relationship on the self. The director of the Stone Center, Jean Baker Miller (1993, p. 30), describes its powerful effect on individual functioning: "Each person feels a greater sense of 'zest' (vitality, energy). Each person feels more able to act, and does act. Each person has a more accurate picture of himself/herself and the other person(s). Each person feels a greater sense of worth. Each person feels more connected to the other person(s) and feels a greater motivation for connections with other people beyond those in the specific relationship."

This is a description of vital and mature living. The Stone Center views the connected relationship as the source of the individual's vitality and overall health. Attributes like *zest* have received little attention in psychology to date, but seem to correspond with Stern's description of *vitality affects* (1985) in infants. Likewise, what Miller (1993) meant by zest is reflected in Hendrix's understanding of *relaxed joyfulness* (1992). These and other observations have led to the emergence of the *connected relationship* as a central organizing construct.

In Imago work, the levels of vitality, energy, and joyfulness that couples express reflect the extent to which their relationship is in good connection. IRT provides a lens through which couples come to realize that their experience as individuals is substantially a function of their relationship: when they are in good connection with

each other, personal energy is high; caught in the throes of disconnection, their energy dissipates.

The Relationship Nightmare

The effects of disconnection are most clearly detected in what has
been termed the *relationship nightmare*. A relationship nightmare
occurs when two relatively mature adults regress to fighting like two-
year-olds. Usually there is overt fighting characterized by intense
reactivity and mutual shaming, but for some couples, the problematic behavior is relatively covert. The relationship nightmare is typically initiated by two events. There is a conscious precipitant that
both members of the couple remember; preceding this is an unconscious precipitant that neither remembers. Both precipitants involve
empathic breaks that are usually produced by shaming. As soon as
such empathic breaks are addressed in the therapy session, clients
can recover their energy and their sense of cohesion.

Although a complete discussion of the relationship nightmare
is beyond the scope of this chapter [Editors' note: see Mason,
Mason, & Hannah, "The Relationship Nightmare as an Expression
of Disconnection," Chapter Eleven in this volume], an abbreviated
example of one might be helpful. For one couple, a nightmare of
two weeks' duration followed the female partner's statement about
her male partner's inadequacy as a male. This was the conscious
precipitant that they both remembered and for which she offered
profuse apologies, which nonetheless did not terminate the nightmare. The unconscious precipitant occurred shortly before her
critical remark to him. The two of them had been mocking the
drunken behavior of the female partner's mother, whom they had
recently visited. Although the female client had joined her partner
in ridiculing her mother, on an unconscious level she experienced
shame. Because shaming is experienced as a threat to the integrity
or cohesiveness of the self, the nightmare was launched as the
female partner's attempt to survive the undermining of the self.

I have observed a similar although less intense dynamic in my
work with individuals. For example, one man came in feeling overwhelmed and unable to cope. We searched for and analyzed the
empathic breaks in his primary relationship. Afterwards, the client
felt once again able to cope, even though the realities of his situa-

tion remained unchanged. In my earlier work with individual clients, I did not focus much on the significance of their relationship. I spotlighted the individuals themselves and concentrated on how they were managing their personal issues, such as their low energy level or their depression. I believed that if a client had such difficulties, then he or she should undergo individual therapy to grow up and become prepared for a relationship. It seemed logical to view the relationship as being in trouble due to the depression of one of the partners, rather than to see the depression as a symptom of a disconnected relationship. I had an almost magical belief, in fact, that individual therapy would make the person mature enough for the relationship or at least mature enough not to be bothered by the relationship—another manifestation of the narcissistic self-sufficiency fantasy. I have since found that focusing on individuals' pathology simply adds to their feelings of shame and isolation, which further lowers their self-esteem as well as damages their relationship. This leads to an iatrogenic increase in the couple's distress: the treatment exacerbates the very condition it is supposed to correct.

Relationships and Traumatic Events

Congruent with a new understanding of the influence of relationships on individual functioning is Stolerow and Atwood's observation (1992) that the quality of one's relationship determines the nature and intensity of the impact of traumatic events on the individual. They note that the psychological effects of events like death, rape, or other trauma are not determined by external or objective factors; rather, reactions vary from person to person and depend on the quality of a given individual's matrix of significant relationships. Stolerow and Atwood's comments suggest an analogy of a psychological immune system that neutralizes threats to the person's integrity.

A respect for the power of relationships can transform each partner's perspectives of his or her own relationship and of one another. A client described this shift by saying that he had discovered a "third partner" in his marriage. Couples begin to realize that when they feel hateful, what they hate is not their partner but the pain of their relationship. They thus no longer have to admit to some intrinsic defect within themselves or their partner. Feeling less shame, they finally become capable of admitting that their relationship problems have led them to behave differently toward one another than they did when they first met. People are tremendously relieved to realize that the horrible ways they act toward their partner do not reflect their true inner self, but rather the intensity of their relationship nightmare. Similarly, couples learn that the relationship exits they use, such as addictions or affairs, are retreats not from the partner but from the distress of the relationship. One woman who came to view her husband's affair in this light was immediately and visibly relieved: "You mean his affair isn't because of my inadequacy as a woman but is due to our relationship?"

Relationships as a Top Priority

Years ago I read Joseph Campbell's *The Power of Myth* (1988), and I recall reacting negatively to the following passage: "I would say that if the marriage is not the first priority of your life, you're not married. The marriage means that the two are one, the two become one flesh. If the marriage lasts long enough, and if you are acquiescing constantly to it instead of to individual personal whim, you come to realize that this is true—the two really are one" (p. 6).

There were two reasons for my negative reaction. First, at that time, I was barely starting to think of my primary relationship as having priority over my career. While I was growing up, I did not consider my relationship and my career as being in competition. But in reality, I spent the majority of my time and energy taking care of my career. A second reason for my response to what Campbell said was my conviction that acquiescing to anyone was repugnant. Later, after having experienced the power of a committed relationship, I considered Campbell's statement on marriage as a number one priority to be descriptive, rather than prescriptive. Campbell did not mean that one must make the marriage one's first priority; rather, if one is in a connected relationship—is truly married—then the marriage is, descriptively, of top priority. I also came to realize that any acquiescence that is made is an acquiescence not to the partner but to the relationship. This position ought to deliver couples from feeling dominated over or submitted to, even though it demands that each partner act for the good of the relationship. One might, on occasion, even have to do something to which one's partner objects, if to do it is good for the relationship. At the same time, acting for the good of the relationship is acting for the good of the self. A commitment to "we-ness" is, in fact, the best way to care for the self.

Moore describes the reality and potency of this "we-ness" as "the mystery of the ineffable 'in-each-otherness of persons,' into which we are drawn, rather than before which we are bowed down" (1989, p. 5).

Empathy as Connective Tissue

Assuming that relationships constitute the core of well-being and vitality, as I suggest here, we view empathy as the connective tissue of relationships and empathic breaks as lacerations. Empathy and its accompanying sense of connection bring about a cohesive centered firmness of the self; empathic breaks and disconnection lead to the self's enfeeblement and fragmentation. This inner cohesiveness, which enables one to "hold" one's own reality, is a reflection of the connection within the relationship; that connection, in turn, is a function of the empathic milieu.

This notion of empathy as the connective tissue in relationships is paralleled in Kohut's description of empathy as "emotional oxygen" (1984, pp. 47–48): without oxygen, we die physically, and without empathy, we die emotionally. The oxygen metaphor is also congruent with Daniel Stern's descriptions of vitality affects (1985).

Kohut refers to a phenomenon familiar to both self psychology and Imago theory when "he depicts empathy as a 'powerful emotional bond between people' . . . and claims that 'empathy *per se*,' the mere presence of empathy, has . . . a beneficial, in a broad sense, a therapeutic effect—both in the clinical setting and in human life in general" (Stolerow, Atwood, & Branchaft, 1994, pp. 43–44).

These statements might alarm those who, fearing codependency, decry the prospect of the relationship as a primary source of personal healing. But a truly empathic relationship precludes codependent caretaking or doing for others what others need to do for themselves. Empathy can energize the other's performance in the world, but it is does not act in the place of the other.

Couples Dialogue

IRT's primary process for the facilitation of empathy is the Couples Dialogue, in which each partner, sensing the empathy of the other, receives the emotional oxygen he or she needs. This leaves the couple feeling energized, peaceful, and at one with themselves.

Mirroring

How does the dialogue facilitate "standing in the place of the other"? The first step is *mirroring*, in which a receiver of a message conveys to the sender what the receiver heard. The mirroring begins with "If I hear you right," or "Let me see if I have gotten that," followed by either a paraphrase or a verbatim repetition of the sender's message. This simple activity serves two functions: it helps the one doing the mirroring to gather accurate information about the partner, and it soothes the one being mirrored, provided that the mirroring is accurate. Accurate mirroring is more difficult than one might imagine, however. Clients are sometimes astonished to find that they cannot mirror accurately or that they were vastly mistaken in what they thought their partner meant. The difficulty of mirroring increases when the receiving partner internally reacts to what the other is saying, but the structure of the dialogue helps diminish that reactivity. Mirroring has the effect of calming and increasing the centeredness of the person being mirrored, unless that person is feeling so emotionally explosive that he or she cannot experience the mirroring.

Marion Chase, the founder of Modern Dance/Movement therapy, became aware of the power of mirroring during the 1940s, when she was working with schizophrenic patients at St. Elizabeth's Hospital in Washington and the Chestnut Lodge in Maryland. She had patients simply move to music according to their own wishes and inner feelings. She discovered that moving with them in a mirroring image led to a calming and an amelioration of their condition (Sandel, 1993).

Self psychology also uses mirroring in its term *mirroring transference*. The mirroring transference is a manifestation of connectedness between the analyst and the client; here, the client either experiences a sense of oneness with the analyst or views the analyst as admiring of the client's specialness. The establishment of the mirroring transference enhances the client's cohesiveness, and an analysis of the transference might, over time, diminish the intensity of the client's need for mirroring. The transference also teaches the client that it is normal to need the affirmation of mirroring. In fact, because our culture shames such needs, many people have problems with the expression of a desire for mirroring. During adulthood, the committed relationship is the primary context in which one can and should experience mirroring.

Inaccurate mirroring ("convex" or "concave" mirroring, to Hendrix), though, can stimulate reactivity. Kohut (1991), describing a female client he was seeing in analysis in the early 1970s, noted a phenomenon observed by many Imago therapists in their couples work. During each session, at about the halfway point, Kohut's client would break into a impassioned diatribe. Whereas others might rush in with a diagnosis of "borderline" or would prescribe medication, Kohut simply observed that "he and the client did not as yet know the meaning of her symptom" (p. 503). After long investigation, they discovered that her outbursts occurred whenever Kohut, in his summaries of what she had told him (similar to the "summary mirror" in IRT), would add an interpretation that went beyond what she had said. Kohut's interpretations shamed the client by undermining her sense of reality; her rages were attempts to survive.

Accurate mirroring also demands paying attention to what is being said nonverbally. During a demonstration of the Couples Dialogue, a woman complained that her partner was not mirroring her, despite the fact that he was mirroring the content accurately. Indeed, he had gotten all her words right, but she was communicating with high energy and intensity; his energy was much lower, and his expressive style was markedly different from hers. Thus, although her partner was mirroring the content of her message well, she did not experience him as present and responsive.

Validation

Validation and *empathy* increase the empathic effect of the Couples Dialogue. Dialogue is designed to clarify and honor the realities of both partners. Validation both demands and leads to a greater awareness of the other's difference from oneself. Achieving such awareness begins with, but is not fully accomplished by, accurate mirroring; its achievement also requires perceiving the other's reality as something not to be changed but to be understood and honored. Validation, then, entails understanding and communicating to the partner why his or her reality makes sense.

Empathy

Empathy, the third step of the Couples Dialogue, is validation of the affective: what you feel is understandable, in light of what you have experienced. The validation of feelings, as opposed to the expression of compassion, is what makes the empathy step potent. Compassion can easily degenerate into parentalistic verbiage that strikes the listener as condescending. But hearing the other validate one's emotional experience can be empowering, enlivening, and healing.

Mirroring, validation, and empathy together create safety and enhance the reality of the self. In the sense of "standing in the place of the other," empathy involves hearing and mirroring the other's story as he or she perceives it, affirming the other's reality, and validating the feeling experience of the other. This three-step process calls the partners into being and vitality through their experience of another "standing in their shoes."

Clients come to understand the power of the Couples Dialogue and the relevance of the Imago process primarily through their personal experiences with empathy. Until the work of Rogers and Kohut, relatively little attention was paid to the role of empathy in relationships. IRT, however, has made empathy the central task of relationship work.

The shift and commitment to empathy represents a shift from a hierarchical to a consensual model of how the truth is constructed and used. In the past, the truth as it was understood by religious and psychological authorities was emphasized: there was but a single truth, and the therapist's task was to help the client understand and come into agreement with it. The therapist's interpretations grew out of that truth, rather than from the therapist's empathic immersion into the client's reality. When interpretations are based on the latter, they become more descriptive in nature, which allows the "truth" to be constructed consensually by the therapist and client together. Meanwhile, the truth of each remains acknowledged and honored. The same principle applies to couples: their two realities need not submit to one another. There are differences in how one knows and even in what is known. The assumption of a single reality inevitably results in the power struggle, which can eventually desecrate and violate the individuals within a relationship as well as nations and religious groups within the greater context of society.

The centrality of empathy for IRT warrants an examination of four dimensions encompassed within an empathic stance—each of which is essential to the exercise of true empathy.

Dimensions of Empathy

Kohut raised the status of empathy from that of a therapeutic procedure to one of a scientific tool of investigation. In *The Restoration of the Self* (Kohut, 1977), he discusses the problem of applying research methodology to psychoanalysis. Most sciences study the world through sensory observations and the use of sophisticated technology. Kohut sees empathy as equivalent to a scientific tool: "Valid scientific research in psychoanalysis is nevertheless possible because the empathic understanding of the experiences of other human beings is as basic an endowment of man as his vision, hearing, touch, taste and smell" (p. 143).

Kohut acknowledges the difficulty of establishing empathy as a reliable investigative tool, but believes that this is no more difficult than demonstrating the reliability of sensory observations used by the sciences. Other fields have had to develop methods to establish reliability, and psychoanalysis is also faced with that task with respect to empathy.

Kohut's observations (1977) are congruent with IRT's use of the Couples Dialogue as its chief method for comprehending the subjectivity of the other. Partners investigate and thus come to know one another through the empathy gained by the dialogue.

The Investigative Versus the Bonding Nature

Stolerow, Atwood, and Branchaft (1994) raise a legitimate concern about the potential conflict between empathy as an investigative tool and empathy as a means of bonding and healing. Kohut likewise differentiated between the bonding and healing qualities of empathy. These observations justify an examination of the way empathy might be employed in Imago work.

If the bonding function of empathy were to be given priority over its investigative purpose, then people would likely focus on what they considered to be bonding, rather than on an accurate understanding of the other's reality. Even if accurate understanding and communication of the other's reality did not appear to be the "bonding thing to do," offering such understanding and communication would allow bonding to occur. If partners did only what appeared to them to be bonding, then neither empathy nor bonding would result. Both empathy and bonding spring from an understanding of how the other person experiences reality.

Empathy is seen, then, as a process incorporating both investigative and bonding functions. If investigative inquiry along with accurate mirroring do not lead to bonding, then the inquiry was inadequate and true empathy was absent. Likewise, if bonding is not grounded in accurate vicarious introspection, then such bonding is spurious and therefore futile.

Due to the potential conflation of the two functions of empathy, Stolerow, Atwood, and Branchaft (1994) suggest using different terminology, for example, *affective responsiveness,* to describe the bonding aspect of empathy. However, this particular term removes the necessary tension that exists between the polarities, and enables each meaning to correct for the other.

Kohut (1991) did add a wrinkle to the bipolar framework of empathy discussed here. He was convinced that empathy could be used for evil purposes as well as for bonding and healing. He suggested that the Nazis' talent for vicarious introspection heightened their capacity to torture and brutalize. Kohut's point here does not conform to his insistence, discussed earlier, that both ends of the polarity must exist for empathy to be present. Though this inconsistency does not negate the integrity of Kohut's model of empathy, an awareness of the potential destructiveness of empathy would probably be wise.[2]

Avoidant Versus Useful

According to self psychology, rage is a reaction to narcissistic injury. Many object relations theorists hold that aggression and rage are not merely reactive but abide within all persons, and that the repression of these drives creates difficulties. For example, symptoms might occur when endogenous aggression and rage have been repressed. For object relations therapists, treatment must uncover these forces and aim them in a healthier direction.

Object relations thinkers might also wonder if empathy, as used by the self psychologist following Kohut's tradition, is actually a manifestation of the therapist's unconscious fear of the client's aggression. Object relations theorists would argue against an empathic stance, because it permits clients to avoid the "real" issues. Some Imago therapists might agree, viewing dialogue as a useless distraction that avoids a necessary confrontation of the partner and that turns the therapist into an ally of the avoidant spouse. IRT has been criticized, in fact, for being soft and nonconfrontational: it is more concerned with validation and empathy than with confronting serious character flaws that are wrecking relationships.

There are, however, three problems with confrontation. First, its use assumes that the therapist or the confronting spouse has accurately determined what the "true" relationship difficulties are, as well as what the pathological or errant spouse should do to rectify those problems. Confrontation fails to consider the different truth of the other. Second, clients are better able to become aware of their character flaws and resulting relationship problems when empathic understanding is present. Empathy enables one to encounter, at a deeper level, the difficulties created by one's own character defects. Third, confrontation produces questionable results. Often, it triggers fear and adaptive compliance with the wishes of the confronter. Compliance then leads to characterological entrenchment as opposed to self-awareness and a commitment to growth. Confrontation usually tears down rather than contributes to the cohesion of the self and the self's capacity to act. Empathic awareness is more likely to produce self-confrontation.

This is not to dismiss all forms of confrontation; rather, if it is to be effective, confrontation must be empathic. A clinical vignette from Kohut's *How Does Analysis Cure?* (1984) demonstrates this quality. A psychiatric resident was in his third year of analysis with Kohut. One day the resident, late for his analytic appointment, explained that he had once again been stopped for speeding. Arrogantly, he had provoked the officer into issuing him an expensive ticket, even though the officer had initially been inclined to let the physician go with a warning. Angrily, the analysand reminded

Kohut of similar incidents that had led to auto accidents. When the resident stopped talking, Kohut indicated to him "that I was going to give him the deepest interpretation he had so far received in his analysis. I could see his utter surprise at this announcement; it was totally different from anything I had ever said to him before. Then, after several seconds of silence, I said, very firmly and with total seriousness, 'You are a complete idiot.' There was another second or so of silence, then the patient burst into a warm and friendly laughter and relaxed visibly on the couch" (1984, p. 74).

Although startling, the announcement "You are a complete idiot" can be seen as empathic and, in fact, as bonding. However, one would not arrive at this conclusion by listing all of the bonding responses Kohut could have made; the statement he made would not strike anyone as bonding. Its empathic effect on the resident, however, was palpable: he relaxed and experienced the release of laughter. It's doubtful that most other confrontations would have achieved a similar outcome.

Is there any other way to understand Kohut's comment as empathic, other than through observing the client's response? Kohut's expression of empathy required an in-depth knowledge of the patient that he achieved through their three years of four sessions of analysis per week. The analytic process would have demanded of Kohut an attitude of inquiry, which would have then led to accurate vicarious introspection. "You are a complete idiot" grew out of Kohut's empathic understanding of this client, who experienced the statement with a deep sense of *being known*. Kohut, standing in the shoes of the resident, knew that the resident possessed a foundational awareness of what it means to be "a complete idiot."

Although the statement "You are a complete idiot" could be judged as confrontational, it differs from typical confrontations in a very significant way: it grew out of Kohut's vicarious introspection into the client's world, rather than out of some external standard. The usual rationale for confrontation is that the client is deviating from our standards, from our notions of reality, or from the norms of others. Confrontation is done to bring the client into line with the truth, rather than to bring the therapist or spouse into a deep comprehension of the truth of the client.

The useful and avoidant applications of empathy fall at two polar ends that are in tension with one another. Empathy might enable the therapist to avoid a wounding encounter with the client, but empathy also requires its giver to have an accurate grasp of the inner world of the other. True empathy requires both supportive responsiveness and precise understanding.

Boundaried Empathy Versus Unboundaried Empathy

Mature empathy can be defined as a developmental achievement in which the individual moves from unboundaried to boundaried empathy. An example of unboundaried empathy is when babies in a nursery begin to cry in response to one baby's cries. Experiencing the crying baby's distress as their own, the other babies empathize, so they too begin to cry. The development of a boundaried self saves the individual from merging with the emotional states of others: the infant no longer has to cry merely because others are crying. This achievement of the boundaried self is necessary for adult functioning, in general, and for therapeutic capacity, in particular.

Kohut (1984), noting a developmental trajectory from unboundaried to mature empathy, suggests the goal to be an attenuated rather than a highly boundaried empathy. Attenuated empathy is necessary for caregiving because to provide containment the mother must allow the child to merge with her. Kohut adds that attenuated empathy sensitizes the mother to the baby's signals of anxiety. Attenuated empathy thus enables the mother to provide containment through holding the infant. Without attenuated empathy, she would have responded to the infant either with empathic flooding, which might have overwhelmed the child, or by walling herself off from the child, which would have deprived the child. Either of these responses by the mother can result in serious detrimental effects on the child, who as an adult might be susceptible to uncurbed rushes of emotion or, alternatively, might wall himself or herself off in self-protection. The capacity for human experiencing through mature empathy would thus be lost. Kohut concludes: "From the beginning of life, therefore—and the analytic situation is no exception—the desideratum is exposure to attenuated empathy, not exposure to total and all encompassing empathy" (1984, pp. 82–83).

Cultural and professional stereotypes depict mature empathy as manifested in a more boundaried and cognitive self: mature empathy is an involvement with the other that maintains a clear sense of separation. Moreover, the male is often considered the prototype of this boundaried cognitive self. In contrast, females are perceived as identifying too strongly with others, leading to emotional overinvolvement and a lack of distinct separation. Such "regressive merging" tendencies are typically viewed as detrimental to an effective empathic stance.

Such gender-based stereotypes are consistent with the cultural assumption that the male way of being is normative for mature humans. Any deviation by women from this norm has often been viewed as a reflection of their inadequacy. As Surrey (1991) points out, because the experiences of women have not typically been incorporated into psychological theories, definitions of maturity based on those theories are incomplete.

Some theorists see women as having problems with empathy because of their lack of sufficient boundaries, which is thought to result from little girls' difficulties with separating from their mother. This analysis, however, is based on theories that fail to take into account the differentness of women's experience. Jean Baker Miller (1991) rejects the idea that girls fail to develop an internal sense of self because they lack the need that males have to separate from the female caretaker. Girls develop an internal sense of self as much as boys do, but the process is different in girls: the development of the self in women takes place within the context of connection, as opposed to separation.

Affirming such gender-based differences, Surrey (1991) suggests that the early developmental representation of the self in females be described as an *encompassing* sense of self, in contrast with the more boundaried or limited self of boys (Miller, 1991). Women do not have greater difficulty in learning boundaries; rather, their concept of self and the nature of their boundaries differ from those of males. Any comprehensive theory of empathy must include such gender-based differences.

Jordan (1991), incorporating the experiences of both genders, views mature empathy as the result not of boundary development but of a process of differentiation. Mature empathy implies not separation but differentiation within the context of connection. Empathy includes the person's capacity to merge while remaining differentiated.

To illustrate, Jordan relates her experience of listening to a young female client relate the details of preparing for her first prom. As the client shared the details, Jordan mentally relived her own first prom. The images evoked by the client's description stimulated and become blurred with Jordan's memories of her own prom dress, her first pair of high heels, and her first stick of lipstick. She likewise experienced her client's feelings of anticipation and excitement: "There is an oscillation back and forth; she is now in her pink dress, now in my green one. As this occurs, I am also observing my own affective state, aware of the process. I am not cognitively confused about who is who, but I feel deeply present and sharing, knowing what she is feeling" (1991, p. 73).

Jordan describes empathy here as a joining with the other. The joining is real on an affective level as well as on cognitive and imaginative levels. Although she acknowledges the importance of the cognitive component of empathy, Jordan argues that "to assume that affective arousal necessarily leads to cognitive confusion is to underestimate the capacity for integrated functioning—a functioning that, we might add, is the essence of mature empathy" (1991, p. 74). For Jordan, joining is prerequisite to mature empathy. The joining process yields a more accurate picture of the partner and thus enables a more empathic response. This is the antithesis of regressive merger: it is an empathic imagining made possible by the capacity to be with, yet clearly differentiated from, the other. One does not lose the self in the process.

This depiction of mature empathy incorporates the feminine experience of developing an encompassing sense of self in the context of connection. Does the male context of separation serve as a handicap to the development of empathy? The significance of separation for males is not well understood. Certainly, there appear to be gender differences in empathic style, with males being more cognitive and females seeming more affective. Marital therapists have noted these differences when working with couples. For example, when a therapist tells a couple that the goal of therapy is the development of increased connection, the woman usually nods knowingly while the male responds with puzzlement and perhaps anxiety.

In his work with couples, Bergman (1991) observed a condition that he calls "male relational dread." When I have related that expression to groups of couples, the women are completely baffled over what the term could mean; the men all nod knowingly. An "encompassing sense of self" undoubtedly connotes something to males that heightens their dread. Consequently, men will tend to engage in a defensive devaluation of the unboundaried self, which they consider to be more permissible for women. Too, men tend to equate intimacy with sexual activity rather than with emotional connection. But after careful investigation, I've found a strong desire for connection underlying much of males' talk about sex. This longing for connection triggers shame for men; it is therefore less embarrassing for men when they talk about their yearning for connection in terms of a desire for sexual satisfaction.

Men need to develop an appreciation of the encompassing sense of self that they have devalued in women for so long and so often. They need to acknowledge this encompassing sense of self as a strength and a way of knowing for women that men, too, can discover and restore in themselves.

At this juncture, the terms *joining* and *differentiation* could replace *merging* and *boundaries*. Although joining and differentiation might seem to be polar opposites, both must be fully present for the creation of maximum empathy. Joining does not imply empathic flooding, and differentiation does not entail cognitive and boundaried nonjoining. The healthy attenuation of empathy calls for diminution of neither joining nor differentiation.

Responsiveness Versus Accountability

IRT's psychoeducational approach and structure might strike some as mitigating against empathic responsiveness to clients. Clients are urged to go to workshops. They must learn and practice the Couples Dialogue. There are relationship guidelines and homework. There are prescriptions for what should happen in therapy, at least during the initial sessions. And clients who appear to be making slow progress might feel pressured to "get with the program."

Although many couples view the structure of IRT as one of its strengths, a rigid framework is incompatible with any approach that uses empathy as its primary tool. Interventions should emerge through the therapist's empathic resonance with the couple, rather than from a theoretically derived methodology that is assumed to be equally good for everybody.

Therapeutic structure is often rejected in favor of empathy—with empathy construed here as a free-flowing responsiveness to clients. Some therapists use such a version of empathy in traditional modes of psychotherapy that are primarily antistructural. Empathy of this nature, however, often simply masks the therapist's own empathic limitations. For example, to ensure that he or she appears warm, nonintrusive, and responsive, a therapist might avoid making strong recommendations to a couple, particularly when one or both partners seem resistant; for example, one partner might refuse to engage in dialogue or to make a no-exit commitment to the therapy. A therapist's avoidance of certain interventions and his or her failure to explore the couple's resistance to those interventions provide clues to possible empathic limitations in the therapist.

Once again, a polarity must be held in tension: in this case, it is a tension between structure and responsiveness. True empathy incorporates both ends of this pole. A therapeutic structure that is nonresponsive to the particular needs of a couple is clearly unempathic. But failure to provide sufficient structure to couples who desperately need such structure is also unempathic. Empathy must include both empathic resonance and accountability. Empathic resonance means that the therapist learns the meaning of responsiveness from his or her clients. Accountability implies the therapist's adherence to the methods and standards developed by colleagues through their own empathic involvement with clients. Accountability along with empathic resonance expands the therapist's empathic capacity.

Understanding the New Paradigm

This chapter began by examining the adult committed relationship within the context of connectivity. A person's individual functioning was seen as dependent on the quality of the person's committed relationship. Next, a new relationship paradigm was described, one that sees the connection within the couple as the primary unit of analysis. This model suggests that individual functioning and well-being are as much a function of the relationship as the relationship is a function of the individuals who are in the relationship. Empathy was then described as the "stuff" and mediator of the connected relationship, and the Couples Dialogue was offered as a prime example of an empathic process and as an ideal facilitator of connection. Finally, four polarities thought to be contained within empathy—polarities that must be kept in balance for the maximum achievement of empathy—were discussed: the investigative versus the bonding nature of empathy, the avoidant versus the useful aspect of empathy; empathy as merging versus empathy as maintaining boundaries, and empathy's responsiveness versus its accountability.

Notes

1. The Stone Center is a group composed primarily of women psychotherapists who study the psychology of women.
2. Indeed, Kohut, in a complex argument that is beyond the scope of this chapter, would argue that even in this instance one could postulate a minimal degree of bonding. Although this certainly seems more theoretical than experiential, Kohut would maintain that there is a bond between enemies that is greater than the bond between the self and nonhumans (Kohut, 1991, pp. 529–530).

References

Bergman, S. (1991). Men's psychological development: A relational perspective. *Work in Progress,* No. 48. Wellesley, MA: Stone Center Working Paper Series.

Campbell, J. (1988). *The power of myth.* New York: Doubleday.

Hendrix, H. (1992). *Keeping the love you find: A guide for singles.* New York: Pocket Books.

Jordan, J. (1988). Relationship development: Therapeutic implications of empathy and shame. *Work in Progress,* No. 39. Wellesley, MA: Stone Center Working Paper Series.

Jordan, J. (1991). Empathy and self boundaries. In J. V. Jordan, A. G. Kaplan, J. B. Miller, I. P. Stiver, & J. L. Surrey (Eds.), *Women's growth in connection: Writings from the Stone Center* (pp. 67–80). New York: Guilford Press.

Kohut, H. (1977). *The restoration of the self.* New York: International Universities Press.

Kohut, H. (1984). *How does analysis cure?* Chicago: University of Chicago Press.

Kohut, H. (1991). *The search for the self: Selected writings of Heinz Kohut, 1978–1981* (Vol. 4; P. H. Ornstein, Ed.). New York: International Universities Press.

Miller, J. B. (1991). Development of women's sense of self. In J. V. Jordan, A. G. Kaplan, J. B. Miller, I. P. Stiver, & J. L. Surrey (Eds.), *Women's growth in connection: Writings from the Stone Center* (pp. 11–26). New York: Guilford Press.

Miller, J. B. (1993). What do we mean by relationships? *Work in Progress,* No. 22. Wellesley, MA: Stone Center Working Paper Series.

Moore, S. (1989). *Jesus, the liberator of desire.* New York: Crossroads.

Sandel, S. (1993). The process of empathic reflection in dance therapy. In S. Sandel, H. Chaiklin, & A. Lohn (Eds.), *Foundations of dance/ movement therapy: The life and work of Marion Chase* (pp. 98–111). Columbia, MD: Marion Chase Memorial Fund of the American Dance Therapy Association.

Stern, D. N. (1985). *The interpersonal world of the infant: A view from psychoanalysis and developmental psychology.* New York: Basic Books.

Stolerow, R. D., & Atwood, G. E. (1992). *Contexts of being: The intersubjective foundations of psychological life.* Hillsdale, NJ: Analytic Press.

Stolerow, R. D., Atwood, G. E., & Branchaft, B. (1994). *The intersubjective perspective.* Northvale, NJ: Aronson.

Surrey, J. (1991). The "self-in-relation": A theory of women's development. In J. V. Jordan, A. G. Kaplan, J. B. Miller, I. P. Stiver, & J. L. Surrey (Eds.), *Women's growth in connection: Writings from the Stone Center* (pp. 51–66). New York: Guilford Press.

Chapter Nine

Imago, Relationships, and Empathy: A Response to Mason

Ted Smith, D.Min.

Randall C. Mason (1996) has written a stimulating and challenging article, one that raises many important issues. [Editors' note: Mason's article appears in this volume as Chapter Eight.] He has drawn many conclusions with which I agree, including the following:

1. Committed primary love relationships have a unique quality that other relationships lack.
2. A good sense of connection can be a powerful agent for individual well-being and vitality.
3. Without a sense of connection, such relationships can exercise a destructive force on the individual.
4. Disconnection leads to the power struggle.
5. The Couples Dialogue used in Imago Relationship Therapy (IRT) is a potent and effective tool for creating empathy, which is needed for connection.
6. Shaming produces empathic breaks, which are destructive to relationships.
7. The difficulties in relationships are not a reflection of the partners' true inner selves.
8. Similarities exist between the couple relationship and the psychoanalytic relationship.
9. Psychology in general and psychotherapy in particular have

paid insufficient attention to the concept and workings of relationships.
10. The old atomistic thinking in psychology is archaic and must
give way to a more relational paradigm.

On other issues, my perspectives deviate from those of Mason.
I will now offer alternative viewpoints on some compelling questions raised by Mason's article. My views are based on my own clinical experience as an Imago therapist as well as on the thinking of
theorists and colleagues in the marital therapy and related fields.

The Primacy of Relationships

Mason states that relationship problems are simply relational in
nature; there is no such thing as intrapsychic pathology. Mason's
position would reverse many of the advances made in understanding the human being since Freud's discovery of the unconscious.
Relationships inevitably reveal hidden pathology and personal
immaturity; only exceptional problems are purely relational. Thus,
although relationship difficulties do not reflect the true inner selves
of the partners, they reveal intrapsychic issues such as early wounding from damaging object relations, inner fears, and powerful
unconscious mechanisms of defense against vulnerability and pain.
Inner pathology consistently interferes with effective dialogue, validation, empathy, connection, and intimacy, so inner issues must
be dealt with to enable effective relating. On this issue I side with
the object relations theorists, who say that effective treatment must
uncover and work with intrapsychic problems (Almaas, 1988; Greenberg & Mitchell, 1983; Scharff & Scharff, 1991). Furthermore, because each partner has his or her own subjective experience of the
relationship as a structure in consciousness, effective couples therapy always and inevitably must deal with those separate structures.

The Importance of Relationships

The quality of relationships and of connection in relationships has
been neglected in psychology, psychotherapy, and healing work. I
heartily concur, therefore, with Mason's emphasis on the importance

of relationships, especially the primary love relationship, for the well-being of individuals. For most persons, the focus of inner ideation and rumination is relationship: relationships from the past, in the present, and anticipated in the future. The issues discussed by clients in individual psychotherapy are typically about relationships, both current and past, particularly early relationships with parents and other primary caretakers.

A psychoanalytic or existential approach to therapy will inevitably focus on the client-therapist relationship. Mason observes that he used to think of the relationship of couples as like the relationship between the analysand and the analyst, but he now sees the psychoanalytic relationship as most like the couple relationship. This seems valid: the intensity of the psychoanalytic relationship may approach that of the primary love relationship. For the last twenty years, Harville Hendrix (1988, 1992) has focused on the extraordinary and intense nature of love relationships and their capacity for destroying or healing. Mason points to breaks in relationship as the source of most emotional trauma. Partners in marital turmoil don't really hate the partner; they hate the overwhelming difficulties they experience in the relationship.

Psychological theory seems stagnantly engulfed in archaic thinking that identifies an (actually fictitious) isolated self. Modern science, however, especially physics but now also biology (Sheldrake, 1981) and the human sciences, has come to acknowledge the primacy of relationships. Imago theory, too, has established the centrality of relationships to human experience. Yet something remains unclear in all this discussion about relationship: What is relationship?

Defining Relationships

Theorists have yet to clearly define the concept of relationship. Historically, psychology has focused on the individual. Family therapy has focused on systems. The primacy of relationship is a relatively new idea, one that has not yet stimulated sufficient study and research. Both philosophically and psychologically, we are at an infantile stage in our understanding of relationship.

I am reminded of a cartoon in which two fish have leaped out of the water. While suspended in midair, one of them points down at the medium they have temporarily left and says, "*That* water, dummy!" As conscious beings we are immersed in relationship—it is all around us. Yet we barely understand what this really means.

When we speak of relationship, we speak almost poetically, rather than scientifically; perhaps we are reduced (or elevated) to this because the nature of relationship is ineffable, or because our immersion in relationship prevents us from speaking about it objectively. By its very nature, relationship cannot be an object. As Heisenberg (1962) showed, attempts to investigate something "objectively" alter or affect what we are investigating. Because of its subjective nature, relationship cannot be concrete, and thus it is impossible to describe it concretely. Therefore, whenever we are investigating the nature of a relationship, we cannot be certain of what we are investigating, because an investigator will always be a part of the relationship he or she is investigating. In couples work, then, the therapist is part of the relationship, because in viewing the relationship, he or she is always part of it. Speaking phenomenologically, there is no such thing or entity as the relationship; the relationship is what it appears to be, whether viewed by a partner or by the therapist.

In addition, we have not established what we mean by the relationship of a couple. Mason echoes Judith Jordan (1991) in stating that from a relational perspective, individual functioning may be seen as a function of the relationship. The individual is inseparable from the relationship. However, it seems an exaggeration to presume that the individual acts only as a function of the relationship. To imply that the individual functions purely in terms of the primary love relationship, without reference to an inner psychic world, is to deny the existence of that inner world. This denial risks a replication of the fallacy, perpetrated by systems theory, that the individual ceases to exist. The individual's present sense of identity has developed out of the relationships of the past, and the inner representations of early object relations projected onto present relationships are a part of those present relationships.

What actually is the relationship? Are Jordan and Mason speaking ontologically or phenomenologically about the present relationship? An outsider or therapist might look at a couple and refer to the relationship, and the partners themselves might refer to it in the same way, but this is where our thinking becomes fuzzy. Is there an actual object or an entity that we can all agree is the relationship? Is relationship itself an entity? We cannot isolate relationship as an object of study, no matter how earnestly we might want to do so. The realm of relationship has an ineffable quality that cannot, by nature, be isolated and identified with precision.

Relationship and Consciousness: An Existential Phenomenological View

We have established that relationship is difficult to investigate and discuss clearly and objectively. This is because relationship is itself a function of consciousness. We are necessarily forced into a phenomenological position: for every individual, relationship arises in consciousness. For a couple, the relationship they are "in" takes form in the consciousness of each partner; that is, the relationship appears as a structure in the consciousness of each individual. This is where they live and how they relate: according to the form that structure takes. Because perception is subjective, each partner's version of the relationship is different. Imago theory affirms this notion, stating that each partner has a different reality, a different world, and therefore a different view of the relationship. Thus, when a couple presents for therapy, there are three relationships there: one in the mind of the husband, one in the mind of the wife, and one in the mind of the therapist.

Three Relationships in One

To illustrate, imagine that a couple has arrived at the therapist's office for intake. Each partner takes turns describing the relationship. It is clear to the therapist that there are two different relationships being described, the one in the mind of the husband and the other in the mind of the wife. Metaphorically, two different movies are running. As Mason (1996) states in psychoanalytic language, every relationship is the interaction of two different subjectivities, a cauldron of transference and countertransference. This means that each partner has a picture of the relationship which is different from that of the other partner, and that these separate relationship pictures are colored by whatever is in the mind of each partner. The mind carries the past, and it is the contents of the past, especially earlier object relations, that give shape to the appearance of present relationships. This is especially true for primary love relationships, which are infused with intense emotion. With increased emotion, subjectivity increases and objectivity recedes.

Thus two relationships enter therapy, along with the third relationship that the therapist observes. Each partner relates to the other as if the picture in the partner's mind is the actual relationship. Each partner attempts to convince the other of the rightness of his or her own perspective, and each partner attempts to convince the therapist of this, also. So when the therapist tries to describe the relationship, he or she is attempting to refer objectively to that cauldron consisting of the interaction of mental images coming from the mind of each partner. This inner ideation—the imagery, impressions, and memory projected outward toward the other partner—constitutes the relationship picture in the mind of each partner. In therapy, unfortunately, this phenomenon interferes with working on one relationship in which connection would be the hallmark.

Using this phenomenological perspective, to speak of the relationship requires that we first distinguish which relationship we are referring to—the relationship in the mind of one partner, of the other partner, or of the therapist. The therapist must distinguish the wife's relationship from the husband's relationship, because the two are surely different. In doing so, the therapist is focusing not on the relationship as it appears to the therapist but on the structure in the consciousness of a given partner. The focus is not on an entity called the relationship at all, but on consciousness and on the image of the relationship held in the mind of that particular partner. As Imago therapists, we claim to be working on the relationship, but we are in fact working on the consciousness of each partner. IRT improves the relationship by helping partners relate differently to one another, but the therapy works primarily through its influence on the minds of the partners. Even when we work with a relationship, we are actually working with the psyches of the partners.

To summarize, the relationship is a complex structure in the consciousness of each partner, a consciousness that is always changing and evolving, both affecting and being affected by the relationship it perceives.

Consciousness and Relationship

I would suggest that consciousness and relationship are not two separate things; consciousness itself is, in some way, relationship, and relationship is consciousness. As William James (1912, p. 12) stated it, "Consciousness and world are inseparable." James concluded that ultimately there is no way to separate consciousness from the world in which it is embedded and which fills it: "All . . . painfully accumulated points of difference run gradually into their opposites and are full of exceptions" (cited in Hunt, 1995, p. 18).

Consciousness is by its very nature relational and dialogic, structured like an interior conversation. Consciousness is not itself an entity; rather, it is always in the process of being transformed by what is in it. "Consciousness has no independent nature of its own" (Cleary, 1980, p. 19). There is no such thing as perception: there is a continually unfolding process of perceiving. "Perception, in fact, does not have an end. Perceiving goes on" (Gibson, 1979, p. 253).

Not only is relationship a function of consciousness, but consciousness is a function of relationship. Consciousness is in fact relationship, a dynamic flux ever in motion, filled with its world from which it is inseparable. Consciousness is not, as cognitive psychology suggests, "a transparent medium empty of all content and limited to the functions of selection and choice" (Hunt, 1995, p. 44).

Relationships, Individuals, Consciousness, and Connection

Mason states that partners in a difficult relationship "no longer have to admit to some intrinsic defect within themselves or their partner. . . . People are tremendously relieved to realize that the horrible ways they act toward their partner do not reflect their true inner self, but rather the intensity of their relationship nightmare" (1996, p. 6). A relationship certainly can become a nightmare for both partners (although often it seems more of a nightmare for one than for the other). But the nightmare itself—the interaction of two subjectivities, a cauldron of transference and countertransference—is fundamentally the product of the projections of each partner.

It cannot be claimed that in a relationship, there is no individual pathology. The relationship is a function and product of the unfolding of the consciousness of each and both individuals. Imago theory upholds this point, seeing dysfunctional couple relationships as the product of damaging early object relations, which result in "wounding" (Hendrix, 1988).

Many theoreticians who have paid attention to the nature of the human being (Almaas, 1988; Edwards, 1982; Hadot, 1995; Hendrix, 1988; Hora, 1986; Hunt, 1995; Linthorst, 1979; Walsh & Vaughan, 1980; Wilber, 1995, 1996; Wilber, Engler, & Brown, 1986) posit that the true inner condition of the human being is essentially uncontaminated by the effects of conditioning. This implies that in a dysfunctional relationship, the condition of the partners is not a reflection of their true inner self; their condition is an indication of all the "stuff" they picked up in earlier relationships, especially in childhood. This inner stuff now forms the personality, a kind of "false self" operating as structures in consciousness, governing and running the person's life, including his or her relationships. Early object relationships are replicated in new relationships (Almaas, 1986; Greenberg & Mitchell, 1983; Scharff & Scharff, 1991). It goes both ways: beginning in infancy, relationships create patterns in individuals, and patterns in individuals create relationships. Relationships create the individual's self- and world perceptions, and such perceptions create the emotional and ideational structures through which new relationships are formed in an unconscious attempt to replicate earlier relationships. It is impossible to decide which came first, then, the individual or the relationship. Relationship and the consciousness of the individual arise together: they are one and the same.

The old atomistic thinking common in psychology is outdated and false. There is no such thing as an individual in isolation, as a separate entity. Just as there is no such thing as an individual apart from relationships, there is also no such thing as a relationship apart from its individual components, which are the individuals who are in relationship. Individuals and relationships are not two different things, but two different ways of viewing the same thing. So when we say "self," we do not mean self-in-isolation, but self-in-relationship.

When psychoanalysis works, it works on the level of relationship. Our primary focus in psychotherapy should be not on relationships per se, but on the understanding that "relationships" and "individuals" are two different levels of one reality.

Connection, Transcendence, and Healing

Considering the goal in couples therapy of establishing deeper connection, a question arises: Can two individuals who are subjectively transferring to each other truly connect? Obviously not! Two projecting partners cannot connect. They are relating not to one another but to their projections onto one another. The very nature of projection blocks connectivity.

Developing Connection

Partners can develop connection through a dialogical process, specifically through what IRT calls the Couples Dialogue. Genuine dialogue has a unique function: it not only introduces the distinct world of each partner but also begins a process of dissolution of the cauldron of transference and countertransference. Dialogue does not view transference as a permanent fixture that must be accommodated. Dialogue does not merely bypass transference. When the Couples Dialogue is truly effective, it dissolves the transference.

Projecting individuals cannot have a relationship with anything other than the object of their projections. Each may believe he or she is relating to the other partner, but each is in fact relating to an inner object projected onto the partner.

Transcending Personality

Personalities are false selves functioning as the distillate of earlier object relations (Almaas, 1987, 1988). Early object relations that manifest as structures in consciousness, as personality itself, express the incompleteness, the insufficiency of those early relationships. Couples have to transcend their personalities—transcend the false self and its subjectivity. If a troubled relationship is the interaction of two subjectivities, the cauldron of transference and countertransference that is at the core of their disconnection, what has to happen for reconnection to take place? Two individuals whose mode of being in the world, whose way of life, is full of projection, especially toward each other, cannot reconnect without growing up, growing beyond the perceptually limiting power of early object relations. Personalities cannot be intimate. Therefore, connection is a form of transcendence of personality, a transcendence of the parts of the character structure that limit relationship. Personality or character structure as it functions for the purpose of self-protection is resistant to relationship (Almaas, 1988). According to T. Wilber (cited in K. Wilber, 1993, p. 170), "The ego is nothing but the contraction or avoidance of relationship."

Completing Childhood and Healing Wounds

In therapy, the dilemma is further complicated by the fact that most people have a tremendous resistance to growing up. In a relationship, partners typically are seeking not equality but a good mommy or daddy so they can avoid growing up (Almaas, 1987). As Imago theory states, partners want the other to become a good parent who won't fail them in the ways the original parents did. In psychotherapy, clients usually want the therapist to be a good parent, rather than an agent who assists them in growing up. Although at times both therapists and partners must function as parents, a major therapeutic goal is for partners to grow up so that their relationships can be healthy.

Mason (1996) observes that we can't make growing up a precondition for entering into a relationship. Yet Imago theory implies that for persons in relationship, not being grown up is part of the problem. The IRT process is not aimed at helping couples accommodate to early object relations while finding ways to connect despite them. The Couples Dialogue and other IRT interventions are designed to help partners stop projecting and start listening to one another. IRT helps partners grow up.

The question of what it means to "complete childhood" generates considerable disagreement among Imago therapists. Does it mean obtaining from our partners what we missed in childhood? If completing childhood (or to use object relations language, completing early object relations) means to finally get what we missed in childhood, then doing so seems to perpetuate childhood by perpetuating the assumptions of childhood—that is, the structures in consciousness that first developed in childhood. If this is what it means to complete childhood, then IRT provides a palliative that prevents growing up and bypasses real healing. If, on the other hand, completing childhood means growing up beyond it—transcending the hold of early object relations—IRT is on solid ground. To fulfill the ultimate goal of couples therapy—that is, growing up—the notion of completing childhood must be interpreted as transcending the bind of childhood structures in consciousness.

The interpretation of this concept will guide the therapist's work with couples. When Imago theory speaks of healing inner wounds, this is not, in my opinion, about soothing or appeasing wounds through skillful relating, but rather about breaking the hold of early and damaging object relations that manifest in the wounds. IRT is ultimately about dissolving the imago, or at least dissolving the personal attachment to the imago, thus creating space for the reality of the partner.

Couple Problems Beyond Relationship

Many couples in therapy reveal problems that are not a function of the relationship. One couple I have been working with has been coming to therapy for about five years. Therapy with this couple has often been difficult. The wife has low self-esteem stemming from childhood abuse by her father. The husband has an abiding rage that simmers just below the surface. The wife has stated her belief that her husband has problems with addictions, problems that appeared unrelated to the relationship. Lately, the wife has been stating that her husband's continuous anger is more than she can bear. The husband blames his anger and addictions on the wife's distance and incompetence. He especially decries what he views as her incompetence with their children, whom he believes are in danger from the wife's neglect. (I see no such danger.)

Although the partners have attempted to use the Couples Dialogue to deal with these issues, the dialogue always breaks down. These are two very intelligent but wounded persons, and the only time they can come close to dialoguing now is when they are in the therapist's office. Even there, the dialogue is not satisfying or healing (and has come nowhere close to addressing deeper characterological issues). No dialogical process is going to heal this impasse, though, because the impasse is not simply a function of the relationship. This couple's relationship reveals deep characterological issues, and its functioning is a demonstration of those issues. The issues extend beyond what the Couples Dialogue process can adequately address. Nothing seems to connect this couple because the individual pathology runs so deep. This is not a case of pathologizing a couple who merely have relationship problems. It is a recognition that, sometimes, problematic issues are about more than the relationship: the problem may be rooted in the deep unconscious of the individuals involved.

As Mason (1996) asserts, "[IRT] provides a lens through which couples come to realize that their experience as individuals is substantially a function of their relationship: when they are in good connection with each other, personal energy is high; caught in the throes of disconnection, their energy dissipates" (p. 4). This statement seems to imply that one's sense of well-being is solely dependent on the relationship. Such a notion should be challenged, because many other intrapsychic factors besides the relationship affect one's sense of well-being and, thus, the capacity to connect. On the other hand, the quality of a couple's connection has everything to do with the partners' individual sense of well-being. If we understand consciousness and relationship as not being separate, we can avoid the simplistic assumption that either the relationship or the individual is the source of the problems.

One issue that is often overlooked involves what the relationship culls out of each individual. If the individual has any pathology, any unresolved childhood trauma, any unhealed wounding, or any defenses against pain, then we cannot claim that the relationship is the sole source of the difficulty in the relationship. The relationship brings those issues to light; it holds up a mirror to each individual, revealing where the unresolved pain is and how the partner's character structure is disabling the relationship. The primary love relationship is much like a powerful Rorschach that reveals the functioning of each partner.

Imago theory must avoid the implication that all problems or issues can be reduced to a relationship problem. When systems theory was first used in family therapy, most systems theorists maintained that the system was the only structure to be focused on. The individual ceased to exist or, at best, existed only as a part of the system. Eventually, the pendulum began to swing back the other way: articles and books dealing with the individual within the system appeared, finally bringing some balance to the perspective. Imago theory should not make a similar mistake. Relationship is an extremely complex phenomenon, and it would be a disservice to the purposes of IRT to imply that we have eliminated the individual and, consequently, the relevance of unconscious and characterological factors in couples therapy. IRT, in fact, both directly and indirectly, addresses characterological issues while it reveals deep wounding from childhood, which now interferes with the relationship.

It would be a mistake, then, to tell a couple that their problems are solely a function of the relationship. Some partners scapegoat their relationship, blaming it for their poor functioning and believing that eliminating the relationship would end their problems. But the relationship reveals the functioning of each partner. Clearly, we must avoid extolling what Mason (1996, p. 3), commenting on Stolerow and Atwood's 1992 work, calls "this mythical self as a computer that somehow thinks and feels independently of its biological and social milieu." But we need to guard as well against the idea of the isolated relationship—relationship apart from the inner worlds of the partners.

Mason (1996) offers an excellent example of the way characterological issues, such as male gender issues, affect the primary love relationship. Bergman (1991, cited in Mason, 1996, p. 15) addresses what he terms "male relational dread." Men generally have this dread, a product of childhood relationships, long before they enter into love relationships and marriage. The dread of relationship is characterological, so that when male relational dread begins to emerge in the man's relationship, it is not true that the problems this creates have their source in the relationship. The relationship simply reveals the underlying characterological issue. This is not, therefore, a relationship problem, although the impact of this problem on the relationship is formidable.

Gaining Perspective

The issues and conclusions discussed here can be summarized as follows:

1. Relationships, especially committed romantic relationships, are a central focus of human beings. Everything in the universe is in relationship.

2. We cannot be certain what we are referring to when we speak of the relationship of a couple, because each partner has his or her view of the relationship, and the therapist has yet another perspective. The nature of relationship demands a phenomenological perspective.

3. Because everything we know manifests in consciousness, relationship is a function of consciousness. Consciousness is relational in its very existence.

4. The controversy about the *individual* versus the *relationship* is bypassed by the realization that these two terms are two different ways of describing the same thing, like two facets of a single diamond.

5. Object relations from early life exist as transferences and projections in the mind. The contents of the mind constitute personality, which in turn interferes with true relationship.

6. Connection depends on the dissolution of the personality traits and defenses that create separation. The old object relations and the imago itself have to be dissolved through therapy for real connection to take place.

7. The primary love relationship serves as a mirror revealing the characterological issues and, therefore, the inner world of the individuals in the relationship.

References

Almaas, A. H. (1986). *Essence: The diamond approach to inner realization.* York Beach, ME: Weiser.

Almaas, A. H. (1987). *Diamond heart, book one: Elements of the real in man.* Berkeley, CA: Diamond Books.

Almaas, A. H. (1988). *The pearl beyond price: Integration of personality into being: An object relations approach.* Berkeley, CA: Diamond Books.

Bergman, S. (1991). Men's psychological development: A relational perspective. *Work in Progress,* No. 48. Wellesley, MA: Stone Center Working Paper Series.

Cleary, T. (1980). *Timeless spring: A Soto Zen anthology.* San Francisco: Wheelwright Press.

Edwards, D. G. (1982). *Existential psychotherapy: The process of caring.* New York: Gardner Press.

Gibson, J. (1979). *The ecological approach to visual perception.* Boston: Houghton Mifflin.

Greenberg, J., & Mitchell, S. (1983). *Object relations in psychoanalytic theory.* Cambridge, MA: Harvard University Press.

Hadot, P. (1995). *Philosophy as a way of life*. Oxford: Blackwell.

Heisenberg, W. (1962). *Physics and philosophy: The revolution in modern physics*. New York: HarperCollins.

Hendrix, H. (1988). *Getting the love you want: A guide for couples*. New York: Henry Holt.

Hendrix, H. (1992). *Keeping the love you find: A guide for singles*. New York: Pocket Books.

Hora, T. (1986). *Beyond the dream*. Orange, CA: PAGL Press.

Hunt, H. T. (1995). *On the nature of consciousness*. New Haven, CT: Yale University Press.

James, W. (1912). *Essays in radical empiricism and a pluralistic universe*. New York: Dutton.

Jordan, J. V. (1991). Empathy and self boundaries. In J. V. Jordan, A. G. Kaplan, J. B. Miller, I. P. Stiver, & J. L. Surrey (Eds.), *Women's growth in connection: Writings from the Stone Center* (pp. 67–81). New York: Guilford.

Linthorst, A. T. (1979). *A gift of love: Marriage as a spiritual journey*. Orange, CA: PAGL Press.

Mason, R. C. (1996). Imago, relationships, and empathy. *Journal of Imago Relationship Therapy, 1*(2), 1–18.

Scharff, D., & Scharff, J. (1991). *Object relations family therapy*. Northvale, NJ: Aronson.

Sheldrake, R. (1981). *A new science of life: The hypothesis of formative causation*. Los Angeles: Tarcher.

Stolerow, R. D., & Atwood, G. E. (1992). *Contexts of being: The intersubjective foundations of psychological life*. Hillsdale, NJ: The Analytic Press.

Walsh, R. N., & Vaughan, F. (1980). *Beyond ego: Transpersonal dimensions in psychology*. Los Angeles: Tarcher.

Wilber, K. (1993). *Grace and grit*. Boston: Shambhala.

Wilber, K. (1995). *Sex, ecology, spirituality: The spirit of evolution*. Boston: Shambhala.

Wilber, K. (1996). *A brief history of everything*. Boston: Shambhala.

Wilber, K., Engler, J., & Brown, D. (1986). *Transformations of consciousness*. Boston: Shambhala.

Chapter Ten

Imago: A Theory and Therapy of Connectivity

Randall C. Mason, Ph.D.

Clinical experience suggests that when couples experience undisturbed connection, the partners feel empowered and energetic. If their connection becomes disturbed, they feel hopeless and lethargic. It is possible for a person to be too clinically disturbed—too depressed, for example—to function well in a committed relationship. In most instances, however, it is the disturbance in the relationship that creates disturbed functioning in the individual. The whole of the relationship is greater than the sum of its parts, and it is the well-being of that whole that creates the well-being of the partners.

Empathy is a prerequisite to the partners' experience of connection; once it is established and sufficiently maintained, empathy fosters a cohesive and centered firmness of the self. Personal cohesiveness, which includes the capacity to hold one's own reality while encountering the different reality of the other, can therefore be attributed to the goodness of the relationship connection.

Imago Relationship Therapy (IRT) uses the Couples Dialogue as the major modality for engendering empathy, differentiation, and connection. Dialogue not only enhances the connectivity of the relationship but also strengthens the differentiation of the individuals in the relationship.

The Meanings of Connectivity

The term *connection* or *connectivity* has been used widely in recent years. Some consider connectivity as an ideal personal state that can be created through intentionality and consciousness, or through maturity and psychic health. In this chapter, connectivity describes a condition that emerges inevitably between persons in long-term committed relationships. The emergence of connection relies on neither intentionality nor psychological processes. Seen from this vantage, the mere attainment of connection is not nearly as significant as the establishment of a good connection as opposed to a disturbed one. Connection can and does in fact exist between disturbed or fragile persons, as it does between healthy ones, and the functioning of the individuals in the relationship serves as a key indicator of the quality of the connection between them.

Ontological

When used in this more specific sense, connectivity has at least four different meanings, which provide distinct frameworks for doing couples therapy. One definition of connectivity is the ontological, in which one affirms that all things are connected: nothing happens in one section of existence that does not affect all things. What is the significance of such an assertion? It provides an answer to the question, Are human beings finally and inherently separate, with a goal to realize and live out that separateness, or are persons inherently connected, so that their optimal condition is living within connection? We can ask the same question in reference to distressed couples: Should we see couples' difficulties as due to surrendering what some would consider their mature individuality and becoming enmeshed with one another, or should we understand their problems as stemming from their difficulty experiencing connection with one another? Is connectedness a sort of add-on, albeit a desirable one, to an otherwise fulfilled self, or is connectedness a prerequisite to self-fulfillment? Does connectivity elicit enmeshment, or is differentiation possible within the context of connection? One's position on these issues underlies the choice of therapeutic goals in doing couples work: Is the goal the attainment of an individuated and self-sufficient self who is thus capable of relationships, or is the goal the attaining of "good connection" in relationship to become more self-competent?

Developmental theorist Margaret Mahler and her contemporaries accepted the prevailing assumption of their time, which was that separation and individuation are the goal. Self psychology, the theoretical position emerging from the Stone Center (for example, Jordan, 1991), and Imago theory (Hendrix, 1988), however, emphasize connectivity.

Experiential

When the experiential meaning of connectivity is applied, it becomes possible for human beings to experience disconnection as well as connection. Using this definition, even though we might be connected in the ontological sense, in day-to-day life we will feel both connection and disconnection. In light of the assertion that connection is an inherent condition existing between persons, it is perhaps best to reserve the term *disconnection* for permanent states, such as a divorce, death, or relationship breakup, and to use the term *connectional disturbance* to refer to the subjective experience of disconnection. Indeed, the connectional disturbance is about a wounding of the connection, rather than true disconnection.

Transitory

One variant of connection could be called "transitory" connection. An example is a conversational interaction about which the participants report enthusiastically, "We really connected." Likewise, people can emerge from business meetings feeling discouraged and disconnected from the other participants. Those with minimal social contacts or poor interpersonal skills may feel a more generalized sense of disconnection from society.

Clinical and Foundational

When applied to clinical work with couples, connectivity refers to the bonds that occur in a couple when there has been the experience of romance, a degree of commitment to the relationship, and a sufficient period of being together to the point of feeling they belong together. Feelings of aliveness, hope, and zest are the more dramatic indicators of a good connection. Such feelings often emerge expansively during the romantic period, making all the more painful any connectional disturbance, which will usually be accompanied by lethargy, depression, and hopelessness. This form of primary connectivity is the main focus of this chapter.

When a couple has been together over a period of time, a second form of connection, *foundational connection,* may be formed. Foundational connection occurs when a couple realizes they belong together and can depend on one another to remain in the relationship. No fight or disagreement will separate them. Living in foundational connection may be unconscious, although its positive effects are experienced consciously. It may take years for a couple to develop this sense of connection, especially when they have gone through divorce in prior relationships or have otherwise experienced a "shaking of the foundations." This special understanding of connection illuminates the most important component of the no-exit decision, which is the *partner's experience of the reality* of that decision. Foundational connection allows one to sink into the safety of the relationship, providing an awareness of belonging together regardless of what happens. The "for better or worse" phrase of the traditional marriage vows is, in effect, a no-exit decision that may lead eventually to an experience of foundational connection. Perhaps the inclusion of that phrase reflects our culture's awareness of the crucial importance of both connectivity and safety to marital and family stability. When experiencing a sense of foundational connection with one's partner, one does not feel vulnerable to being abandoned to one's own resources. Thus, foundational connection produces a feeling of being safe in the world.

There are at least three groups whose experience is different than that of the connected couple. One example is those who are living in a parallel relationship, generally feeling empty and hopeless about the future. Their condition develops when the connectional disturbance has become so painful that the partners shield their vulnerability through an emotionally walled-off cordiality, yet they are unable to separate, perhaps due to foundational connectedness. In such relationships, there is a cessation of day-to-day experience of connectedness, although foundational connectedness might remain. The second group would be those who experience a recovery of energy and capacity for living after experiencing a permanent disconnection through death or divorce. The lost connection might have felt so constricting that at least one spouse felt trapped by his or her long-term relationship. This is often the case for widows or widowers who, after mourning of the loss of the spouse, begin to express significantly more energy and zest in the world than they did when the spouse was alive. Of course, not all bereaved individuals experience this; for some, bereavement has the opposite effect. The third group would be single persons. The person may seem to be functioning well enough, but feels an underlying sadness and an unmet longing deep within. The single state might indeed be best for some, but what the single person often experiences is the absence of connection.

A Different Kind of Relationship

I maintain that Imago couples work occurs within the context of this comprehensive understanding of connectedness and connectional disturbance. IRT can, in fact, be encapsulated as the investigation, formation, and maintenance of connection in committed relationships, so that the primary task of an Imago therapist is to facilitate the couple's experience of connectedness.

The dialogical exercises are relevant and effective in accomplishing that task. Recently, a couple reported to me how connected they'd felt since using the Couples Dialogue the prior week in dealing with a conflict. They were proud both that they had done it and that they had done it well. What amazed them, and what is part of the phenomena of connectivity, is that after the dialogue, their positive feelings had continued, but they were unable to remember what the conflict had been about, what they had discussed, or what the resolution of the conflict had been.

Many couples (and many therapists) are unaware of the qualitatively different impact connected romantic relationships, in comparison with other types of relationships, have on one's everyday life. Again and again, I have heard spouses express confusion that their partner can smile and be happy around everyone else but the spouse. Some are amazed at how the effects of the loss of a partner through death, divorce, or breakup can still be devastating many months later. Many people realize only after their relationship is over how unique and irreplaceable the connected relationship is. Males and females may experience its importance differently, however. When the notion of connectivity is presented in therapy, for example, women immediately intuit the notion of being connected; men, in contrast, seem to grasp more clearly what disconnection feels like.

The contention that connected relationships are different from all others is actually not new at all. The difference has been intimated by poets—who have always known that heartbreak and loss lead to death—and in the everyday language of people: one often hears the bereaved speak of the death of a spouse as a loss of a part of themselves. One would reject such a statement as a reflection of physical reality, because common sense tells us that the self resides within the physical limits of the body, and of course, the person hasn't lost anything within the body. Likewise, the statement that the "two shall become as one" might be interpreted as either a moral imperative or a romantic ideal, but would certainly not be construed as a description of physical reality.

From the perspective articulated here, however—the perspective of the primacy of the connected relationship—both the expression of the bereaved spouse and the assertion that "two shall become as one" are, in fact, descriptive realities. The idea that the self includes more than what lies within the limits of the body, in sharp contrast with the popular atomistic postulate of separateness, serves as a transitional point for investigating the phenomenon of connectivity.

Moving from a Discrete Self to an Expanded Self

Central to an understanding of connectivity, then, is the assumption that the self within a connected relationship extends beyond the limits of the physical body. Although novelists and poets have long known this, a realization of a more scientific nature occurred when the English school of ethologists began noting the phenomena of "bonding" in the world of animals.

Bonding

The ethologists observed that extended periods of mourning were not confined to humans; birds would show acute reaction to separations and searched for lost mates for a long time. Bowlby was the first major theorist to give serious consideration to this phenomenon, which he referred to as attachment and is referred to here as connectivity. Bowlby's writings (1969) were followed by Weiss's work (1975) on marital separation and by that of Parkes (1974) and Parkes and Weiss (1983) on the experience of the bereaved spouse. Both Weiss and Parkes, as a part of the Harvard Bereavement Study, used Bowlby's studies of animal responses to loss as a paradigm for their understanding of loss of a spouse. They noted the distinctive long-term effects of a breakup of a primary relationship, implying that such relationships are unique from all others.

Bonding thus includes a linkage formed with another, a bond that is more permanent than transitory and one that creates the other as part of the self. This conceptualization of bonding suggests that the bonded relationship demands a different mode of understanding than that used for other relationships.

Transference

Heinz Kohut (1971) observed that many of his clients began to improve only after they had established a sort of merger or twinship with him. Kohut wrote about a variety of transferences, all of which involved a sense of oneness between the patient and the therapist, and all of which contributed to the well-being and cohesion of the patient. He described, for example, the *mirroring transference,* in which the client views the therapist as responsive and admiring of the client's specialness, thus contributing to the client's cohesiveness and energy. This mirroring transference seems to make possible a greater sense of self-esteem in the client, providing the client with an enhanced capacity for carrying out life tasks. In the *idealizing transference,* the client experiences both the therapist's greatness and his or her capacity to protect. The idealizing transference produces a calming of the self, akin to that of a mother holding and rocking her infant, and a repository of ideals that the individual cannot hold alone. The *twinship transference,* an experience of sameness or fellowship with others, also seemed to enhance the client's capacity to act in the world. Kohut came to understand that through such transferences, he provided a valuable function in the life of his patients: he was needed as a part of the patient's self. Kohut noted that describing himself as an external object to the patient was seriously misleading, as he became, in fact, a part of the patient's self. From such observations arose the concept of the self-object.

The notion of self-object doesn't imply necessarily any confusion that another is part of oneself. Rather, the term refers to others who fulfill certain roles that are essential to one's psychic health. Adequate and undisturbed self-objects make possible a centered and calm cohesion of the self, even in the face of trauma. Disturbances in self-object relations lead to a loss of self-cohesion and in some cases to psychotic fragmentation. By working with the self-object transference with the therapist, clients become aware of disturbances in their self-object relationships and learn new ways of dealing with such difficulties.

Self-Objects: Pathology or Necessity

The expanded self, in which the inclusion of others as part of the self is essential to optimal functioning, incorporates self-objects as crucial components. To further clarify the term and to distinguish it from the "objects" of those who see the self as discrete, begin by envisioning a box, labeled "the self," drawn in the center of a page. Six to ten boxes surround the center box; these boxes can be labeled mother, father, sister, crib, bottle, and so on, with the implication that each box is discrete from the others. Within this framework, the task of the self at the center is to determine how and when to attach to the peripheral objects. Applied to the experience of the human infant, this schema considers the infant as separate and its task as attachment.

Moving instead to the framework of self-objects, the central box is no longer labeled "the self"; instead, a circle is drawn around all of the objects. Now this circle is labeled "the self," and all the objects encompassed within are called self-objects. Applying this model to the situation of the infant, the infant is seen as already attached and connected, and its task is differentiation. Disconnection is in no way a prerequisite to differentiation which, in fact, is possible only within a state of safety experienced in connection.

Some of the early self psychologists seemed to construe the therapeutic goal as the attainment of autonomy and individuation, apparently without realizing the implications of such a formulation. Self-objects were to be eliminated through maturation, with intensive therapy used as necessary in cases of maturational failure.

Discussions of self-objects were based on a pejorative view of narcissism: narcissism was a pathology to be outgrown so that the adult purity of object love could emerge. Within this context, many physical objects in early childhood came to be experienced as separate from the self. With further maturation, everything physical, including other human bodies, would become other than the self. Even on the emotional level, other persons were viewed as separate from the self. Therapy was most warranted when patients treated as self-objects those who were, to the observer, clearly separate objects. Patients seemed to have the greatest difficulty giving up self-object relations with parents, children, and most of all, the spouse. Through delivering the patient from having self-objects, therapy made possible the completely individuated, separated, and adequate self.

For a period of time, the new understanding of self-objects co-existed side-by-side with the old assumption of individuation and autonomy. In retrospect, the therapeutic ideal of individuation and autonomy can be seen as itself a narcissistic fantasy, one in which the person has fully matured when he or she is "captain of one's soul" and impervious to others. Marital counseling was therefore aimed at helping the individuals grow up and thus become immune to the activity or negativity of the spouse. Many have testified that they tried desperately to make this model work but were unsuccessful. Spouses continued to be highly vulnerable to the relationship with the spouse. Even extensive therapy could not alleviate susceptibility to the power of one's central relationships. Eventually, self-objects came to be viewed not as pathological but as a normal part of the self. Attempts to eliminate self-objects were found to be "crazy-making." Because one is inescapably affected by the spouse and other self-objects, one must learn to deal successfully with self-objects—not seek immunity from them or try to eliminate them. The ideal was now a differentiation that incorporated a continuing connection to self-objects along with a differentiation from the actual self of the other. Surrey (1991, pp. 59–61) has used the term "'relationship-differentiation' as a contrast to the idea of separation-individuation." From this type of discussion has emerged the term *differentiation within connection*. This shift toward a positive evaluation of the self-object led to other revisions as well. Kohut described narcissistic issues as a component of all human difficulties, rather than as features of certain diagnostic categories that result from very early trauma. He made the startling suggestion that narcissistic problems arise from insufficient rather than too much narcissism. Finally, neither narcissism nor self-objects were earmarked for elimination; rather, both were targeted for enhancement.

The Expanded Connected Self

A discussion of the expanded connected self may clarify the nature of the connected relationship as distinct from other relationships. The substance of connected relationships is, at its essence, composed of self-object ties. Self-object relationships serve as the basis for the difference between connected relationships and other relationships, and thus provide a framework for understanding the nature of connectivity.

Some would argue that, even granting the now popular acceptance of self-objects, the self-object is actually no more than a purely intrapsychic representation of the other person lodging within one's brain. However, if the self-object is confined to the brain, why is the whole self so vulnerable to the autonomous activities of a self-object that exists outside the body? One is, it seems, as vulnerable to an external self-object as one would be to an internal liver disturbance.

The argument here is more radical than one might immediately discern, because it asserts a fundamental *continuity* between one and the other—between self and self-object, between the internal and the external. Kohut considered self-objects to be as essential to the maintenance of the self on the psychological level as oxygen is on the biological level. The oxygen in our bodies is not discontinuous or discrete from external oxygen; it is at once both internal and external, a part of the physical self that interchanges continuously with the environment. Likewise, the internal self-object is not discontinuous or discrete from the external self-object but exists both internally and externally. If poison or some other pollutant is introduced in the external oxygen, we will die. If there is a rupture between the self and the self-object, we deteriorate. Goldberg (1995, p. 41) describes the phenomenon like this: "A map of a patient's psyche is a system that extends to the self-objects that constitute the patient's self."

Clinical Implications

Self-objects, then, provide for crucial functions of personal well-being, such as the cohesion of the self, the capacity for energy and ambition, and the capability of being calmed and centered through idealized self-objects. With the fulfillment of these functions, the connected relationship gains the power to accord structure to the self.

Goldberg uses the term "as if by magic" (1995, p. 38) to capture the manner in which this provision of structure alters the therapeutic relationship. What Goldberg seems to be implying is that symptoms are alleviated independently of any procedure that addresses the presenting symptoms or any specific content that is discussed. Change occurs, rather, "as if by magic" through the formation, by the patient, of the self-object relationship with the analyst.

Case Examples

Goldberg (1995) presents two cases to illustrate this quality. In the first (p. 39), a young man seeks treatment to decide if he should announce his homosexuality; he is having homosexual fantasies but not homosexual activity. The four-sessions-a-week treatment facilitates the formation of a self-object tie and thereby a connected relationship with the therapist. Shortly after the treatment commences, and with the formation of a self-object transference, the homosexual fantasies end "as if by magic." This is, of course, a situation in which the patient is most likely not homosexual, and the fantasies are a mask for self-object deprivations.

The second case (Goldberg, 1995, pp. 50–51) is one in which there was amazing improvement. The patient began with a borderline condition (as traditionally understood), progressed to a more narcissistic condition (also as traditionally understood), and then on to Oedipal explorations. Finally, there was the termination of an apparently successful analysis. Following termination, the patient would from time to time write the analyst. The analyst noted throughout the chronology of the letters a reversal of treatment progress, with the patient first moving back to the Oedipal, then to the narcissistic, and finally to the borderline condition, one that was tinged with paranoid overtones. Apparently the analytic situation had provided a connectivity that led to improvement, and the absence of treatment led to the loss of the connected relationship and the reemergence of the original difficulties. Would such a person, to remain free from symptoms, be doomed to treatment for the rest of her life? Not at all: therapy failed over the long run because the treatment did not specifically address self-object issues. The client needed to develop greater attunement to such issues to become competent in achieving and maintaining satisfactory self-objects. Although the analyst provided adequate self-object relations during analysis, the patient had not processed or experienced the significance of the therapist's doing so.

Following the termination of analysis, there was a break in self-object relations of which the client had no conscious understanding; thus she was incapable of responding in a way that would have maintained an adequate self-object milieu.

The self uses self-objects as a sort of internal structure, a structure that could have moved the latter patient from a borderline to a post-Oedipal state. Structure affords the capacity to actualize the self in the world—to live with focus, direction, and energy. With ruptures in self-object relations, the structure is lost, and the person sinks into a depressed or fragmented state. The patient's gradual loss of the structure that had been provided by the self-object relationship with the analyst led to her deterioration. As Goldberg (1990, p. 126) notes: "Self-objects are the others that allow one to achieve and maintain an individual integrity. They are what makes us what we are, our very composition."

Parallels to Couples Work

Goldberg's discussion of the impact of the analyst-patient relationship has its parallels in couples work. Couples come in for counseling with a connectional disturbance, presenting with many complaints about themselves and their partners. Early work in IRT is designed to establish good connection through having clients observe certain rules of interpersonal safety and discuss issues in a dialogical manner. Such methods engender an empathic reimaging of the partner, which fosters healing of the connectional rupture. Within weeks, there may be a marked shift in the relationship; complaints decrease, and the couple reports an improved enjoyment of one another. At this point, none of the issues the couple presented with have been necessarily resolved or even discussed, but the issues have diminished in intensity. The negative thinking and difficult behaviors of the couple vanish "as if by magic." There has been a restoration of connection, although another rupturing event may bring the symptoms back. This restoration of connection does not signify the end of couples work, but makes an end possible. Perhaps a number of unconscious issues must yet be considered, but the couple progresses most rapidly once good connection is reestablished.

Imago: A Theory of Connectivity

The potency of Imago theory and therapy has been demonstrated in the personal and professional experiences of therapists and clients. Clinicians from a variety of schools laud Imago theory as congruent with the personal framework they espouse. Naturally, some would like to interpret Imago theory as an extension of the major framework from which they have been operating. Thus, one might hear that Imago is desirable because it is an intrapsychic theory. Some are gratified because they understand Imago as a family systems theory, while yet others are pleased because Imago is an interpersonal theory.

All three of these different perspectives are related to Imago theory, but Imago does not find a comfortable home in any of the three. I would suggest instead that IRT is focused on issues of connectivity and is a theory and therapy of connectivity. Connectivity represents the guiding framework for Imago work; neither connectivity nor, therefore, IRT can be subsumed under frameworks such as the intrapsychic, behavioral, interpersonal, communications, or family systems. All these frameworks are significant within their own sphere, and they address connectivity in an adjunctive sense, but for none of them is connectivity the central focus. In IRT, our task is unequivocal: connectivity is the orienting focus of our work with couples.

Such a studious distinction between Imago's perspective on connectivity and that of other frameworks keeps the cannibalistic tendency in check. The cannibalistic tendency is the propensity of theories to eat up or digest other theories or frameworks by incorporating other theoretical explanations into one's own. An example would be for systems people to note that all things can be understood through systems theory; after all, even the so-called intrapsychic is a system. Similarly, the psychoanalytic school might reciprocate by insisting that what is assumed to be a system is better explained using an intrapsychic framework: "It is, after all, pretty much all Oedipal." The cannibalistic tendency could thus reduce the notion of connectivity to whatever a particular theory deems it to be. Were this to occur, the new vistas that could open up within the context of connectivity would vanish along with the potential array of therapeutic innovations.

The theories mentioned here are not studying different aspects of the self or of families. What distinguishes these frameworks from one another is not what they study, but rather the different lens they use to view the same reality. The psychoanalyst might be interested in the relationship of connectivity to the superego, drives, or self-esteem and might clarify how changes in any of these aspects of the person might change connectivity. The family systems theorist would address how the systemic context affects the formation and behavior of any part of the system; changes in any part, including connectivity, can lead to changes in any of the other parts. Both frameworks make important contributions to an understanding of connectivity, but connectivity cannot be reduced to what is seen through the lens of these or any perspectives.

Perhaps this point can be clarified by suggesting that, like the two "true" realities of romantic partners, two or more theoretical frameworks can view reality differently, both realities can be "true," yet each framework's explanation of reality is incomplete. Family systems, psychoanalytic theories, interpersonal theory, and others investigate and explain phenomena that are formative to the development of connectivity and thus contribute a valuable component of our knowledge about connectivity, although they may leave connectivity imperfectly explained. Family systems theory, for instance, presupposes connections within systems and describes what happens in systems when connections are absent. Family systems theory, therefore, can help us understand the impact of the system on those connections that belong to the system. Interpersonal or relationship theories also contribute their portion of our understanding of connectivity. Sullivan (1953), for example, clarified how one person can affect the other in ways that may lead to certain kinds of internal structure, such as the "bad me" and the "not me." He noted how the anxiety of one person could be picked up by the other and become part of the other. Yet interpersonal theories still propose a discrete separateness of the two persons, entertaining no notion of the expanded connected self. Psychoanalytic theory helps us understand the makeup or structure of the various components (persons) who are connected as well as the impact of previous connections (relationships) on the persons in connection.

Although these elements are very important to an understanding of connectivity, they fail to focus on the features or dynamics that are intrinsic to connectivity itself. Further exploration is needed to comprehend the manner in which connection unfolds in a committed relationship and how a positive ongoing connection between two persons creates each person anew. A deeper examination of the processes and outcomes associated with Imago theory and therapy offers promise of a more complete explanation of the nature and activity of connectivity.

New Perspective on Connectivity

This chapter focused on the phenomenon and nature of connectivity. Different forms of connectivity and the power of connectivity on individual health and functioning were described. An examination of the nature of connectivity suggested that connection takes place not between discrete objects; rather, those who are connected become part of one another—that is, they are self-objects for each other. There is a continuity between these selves, even as oxygen within the body is continuous with that outside the body. These discussions suggest a new perspective on the nature of connectivity in relationships, a focus that is distinct from those of the intrapsychic, family systems, or earlier relational theories that posited a discreteness to the selves.

In response to an earlier version of this chapter, Hendrix maintained that despite its emphasis on connectivity, the argument of this chapter had been developed within the context of the individual. To a large measure, this contention is accurate.

Given all that, one could argue that it is at the end of this chapter that the beginning point has been reached. The discussion has evolved to the point where it is now rooted within the context of connectivity. The questions and the focus now shift: for example, what are the relationship characteristics that reflect connectivity? How does the nature and quality of the history of relationships, as opposed to the history of the self, determine the capacity for present connectivity within the relationship? Which relationship variables contribute to empathic ruptures and which enhance empathic capacities?

In conclusion, this discussion has far wider implications than those for committed relationships, although these are crucially important. However important the Industrial Revolution was to the development of our culture, its emphasis on the individual led to the breaking of connections. Some would insist that our civilization's future hinges on the solidity of marriages and families today. If that is so, then the concern of Imago therapists about whatever solidifies connection within families is of tremendous importance.

References

Bowlby, J. (1969). *Attachment and loss: Vol. I. Attachment.* New York: Basic Books.

Goldberg, A. (1990). *The prisonhouse of psychoanalysis.* Hillsdale, NJ: Analytic Press.

Goldberg, A. (1995). *The problem of perversion.* New Haven, CT: Yale University Press.

Hendrix, H. (1988). *Getting the love you want: A guide for couples.* New York: Henry Holt.

Jordan, J. V. (1991). Empathy and self boundaries. In J. V. Jordan, A. G. Kaplan, J. B. Miller, I. P. Stiver, & J. L. Surrey (Eds.), *Women's growth in connection: Writings from the Stone Center* (pp. 67–80). New York: Guilford Press.

Kohut, H. (1971). *The analysis of the self.* New York: International Universities Press.

Parkes, C. M. (1974). *The first year of bereavement.* New York: Wiley.

Parkes, C. M., & Weiss, R. (1983). *Recovery from bereavement.* New York: Basic Books.

Sullivan, H. S. (1953). *The interpersonal theory of psychiatry.* New York: Norton.

Surrey, J. (1991). The "self-in-relation": A theory of women's development. In J. V. Jordan, A. G. Kaplan, J. B. Miller, I. Stiver, & J. L. Surrey (Eds.), *Women's growth in connection: Writings from the Stone Center* (pp. 51–66). New York: Guilford Press.

Weiss, R. (1975). *Marital separation.* New York: Basic Books.

Chapter Eleven

The Relationship Nightmare as an Expression of Disconnection

Randall C. Mason, Ph.D.

Margaret Mason, Ph.D.

Mo Therese Hannah, Ph.D.

One of the things I've learned from years of conducting Imago Relationship Therapy (IRT) is that couples are in far more pain than I once thought. This realization crystallized for me during a session when, after listening, mirroring, and validating both partners because they weren't able to mirror and validate each other, I found myself saying to the couple, "God, that really sounds like a nightmare." What sounded like a nightmare to me was the reality of their lives.

Definition of the Relationship Nightmare

I realized then that the term *nightmare* was not just a colloquialism; it was an accurate statement of what goes on between partners. The relationship nightmare is, in fact, an altered state of consciousness,

---

This chapter is based on a clinical training given by Dr. Mason. It was written after his death through a collaboration between Margaret Mason and Mo Therese Hannah.

like the psychosis that emerges while you're sleeping and wakes you up. It is a dreamlike state that comes on suddenly when you've released control of your ego. The nightmare also involves a regression or, in the language of self psychology, a fragmentation. The nightmare involves the regression of two perfectly mature adults who in their day-to-day life are viewed by those around them as healthy persons. They begin to fight like two-year-olds: they stomp their feet; they threaten, "I'm never coming back"; they yell, "I can't believe you did this," and "Ten years ago, I should have known better than to ever have gotten involved with you." Self psychologists who talk about this fragmented state describe it as being off balance. The opposite of fragmentation is cohesion: a feeling of the self being together. Cohesion means that when you're walking down the street, you feel as though you've got everything together, that you're in charge of your life. Fragmentation means that you have lost that sense. One man who came to see me was a clergyman who had broken up an affair the night before. He said, "It feels like my arm is not a part of me. It is dead." He had gone into a fragmentation because of a loss of that relationship.

So in this altered state of consciousness called the relationship nightmare, we have regression and fragmentation. In this state, you are sure that you have met the enemy, that the enemy is your spouse, and that to have any chance at future happiness, you must get away from this person for the rest of your life, no matter what the cost. This nightmare continues until it somehow ends and then, within perhaps a ten-second period, you say, "How could I have ever thought those things about this wonderful person with whom I'm in a relationship?" And you keep thinking that until you are in the next nightmare, at which point you knew that you were fooled, that you must have been in complete denial all along.

That is why I now ask couples, in the very first session, "Do you have a nightmare relationship?" I do this because I've learned that if I don't, people will present themselves in therapy like good little boys and good little girls who are fully mature. That way, the therapist will appreciate the rightness of their position and will go on to chastise their partner appropriately.

Now, when I ask that question, I sometimes hear, "Oh, no." That's when I tell the couple that there are covert nightmares as well as overt nightmares. I describe a covert nightmare as times when the partners are not saying or doing anything nasty or harmful, but they are thinking about such things. Once I describe the covert nightmare to them, many couples admit to having this type of nightmare, and within a few sessions, they begin talking about how this sets off some of their fights. I've also found that when I say, "Talk about the nightmare for two or three minutes," the couple seems to breathe a sigh of relief, as if they experienced my acceptance of this as a form of mirroring and validation.

Treating the Relationship Nightmare

To understand how to intervene in the nightmare, we first need to use microanalysis to pinpoint what triggered the nightmare. To contrast microanalysis with macroanalysis, microanalysis involves minute, time-contained, concrete incidents; macroanalysis refers to the bigger events that occurred during the past month or the past week. In microanalysis, we're not talking about major issues, such as whether the person is a diffuser or an isolator, a maximizer or a minimizer, psychotic or nonpsychotic. We're talking about small but very concrete events.

A Relationship Nightmare Example

One couple with whom I was working came in the Monday after Thanksgiving. They were very proud of themselves, because they had been successful at getting through Thanksgiving at the home of the wife's mother. This mother and the rest of the family were severe alcoholics, so there would be fifteen to twenty people who would be sloshed by two in the afternoon. Every prior Thanksgiving, the couple would go and stay all day, out of loyalty to her family, but they would end up getting into a huge fight afterward. This year, they planned ahead of time to stay for a much shorter period. They were very happy, because this had worked. During the session, the man was sitting with his leg crossed across his knee. Then he said, referring to his mother-in-law, "Randy, you should have seen her." He slapped his knee and told about a couple of incidents that had occurred when the mother-in-law was drunk on Thanksgiving Day. Then the wife added a couple of incidents. About ten minutes later, she turned to me and said, "Randy, when can I expect to have a man for a husband?" I had gotten so carried away with all the laughter that it wasn't

clear to me what had just happened, in terms of the mechanics of the nightmare that had just begun. I even called them up two hours after the session,
because I didn't want them to stay in a nightmare.

Anatomy of the Nightmare

What is the anatomy of this nightmare? First of all, it always starts
with an unconscious precipitant. What was the unconscious precipitant here? You cannot shame her mother without shaming her.
We know that she was unconscious of this precipitant, because consciously, she agreed with her husband about her mother's behavior. The wife was experiencing shame, which goes directly to the
old brain. It's the old brain that says, "Randy, when can I expect to
have a man for a husband?"

In a nightmare, you will have two shaming precipitants: the unconscious one and the conscious one. Next comes the core scene.
During the core scene, characterological factors in the couple intensify; they regress and act it out as though they were two-year-
olds. So if the man is, say, a bit anal-retentive, he will decide that
he isn't going to give anything to her for any reason, under any
conditions, for evermore. If she happens to be a controller-definer,
then during the core scene, she will lay down the law. One of the
spouses will make a retaliatory comment that will shame the other
person, after which he or she will feel satisfied for a while. Next,
the other partner will think up a retort, which he or she will use to
shame the other person. And it will go on from there.

The final step goes in one of two directions: either the nightmare will end in some way that will lead to growth and reconnection, or it will cause a scarring, a build-up of an inner wall that makes
your partner alien to you and you alien to your partner. When the
wall gets thick enough, the couple has developed a parallel relationship.

Treating the Nightmare

So, what do you as the therapist do with the nightmare? First, you
make an assessment. You listen to the content, to why the nightmare is justified: how awful the other person is, how much he or
she isolates or diffuses. Later on, you can use that material to assess
and work on the character structure of the partners. After you've

listened, mirrored, and validated each of them, your first question should be, When did this begin? You have to uncover the conscious precipitant—the remark, the physical posture or superior stance that caused the other person to react. Almost all the time, both partners will be aware of this, which is why it's called the conscious precipitant. Of course, they will not be aware of the unconscious precipitant, which is the most important thing to uncover. To do this, your next question should be, What happened during the half hour before that? Once you get that out in the open—the feelings of shame, of being rejected, of being inconsequential—the nightmare will come to an end.

When the nightmare is over, you can start to work with the couple on their character issues, but until the nightmare is over, there isn't enough safety, because each of them are in the face of the mortal enemy.

Clinical Examples

Relationship nightmares can affect couples in a variety of ways. The following cases are some examples.

The Case of the Missing Ring

A pastor and his wife had been loaned a cottage for a vacation. While they were on their way to the vacation, they talked about whether or not their finances were in good enough shape to buy an engagement ring for the wife. They had been married for twenty-five years. The children had been put through college. Everything had gone well, but they had always decided that there were more important things to spend money on than an engagement ring. On the way to the cottage, when they discussed the issue of the ring, they again decided to postpone buying one. When they got up to the cottage and plugged in their TV, the picture tube blew. Later on that evening, the husband said, "We're going to be up here for two weeks; I guess we'd better go get another TV." And she said, "Better buy an engagement ring!" That was the beginning of the nightmare that went on for two weeks. She was very apologetic, but they couldn't find their way out. So in our session, we investigated. I said to her, "What feelings did you have when you said that?" She replied, "I don't understand it. It doesn't make any sense to me that I said that." I said, "Well, did making the decision again not to buy the ring play any part?" She responded, "Oh, no. No, that doesn't play a part. That was a decision he and I made together. I believe in the decision we made; that doesn't play any part." Then I said, "Tell me about the little eight-year-old girl inside you. What does she think about a woman who hasn't gotten an engagement ring?" Then the tears started to come, and just like that, the nightmare was over. At that point, he could reimage what had happened between them, and she could reimage it, too.

The Canoe Ride

The second case involves an engineer and his wife. They had gone out for a canoe ride, and afterward they had been talking about how wonderful their life had become since starting therapy. They got out the Thermos jug and were having a cup of coffee. She said to him, "You know, things are so much safer in our relationship now; I can't believe it." Then she referred to how she had been sexually abused as a child and said, "I really feel like I'm healing, so I've decided that we should just go without sex for another year, six months to a year, and allow the healing to take place." He replied, "I agree with that completely. I want you to heal." About ten minutes later, he sort of mumbled, "I should have just started with an affair twenty years ago, so this issue wouldn't have to come up anymore." Of course, they now were off into a big nightmare. He continuously apologized for saying such a dreadful thing. He kept repeating how much he really wanted her healing. Finally, I said to him, "Is that the only thought you had?" He answered, "That's all I can think of." So I said, "Nothing even in the back of your head, something that may have come to your mind? Not even a little irritation?" "Well, maybe a little irritation, but I don't understand why I would be irritated by that." And I answered, "You're not irritated when the queen speaks?" What he had experienced was that the queen had made a unilateral decision that he was to live with, and she was not even going to consult him about it. Inside of five minutes, she apologized for acting like the queen, and the nightmare was over.

The Affair

The third case involved a physician and his wife. It had been discovered that he had had an affair with an intern whom he had supervised ten years earlier. He was losing his position at the medical school because this had been made public. His wife was maximizing, saying, "For ten years, this secret has been hidden. He has been leading a double life." In the session, she turned to her husband and said, "Can I tell [Randy] about everything, including the sex?" Her husband responded, "Well, you might as well. You do it at home all the time; you might as well do it here!"

At that point, she stood up and started to leave the room, saying, "The therapist I used to see told me that I didn't have to stay in the room when he was
acting that way." I responded, "Could you just sit down for a minute and tell
me what he's done that makes you want to go out of the room?" So she started
to talk again about the affair. I said, "Well, we've known about that affair for
two months. Something else is going on right now. What else has happened?"
It slowly came out that he had talked with another therapist on our staff about
how to publicly announce what had happened. He had come out and
announced to his wife what he and the therapist had decided should be done.
In other words, the king had spoken; his prime minister had sent word to the
queen about the future, her future, with all of their friends and work colleagues. Was the wife important enough to consult? Not in his world. That was
the source of the nightmare.

The Misinterpretation

Another couple who had been in our (Randy and Margaret's) couples workshop came in for therapy three weeks later. They told me that they had gone
home after the workshop and talked for three days like they never had before
in their twenty-five-year marriage. They were sharing things; they were with
each other fully. But in the midst of this, they had gotten into a nightmare that
they couldn't get out of. So we began to look for the precipitants. As far as she
was concerned, the precipitant was that he tried to have sex with her. She was
absolutely insulted by this, because right after the workshop, she had asked for
a moratorium on sex, and he had agreed to the moratorium. The day the
nightmare started, after they had spent two hours talking, he reached out and
held her in his arms, and he began to move his hands over her. That was the
event that led her to tell him how disgraceful he was, how he didn't live up to
his promises, and how everything was now down the drain.

As we explored this further, we discovered that about a half hour before the
nightmare began, he had misinterpreted something she'd said, and this had
caused him to have an empty feeling inside. They had been interpreting the
problem as if it were due to his sexual aggression. In fact, he was in denial of
his need for connection with her. He felt so much shame over the emptiness he
felt and his need to reach out to her that he was covering it up by talking about
his need for sex. Before he left for work, then, he was trying to reconnect with
her, not to have sex with her. When they discovered this, she said to him, "Well,
if you'd only said that to begin with, we wouldn't have had this nightmare."

Short-Circuiting the Nightmare

To avoid getting into a nightmare in the first place, a couple has to stop using all methods of shaming each other. One of these methods is "constructive criticism," another is put-downs, and a third is kidding. You might want to say, "Well, you ought to be able to kid with your partner." But your partner is probably the one person you can't kid with, because your partner is the person who is most vulnerable with you.

Another thing that couples need to give up is righteous superiority. This is always the factor that causes the shaming of the other. Mirroring and validating counteract the righteous superiority, because these show your partner that you take him or her seriously as a person.

I remember one time when Margaret and I were in a nightmare, and we didn't know what to do. All of a sudden, she said to me, "So if I hear you right . . ." And she was able to summarize everything that was going on with me. The nightmare was ended from my side, and then I did it back to her, and the nightmare ended for her.

You also can end a nightmare by reimaging your partner's rage. You can see your partner not as rageful but as feeling helpless and as truly wanting to get it right. If you keep this thought in mind, you'll begin to soften.

Now, of course, the difficulty of doing all this is that when you're in a nightmare, damned if you're going to mirror and empathize with and reimage that terrible person. But as time goes on, you'll realize that it's better to do that than to continue with the nightmare.

Chapter Twelve

Envy's Manifestation in Individuals and Couples

Implications for Imago Therapy

Bernard J. Baca, Ph.D.

When a couple arrives for relationship therapy, they are usually in the midst of what Hendrix (1988) describes as the power struggle. The power struggle refers to each partner's attempts to coerce the other into perceiving and acting in a certain manner. As Hendrix puts it, in an effort to protect one's own existence, one tries to diminish the partner's reality. This conflict sometimes takes the form of a so-called core scene, in which the partners repeat the same fight in subtly different ways throughout their relationship.

Hendrix (1988) identifies three factors that fuel the couple's power struggle:

1. Our partners make us feel anxious by stirring up forbidden parts of ourselves.
2. Our partners have or appear to have the same negative traits as our parents, which adds further injury to childhood wounds and thereby awakens our unconscious fear of death.
3. Partners project their own negative traits onto one another. Hendrix's model (1988) for partner attraction and selection pinpoints the primitive defense mechanisms of denial, splitting, projection, and introjection. The parts of each partner that are denied, split off, projected, and introjected form the imago.

Imago and the Power Struggle

The imago is the unconscious template for partner selection. It is formed by the character traits all human beings develop to cope with childhood wounding. These character traits are projected onto the psyche of the other, who takes them in through the process of introjection. The defensive sequence of denial, splitting, projection, and introjection is repeated throughout the couple's relationship. At each new level of development, the couple repeats this process to master or work through their childhood experiences (Hendrix, 1988; Scharff & Scharff, 1987).

Hendrix (1988) suggests that couples project onto their partners three aspects of themselves: the denied part, the lost part, and the disowned part. In object relations terms, this would be called splitting. Simultaneously, projection occurs as one partner projects the part-objects of the self onto the other (Scharff & Scharff, 1987). Finally, the other takes in or introjects these split-off parts. The stage is then set for feelings of envy toward the other for having characteristics that each (erroneously) believes is missing, denied, or disowned in the self. So, initially, the parts one partner denies, splits off, and then projects onto the other are, in fact, parts of the self (hence the term *part-objects*) that have been denied, lost, or disowned. The introjection is retained within the partner on whom it is projected, as it is a mirror for his or her psyche (Scharff & Scharff, 1987). The projecting partner then becomes envious of the other for having that which the projecting partner lacks. Meanwhile, this same process is occurring in the other partner as well.

During the initial courtship phase, only the more conscious and positive aspects of the self (established through the projections and introjections of childhood caretakers) are projected onto the psyche of the other (Hendrix, 1988). After courtship, the unconscious or denied (usually negative) aspects of the self are projected onto the partner. The projector then does not have to deal with these denied, lost, or disowned aspects. In fact, each partner has found in the other the capacity to hold these split-off negative qualities. Further, the projector perceives these aspects as though they were the partner's sole characteristics. This provides a rationale for the projector to reject the other for having the very characteristics that the projector denies or has lost. Both partners engage in this unconscious process simultaneously; each is doing the same thing to the other.

This phase of the relationship is known as the power struggle (Hendrix, 1988). One partner attempts to get the other partner to adhere to his or her own perspective. Hendrix (personal communication, 1993) describes this stance as, "You and I are one, and I am the one."

Envy

According to Hendrix (personal communication, 1993), the power struggle is an empathic failure on the part of each partner. It is a mirror of the empathic failure that each member of the dyad experienced in his or her own childhood with his or her significant caregivers (Scharff & Scharff, 1987). Ironically, during the power struggle, each member of the dyad is attempting to secure empathic communication with the significant other, but the method being used to establish this connection is guaranteed to fail. As Hendrix states (personal communication, 1993), what you most want from your partner is what he or she will have the greatest difficulty providing. In addition, according to Hendrix, even when one partner becomes able to provide whatever the other most wants, the receiving partner often becomes terrified and rejects the gift.

For Boris (1994), this behavior of rejecting what one wants is the basis of envy. Hope is the schema that each human has possessed since the womb; it is the notion that each person knows what would constitute optimum care from his or her parents. For most people, this hope was not adequately fulfilled, and what they received was not satisfying. The actual attempt at satisfaction is what Boris calls desire.

Hopes and Desires

What occurs for most people, then, is a disparity between what they actually needed (hope) and what they actually received (desire). According to Boris (1994) and Klein (1984), if there is a substantial disparity between the original hope and the actual desire, then hope prevents the desire from satisfying. This is envy, and envy prevents desire from satisfying. The psychic process is that when hope is thwarted, outrage occurs, leading to envy, which manifests as spite and revenge (Boris, 1994). The loved object, which is based on the mental schema or representation of earlier loving-caring objects, begins to represent the lost object. That object was experienced as inconsistent in its love (Scharff & Scharff, 1987). Re-experiencing this inconsistency sets up the following scenario: obtaining the love-supplying object—the parental imago in the form of the partner—triggers the infantile experience of inconsistent love, which is ambivalence. When the partner possesses the inconsistent love object, whether actual or fantasized, the experience of simultaneously hating and loving the possessed object occurs. Hence the person wishes both to hold the object and to destroy it for triggering the suffering caused by the inconsistency, which of course is based on the past.

Greed

A catch-22 situation now exists: either solution to this dilemma, to accept or to reject the loved-hated object, is horrible. The dilemma then gives way to greed. Greed is the acquisitive expectation of having and controlling the object of one's desire, if by no other means than by controlling its desirability (Boris, 1994). This means that once one has the object one wants, one can engage in a variety of psychological actions to change, reduce, increase, or eliminate the object's attractiveness.

Thus, through denial, splitting, projection, and introjection, the couple uses their unconscious childhood maps in relating to each other (Scharff & Scharff, 1987). This lays the groundwork for the power struggle.

An Unconscious Process

During the power struggle, each partner attempts to project the unwanted part-objects of the self onto the other. This process is primarily unconscious; that is, the partners are not fully aware that they are engaged in these internal defense mechanisms. They see their partner as the problem, without realizing that what they see in their partner is merely a reflection of themselves. There is a goodness of fit between partners that is intrapsychically established and interpersonally reinforced (Scharff & Scharff, 1987). This suitability of partners is rooted in early infantile maps that have historical, psychological, and physiological roots (Grostein, 1993; Scharff & Scharff, 1987). The depth of the goodness of fit, based on infantile-toddlerhood psychic projections and introjections, is the basis for both the intensity of the attraction and the proportional intensity of the power struggle. Substantial infantile-toddlerhood injury yields intense attraction, which produces an intense power struggle (Scharff & Scharff, 1987). But the basic glue holding this process together is envy based.

Boris (1994) argues that as all infants enter the world, they have a preconception of what they want and need from their caregivers; this is a hope intrinsic to the human organism. What the infant receives from the parenting source (introjected parental whole- and part-objects), once it is in the world, is desire, according to Boris. The expectation is that the hope and the desire will become congruent and will overlap. The disparity between the hope (what the infant or toddler intrinsically knows it needs) and the desire (what it actually gets) is the basis for greed (Boris, 1994; Klein, 1984). If the disparity between hope and desire is great, the person will never allow desire to be satisfied. In greed, then, hope essentially attacks desire and makes unsatisfactory anything that is experienced. Consequently, the greedy person will constantly seek to reduce, replace, enhance, or change the experience to achieve elusive and ultimately unobtainable satisfaction (narcissistic gratification) (Boris, 1994; Kernberg, 1975; Klein, 1984; Scharff & Scharff, 1987).

Sameness and Differentness

Boris (1994) suggests that humans have a need to pair and to couple. According to Boris, pairing is based on the sameness, that is, the similarities, of the two. This notion of sameness corresponds to Hendrix's notion (1988) of the romantic phase, in which the couple discovers, to their delight, their similarities. On the other hand, as Boris suggests, the couple develops also on the basis of their differentness. The couple's need for both sameness and differentness is the backdrop for the power struggle. Each partner is attempting to validate his or her own differentness as well as sameness, without being rejected for either. Invariably, one person is attempting to establish the sameness (usually the one who expends the energy, or the maximizer), while the other is attempting to establish the differentness (usually the one who constricts the energy, the minimizer). The partners are attempting to satisfy both their need to be the same and their need to be different from each other. This results in a push-pull between these two needs. What occurs then is that each one becomes envious of the other, both for being the same as oneself (which obscures the differentness) and for being different from oneself (which undermines the sameness).

As an example, the infant first believes that its mother is the same as itself, only gradually becoming aware that she is different. The desire for sameness and differentness triggers envy, regardless of which position (sameness or differentness) each person in the relationship is experiencing.

When partners in a committed exclusive relationship are in the midst of the power struggle, the basis of their conflict is envy. That is, one partner, due to the denied, lost, and disowned aspects of the self, perceives the other as inherently better (or worse) than the self. The projection of one partner's own lack onto the other is envy.

The Significance of Envy

Envy, according to Schoeck (1966), is the feeling of displeasure and ill will at the (perceived) superiority of another in happiness, success, reputation, or the possession of anything desirable (pp. 18–19). It contains feelings of inferiority as well as spite—a wish to destroy the coveted assets. Further, envy develops in an age of scarcity (Boris, 1994), when a person feels deficient, defective, and filled with hate. The perception is not that we are merely left wanting; it is as though we were judged and found wanting. Because envy develops in an age of scarcity, the old reptilian brain of self-preservation is continuously activated (Hendrix, 1988). Envy is difficult to contain because of its ubiquitousness and its primitiveness (Klein, 1984). Envy is a basic component of self-preservation: self-preservation occurs because comparison, which is envy, has occurred (Boris, 1994).

Schoeck (1966) adds that envy is a drive that lies at the core of man's life as a social being, occurring as soon as two individuals become capable of mutual comparison (p. 3). So envy carries the need to destroy through spite, ill will, and hostility the (perceived) superiority of the other (Boris, 1994). This comparison, in which one is a have and the other a have not (Boris, 1994), is envy. Extending this notion to the couple relationship, one person is envious of the other because the other possesses an aspect of the self that one has denied, lost, or disowned.

Furthermore, Spillius (1993) believes that envy is especially likely when one is dependent on another. This dependency is intrinsic in the infant-caregiver relationship and is extended to all other significant interpersonal relationships, including romantic ones. When dependency occurs, envy is present. Projection is, again, the vehicle used to deny and split off one's dependency and to place it onto the other, triggering envy.

Envy has been described in the psychoanalytic literature, particularly by the British object relations theorists as well as the more contemporary theorists in the United States (Scharff & Scharff, 1987). Freud dealt with envy, as did other analysts, including Abraham (1919), Eisler (1922), and Horney (1936). All of these were written in the therapeutic context between analyst and patient.

Envy in Couple Relationships

Little is written about envy in a committed and exclusive couple relationship. In her book *The Narcissistic/Borderline Couple: A Psychoanalytic Perspective on Marital Treatment,* Lachkar (1992) defines envy using the British object relations conceptualization, but she does not describe in detail how envy occurs within a couple relationship—what it looks like and how to deal with it therapeutically. Searles (1994) also defines envy but places it only within the classical psychoanalytic patient-analyst dyad. Kernberg (1975) and Morrison (1989) have essentially mirrored Klein's original contributions regarding the analytic relationship. None has extended these notions in any meaningful way to the couple relationship.

Self-Envy

In envy there is a feeling of impotence, which can be masochistically turned against the self. Lopez-Corvo (1995) writes about this form of narcissism gone awry. His thesis is that all envy is ultimately self-envy. Often, when coupling occurs, each partner believes that the other is the best person for him or her. Although this might appear to provide narcissistic gratification, in fact, the opposite often occurs. Persons seek narcissistic gratification precisely because they were not adequately mirrored, validated, and empathized with (Hendrix, personal communication, 1993). Lopez-Corvo (1995) views the repetition of narcissistic fusion, reparation, failure, loss of the object, anxiety, and the need to search again for fusion with the lost idealized object as an insidious attack on the self for getting what it wants, resulting in damage to the self.

In the therapeutic process with couples, this repetition described by Lopez-Corvo is the core scene that couples play out. They have conflict over the same issues in a variety of contexts. Furthermore, this repetition resembles the transition between the romantic phase of the unconscious relationship, in which both partners are in relative bliss over their sameness, and the power struggle (Hendrix, 1988), with its focus on the partners' differentness. The basis for this process is, again, self-envy (Lopez-Corvo, 1995).

Lopez-Corvo (1992) defines self-envy as the attack by a part of the self, usually related to childhood self-objects, against another part of the self, identified as a creative and harmonious mother-father or parent-sibling relationship, also within the self, which is now projected as a means of avoiding superego accusations (p. 720). These accusations essentially are an internal warning system (a form of conscience) that the internalized infant experiences as terrifying. Later this internalized infant in the adult must avoid these accusations; to do so requires a splitting process.

Lopez-Corvo (1995) states that once the ego experiences the narcissistic fusion with the longed-for ideal object within the self (much like what occurs in adulthood during the romantic phase of a relationship), powerful feelings of envy form the internal representation of an excluded child self-object. These internalized experiences in the unconscious are triggered, and the adult now experiences the warmth of connection while simultaneously experiencing the exclusion that results in frustration. The desire to have two contradictory experiences at the same time leads to greed—the wish for them both (connection and exclusion) simultaneously, eventuating in envy, which is actually self-envy.

Envy is different from jealousy in that envy wishes to destroy the envied object; jealousy seeks only to remove the coveted object and transfer it to oneself, not to destroy the asset itself (Schoeck, 1966).

Ironically, the love relationship harbors the cycle of envy. This envy often precipitates a yearning to obtain that which we should have had during childhood but did not. As Boris (1994) puts it, incoming supplies that appear to satisfy our psychological needs might ameliorate our envy and induce gratitude. Ironically, however, such gratitude also lays the groundwork for our admiration of what others have. But even as we are provided for, we nevertheless covet the facility by which we could supply ourselves and others.

Just as the infant wishes to obtain and internalize the mother's breast and control the supply, it cannot. The infant's reactions are envy based, due to its self-perceived failure to feed both itself and its mother. Likewise, this frustration and the resulting self-envy occur in adult intimate relationships. When adults receive from their partner what they always wanted, which is based on their infantile-childhood psychic needs, self-envy is triggered.

Envy as the Basis of Conflict

Envy does not cease to be envy when it is transferred from objects to attributes of another human being, according to Boris (1994), who suggests that envy may be the active realization that one is not good enough, in comparison with someone else. The basis for conflict in an interpersonal relationship (including a committed and exclusive couple relationship) can be traced to envy. One partner is envious of the other for triggering dependency needs, resurrecting past injuries, carrying split-off self-objects, and so forth that are in fact located within the psychic structure of the envious person. Such pain triggers other parts of the human brain, such as the reptilian brain, which, according to Hendrix (1988), reacts with flight or fight. Further, when a couple is in the midst of the power struggle, they are by definition in an unconscious reptilian brain mode. Hence they are incapable of integrating the good parts and bad parts of their own selves, which each partner projects onto the other and reflects on the other. The projected-upon partner becomes either the all-bad object, the all-good object, or some combination of these. The projecting partner must take steps to eliminate the threat by fighting, fleeing, submitting, or freezing, thereby denying his or her own envious feelings (Hendrix, 1988). Complicating matters further, this process is taking place simultaneously in the projected-upon partner.

The Six Manifestations of Envy

The following are six ways in which envy becomes evident in relationships, according to Spillius (1993), whose ideas are based on Klein's contributions on envy.

1. Denigration of the good qualities of the object, which then provokes less admiration and dependency. By deeming the envied person as less positive, the envious one retains his or her sense of an intact self. This produces a reduction in the gap between the envied and the envious. In a couple, one partner might constantly criticize the other's positive characteristics to reduce the disparity between the positive values of the envied and those of the envious.

2. Projection of envy, leading the individual to see himself or herself as a nonenvious person surrounded by envious, destructive people. This might resemble a variation of the martyr role. In this scenario, the martyr is actually the destructive perpetrator but ameliorates his or her negativity by projecting his or her envy out to others. This allows the projector to claim that he or she is free of envy: the envy is contained in those around him or her. In a marriage, this dynamic might have one partner believing that he or she is somehow better than others, especially the partner. This attitude absolves the projector of any negativity, which is instead projected onto the partner and others.

3. Idealization of the envied object, so that comparisons with oneself become irrelevant. This could also take the form of a denigration of the envied object and an idealization of some other object. Or some aspects of the envied object might be denigrated and others idealized.

One way of dealing with one's envy toward the partner is to make the other so perfect that any comparison would be absurd. In a couple, one member would express envy by extolling the other's perfection. This would prevent any envy from entering the envious partner's psyche.

In another variation, splitting occurs when the envious partner splits off his or her own envy and projects only good aspects onto the partner. The envious partner then idealizes the other but tempers this idealization with negative components that are also projected onto the partner.

4. Identification with the idealized object or aspects of the object. Through projection and introjection, the envious partner feels that he or she possesses the admired attributes. Again, splitting and its associated defenses of projection and introjection are operating. In this case, the envied object becomes part of the self. For example, in working with a couple in therapy, the therapist might notice that one member of the dyad appears to have all the good aspects, whereas the other partner has none. This often occurs with couples who have early infantile emotional injuries and use primitive, all-or-none splitting, as is seen in narcissistic-borderline couples (Lachkar, 1992). In such couples, one partner appears to be the psychologically stable one; the other suffers from severe mental illness. Both are developmentally—psychologically and emotionally—at the same level (Scharff & Scharff, 1987). However, their apparent manifestation of mental illness is complementary; one shows his or her illness through the other (projection and introjection). The therapist must engage such couples very slowly and deliberately to avoid further decompensation or switching of the pathology.

5. A stifling of feelings of love with a corresponding intensifying of hatred, sometimes expressed as indifference or emotional withdrawal. In some couples, one partner, often initially the minimizer, has withdrawn love. The other partner then substitutes overt indifference or withdrawal for overt love, which covers up feelings of hatred toward the other. This is used to defend against the minimizer's envious feelings toward the maximizer.

6. A form of masochistic defense in which the individual believes himself or herself to be omnipotently hopeless. Consequently, the envied object, who cannot cure the other partner's despair, is proven to be worthless. This process effectively negates the envied partner by making him or her impotent, thereby reducing the envy of the hopeless one.

Paradoxically, this might occur when the therapist has done outstanding therapeutic work. The therapist is mystified when the couple gives up in despair and terminates their commitment to couples therapy. The desire of both partners to be better than the other wins out, and the relationship suffers.

In summary, envy is present whenever comparison occurs. Envy is at the core of the search for the ideal partner. Such dynamics must be understood and managed by the therapist and, of course, the couple.

References

Abraham, K. (1919). A particular form of neurotic resistance against the psycho-analytic method. In D. Bryan & A. Strachey (Trans.), *Selected papers on psychoanalysis*. London: Hogarth Press.

Boris, H. (1994). *Envy*. Northvale, NJ: Aronson.

Eisler, M. (1922). Pleasure in sleep and the disturbed capacity for sleep. *International Journal of Psychoanalysis, 3,* 30–42.

Grostein, J. (1993). *Splitting and projective identification*. Northvale, NJ: Aronson.

Hendrix, H. (1988). *Getting the love you want: A guide for couples*. New York: Henry Holt.

Horney, K. (1936). The problem of negative therapeutic reaction. *Psycho-analysis Quarterly, 5,* 529–544.

Kernberg, O. (1975). *Borderline conditions and pathological narcissism*. Northvale, NJ: Aronson.

Klein, M. (1984). *The writings of Melanie Klein: Vol III. Envy and gratitude and other works*. London: Hogarth Press.

Lachkar, J. (1992). *The narcissistic/borderline couple: A psychoanalytic perspective on marital treatment*. New York: Brunner/Mazel.

Lopez-Corvo, R. (1992). Interpretations about self-envy. *International Journal of Psychotherapy, 73,* 719–728.

Lopez-Corvo, R. (1995). *Self envy: Therapy and the divided inner world*. Northvale, NJ: Aronson.

Morrison, A. (1989). *Shame: The underside of narcissism*. Hillsdale, NJ: Analytic Press.

Scharff, D., & Scharff, J. (1987). *Object relations family therapy*. Northvale, NJ: Aronson.

Schoeck, H. (1966). *Envy: A theory of social behavior*. Indianapolis: Liberty Press.

Searles, H. (1994). *My work with borderline patients*. Northvale, NJ: Aronson.

Spillius, E. (1993). Varieties of envious experiences. *Journal of Psycho-Analysis, 74,* 1199–1212.

Chapter Thirteen

The Conscious Self in a Creational Paradigm

Sophie Slade, Ph.D.

As I started writing this chapter, I had just finished reading Joseph Jaworski's book *Synchronicity: The Inner Path of Leadership* (1998). The book had a powerful impact on me, especially the last chapter, in which he acknowledges that his own writing originated in his and his father's experiences with Watergate as well as in response to what occurred during the Holocaust. For me, this gave rise to such questions as, How could this happen then, as it continues to happen now, in different ways? How can we create a different world where these kinds of things do not happen?

So I write this knowing that my voice, like a snowflake, weighs nothing more than nothing, but that all the snowflakes together make the bough fall. I know too that, as Kurt Kauter (1981) stated it, "perhaps there is only one person's voice lacking for peace to come to the world." Mine is but one voice among many who wonder how we could create better human relationships and why that is so difficult to do.

The Healing Power of Relationship

Imago Relationship Therapy (IRT) is an integrative therapeutic approach to working with couples. Having arisen from developer Harville Hendrix's experiences with his own first marriage and divorce, Hendrix and his wife Helen LaKelly Hunt further elaborated IRT on the basis of Hendrix's work as a couples therapist and teacher of marital therapy (1988, 1996).

Later, Hendrix (1992) applied Imago principles to working with single persons who wanted to prepare themselves for committed partnership. The thesis was that although singles can work on their own personal growth, they are not able to receive healing outside of a committed relationship. These pronouncements were experienced by many within the Imago community as wounding, as they inferred that singles were somehow "less than" or more limited than those in a couple relationship. Although this take hardly indicates that the theory is "wrong," it certainly may signify that further examination of the theory is needed.

Healing Childhood Wounds

It makes theoretical sense to me that the deepest levels of healing of childhood wounds occurs when a partner who resembles our childhood caregivers, and who therefore is capable of eliciting similar feelings in us, is willing to grow beyond the limitations of his or her defensive character structure in order to satisfy our unfulfilled childhood needs. It also makes sense to me that a committed partnership challenges us to change our defensive character structure in ways that a less committed relationship would not.

Imago theory provides an elegant and appealing reformulation of the "repetition compulsion": for Imago, the reexperiencing of childhood wounding in our romantic relationship provides us with new possibilities for healing and growth. Through consciousness and intentionality, the nightmare can become the dream. It is only when we receive in adulthood what we did not get from our parents during childhood, and from someone who "looks like" our parents, that we are able to grieve over what we lacked in childhood and to accept, with compassion, that our caretakers did the best they could but nonetheless wounded us.

However, I also maintain that an overreliance on the partner as the source of healing carries the danger of focusing too much on changing the partner rather than the self, although this is not Hendrix's intention. It seems much easier for us to look at what our partner needs to do to meet our needs than to look at what we need to do to provide healing for our partner. I believe that Imago theory has often been misinterpreted, whether consciously or unconsciously, as justifying the abdication of personal responsibility for doing one's own healing work. Perhaps that has even been some of IRT's appeal: the idea that I'm finally going to get the love I want, rather than that I'm finally going to learn how to give the love my partner wants. The emphasis on couple relationships and on the dichotomy between couples and singles may have inadvertently detracted from a focus on the self and on one's own personal responsibility for being conscious and intentional in all relationships.

Probably all our relationships have the potential to be wounding or healing to us, given that we have the capacity to transferentially project our parental imago onto just about any object, person, or institution. Even more important, I believe, is the awareness that we can be either wounding or healing in all our interactions with others.

In his book *Giving the Love That Heals,* Hendrix (1997) demonstrates the applicability of his approach to the parent-child relationship. If, as Hendrix proposes, a parent can be dialogical with a young child who is incapable of adulthood intentionality, then it must not be essential for others with whom we are interacting to be aware and consciously committed to dialogue in order for us to be intentional toward them. We all have the potential to listen to another in a way that represents the spirit of "visiting the other's island with an empty back-pack" (H. Schleifer, personal communication, 1998). When in the role of the "sender," we all have the potential to express our truth in a way that emphasizes that it is about us and our "island," rather than about criticisms of the other. Whenever fulfilling these responsibilities in our interaction with another, we are in dialogue. Thus it takes only one person to be in dialogue. By this, I do not mean that every interaction with another human being must be dialogical. However, the applicability of the Imago approach to relationships goes far beyond the couple relationship; it extends to practicing a relational way of being in the world.

Personal Responsibility

For most of us, being in an interaction with an intimate partner who is committed to our healing and who is conscious and intentional in his or her expression of that commitment is probably the exception rather than the rule. Many of us who have participated in IRT or Imago trainings are with partners who are more committed to changing us to meet their needs than they are to the Imago process. Even that small proportion of couples in which both partners are very committed to the Imago process are forced to interact, at times, with a reactive, reptilian partner, rather than an intentional partner.

I therefore believe that each of us, whether single or married, holds 100 percent personal responsibility to be conscious and intentional in our relationships. When we say things like, "I will if you will" or "I can't because you won't" or "Why should I if you haven't," we actually are taking 0 percent responsibility, not 50 percent, as some of us believe.

The tool of Couples Dialogue can be used in all relationships, and it can be used unilaterally. I would like to see both the sender and the receiver roles taught this way—as an individual process as well as a couples process. The couples processes of re-visioning, re-imaging, holding, making Behavior Change Requests, and containment (Hendrix, 1992) could be adapted for unilateral use by individuals, whether or not they are working with a partner who also is "in the process." The singles processes of saying goodbye to old relationships and to old forms of relating, of identifying the defensive character structure, and of developing a personal growth plan (Hendrix, 1994) could be integrated into the work with couples. All who are interested in better relationships could be taught these basic skills, whether they come with a committed partner or not. More specialized additional work could then be added for those working with a partner (broadly defined as anyone with whom they have a significant relationship) and for those who are working independently, whether or not they are in a committed relationship. This increased focus on personal responsibility within a relational paradigm would remove the false dichotomy between couples and singles and place the responsibility firmly where it belongs—on the self, rather than on the partner. All of us are, after all, individuals who are in relationship.

Being Conscious and Intentional

Why do so many of us find it so difficult to be conscious and intentional in our relationships, to stay dialogical in the face of the other, to take the responsibility for being healing and safe rather than making it the other's responsibility? According to Imago theory, in order to be intentional and dialogical, we have to override our reptilian brains and at least temporarily discard our defensive character structure. One factor that makes this more or less difficult to do is the severity of the wounding we experienced in childhood. Those of us who have faced a very real threat of death, whether through our own serious illness or through abandonment or abuse by a primary caretaker, had to develop a more rigid and intractable defensive character structure. As a general rule, the more severe the threat, the more extreme the defenses, although there do seem to be exceptions. Also, the earlier in life we experienced the threat, the less available is the defense to consciousness awareness.

I also believe that the difficulty is proportional to the amount of threat we perceive in our current situation. This threat may be of fear, shame, guilt, or other bad feelings within the self. For example, I currently find it much easier to be conscious and intentional with my partner than with my teenage son. I have done a lot of therapeutic work with my partner, and for the most part, even my old brain seems to experience him as safe. With my son, who is having to make many choices over which I have no control, and in an environment over which I have no control, I feel much more fear, guilt, and shame over my parenting of him, especially when I experience him as making mistakes. It seems so much harder for me to stay dialogical with him than it is to automatically defend myself from these uncomfortable feelings, which I do by becoming controlling or shaming of him. I also find it much easier when the other person in the interaction is committed to being a safe and healing person to me. My son, however, has no awareness of, or commitment to, being a healing person to me. I imagine that his degree of reactivity to me, and vice versa, are factors; my son's old-brain sensitivity certainly seems to trigger my own reactivity. He is currently my greatest challenge and growth gift on my journey of intentionality.

A Creational Paradigm of Relationships

Through my interactions with my son and my role in creating his environment, I am also continuously "creating" my son. I am well aware that my way of being with my partner, and the work we have done together, have influenced the person he is today. Likewise, he has helped create me. Each of us has been created as we are today by the sum of many different influences, especially our parents, our primary partners, and ourselves. I imagine that the interactions and events of the future will continue to create me, that in twenty years I will not be the person I am today. I have not yet been created; I am in a continual process of creation.

Wade Luquet (2000) stated that a culture's creation myths influence how people relate to each other. Our Judeo-Christian origin myth is that the world was created in six days and then, on the seventh day, God rested. Finished, over, and done with, sort of surveillance and maintenance duty from there on in.

Over the past couple of hundred years, however, this origin myth has been seriously challenged. Galileo shifted us out of the center of our universe, but perhaps Darwin's theory of evolution dealt the first major deathblow to the Genesis creation myth. Einstein's theory of relativity replaced absolutes with perceptions, and quantum physics proposed that everything that exists is interconnected, with each piece a part of the whole, each being in relationship with, and affected by, everything else. The Hubble space telescope shows us images of stars being born in a universe constantly in a process of creation. Developmental psychology is a relatively new field that examines the multiple influences affecting the creation of each human being. During the past few decades, as indicated by developments within the field of adult psychology, it has become generally accepted that adults are not complete, fixed human beings but continue to evolve across the life span.

Our myths have not caught up with our present conceptualizations, however; they continue to shape the ways in which we relate to each other and to our world. We continue to behave as though relationship were a fixed entity rather than a creative endeavor in which each of us plays the role of creator. Our fairy tales reflect the "created and finished" orientation toward relationships when they end with the prince and princess marrying.

We need new myths and stories that reflect the recent developments in diverse areas of thinking, stories that mirror the ongoing creative process of the universe as it manifests in our lives and in our relationships. Such new myths and stories can arise only within a democratic structure, in which individuals have developed a collective awareness of their role in the political structure and of their responsibility for creating their own government and thus their future. Perhaps the rising interest in more organic, personal forms of spirituality will give rise to such new myths, which eventually will become outdated when what we are continuously creating replaces what has been created.

I believe that we are not just evolving, as Darwin suggested; each of us is a creator of the future of the universe; we are a part of the creative energy. According to this creational paradigm, I am not merely relating to others; I also am creating them. I am no longer trying to change the other; I am creating the other through my way of being with him or her. The way I behave in relation to my partner and to my son has an impact on them and on what they create in their interactions with others.

I invite you to imagine a world where people take seriously their responsibility for being creators of the future, a world where people take responsibility for being creators of their partners, of their relationships, and of each person with whom they interact. Perhaps, in such a world, the terror would become the terror of our own awesome responsibility and of our divine nature, rather than the terror of the other.

References

Hendrix, H. (1988). *Getting the love you want: A guide for couples.* New York: Henry Holt.

Hendrix, H. (1992). *Keeping the love you find: A guide for singles.* New York: Pocket Books.

Hendrix, H. (1994). *Keeping the love you find workshop manual.* New York: Institute for Imago Relationship Therapy.

Hendrix, H. (1996). The evolution of Imago Relationship Therapy: A personal and professional journey. *Journal of Imago Relationship Therapy, 1*(1), 1–17.

Hendrix, H. (1997). *Giving the love that heals.* New York: Pocket Books.

Jaworski, J. (1998). *Synchronicity: The inner path of leadership.* San Francisco: Berrett-Koehler.

Kauter, K. (1981). *Thus Spake the Caribou.* Germany: Greifenverlag.

Luquet, W. (2000). *Marriagenesis: The evolution of marriage.* Unpublished dissertation, Union Institute, Cincinnati, Ohio.

About the Editors

Harville Hendrix, Ph.D., is the author or coauthor, with his wife, Helen LaKelly Hunt, of six books, including the best-sellers *Getting the Love You Want: A Guide for Couples* and *Keeping the Love You Find: A Personal Guide.* Imago Relationship Therapy is a product of their partnership, and they cocreated, along with other Imago therapists, Imago Relationships International, an international nonprofit organization that offers training and support to approximately two thousand Imago therapists in twenty-one countries. Dr. Hendrix is a pastoral counselor and has been a frequent guest on many national television shows, including fourteen appearances on the *Oprah Winfrey Show*, one of which won Ms. Winfrey an Emmy Award as the "most socially redemptive" program for daytime talk shows.

Helen LaKelly Hunt, Ph.D., is coauthor of several books with her husband, Harville Hendrix, including *Giving the Love That Heals: A Guide for Parents*, and is the author of *Faith and Feminism: A Holy Alliance.* She has been active in the women's movement for the past eighteen years and is founder and president of the Sister Fund, a private women's fund dedicated to the social, political, economic, and spiritual empowerment of women and girls. Helen has been recognized for her leadership in building the women's funding movement and has received numerous awards, including the National Creative Philanthropy Award from the National Network of Women's Funds (1990) and Gloria Steinem's Women of Vision Award through the Ms. Foundation for Women (1993), and is an honored inductee in the National Women's Hall of Fame in Seneca Falls, New York (1994).

Mo Therese Hannah, Ph.D., is associate professor of psychology at Siena College in Latham, New York. She is the managing editor of the *Journal of Imago Relationship Therapy* and has coedited several books, including *Healing in the Relational Paradigm: The Imago Relationship Therapy Casebook* (with Wade Luquet), *Preventive Approaches to Couples Therapy* (with Rony Berger), and *Building Intimate Relationships: Clinical Applications of the PAIRS Program* (with Rita De Maria).

Wade Luquet, Ph.D., is associate professor of sociology at Gwynedd-Mercy College in Gwynedd Valley, Pennsylvania (outside Philadelphia). He is the author of *Short-Term Couples Therapy: The Imago Model in Action* and coeditor of *Healing in the Relational Paradigm: The Imago Relationship Therapy Casebook* (with Mo Therese Hannah). He has also authored numerous articles and book chapters on the topics of couples therapy, social work, and sociology. He maintains a private practice in North Wales, Pennsylvania.

About the Contributors

Bernard J. Baca, Ph.D., earned an MSSW from the University of Wisconsin at Madison and a doctorate in clinical psychology from Union Institute. He maintains a private practice integrating object relations and Imago Relationship Therapy (IRT), teaching and supervising at Christian Theological Seminary in Indianapolis, and conducting training and workshops for other professionals. Dr. Baca was selected by colleagues as one of the thirty-seven outstanding psychotherapists in Indianapolis and featured in the March 2003 issue of *Indianapolis Monthly Magazine.*

Mona R. Barbera, Ph.D., is a psychologist practicing couples and individual therapy in Providence, Rhode Island, and Boston. She is trained in IRT and Internal Family Systems Therapy. Her publications include *Projective Redemption in Couples Therapy.*

Randy Gerson, Ph.D. (deceased), was associate professor in the Department of Psychiatry and Behavioral Sciences at Mercer University School of Medicine until his death in 1995. In addition, he was director of Atlanta College for Systemic Thinking. He is author of *Genograms: Assessment and Intervention* and numerous articles and book chapters on topics related to couples and family therapy. His work regarding genograms included creation of software for constructing and analyzing family patterns.

Randall C. Mason, Ph.D. (deceased), was a certified Imago therapist and the founding director of the Center for Religion and Psychotherapy of Chicago, created to provide services to clients, training in pastoral psychotherapy, and research in the area of religion and psychotherapy. He was a diplomate in the American Association of Pastoral Counselors, and a certified clinical instructor of IRT.

Stephen R. Plumlee, M.Div., Ph.D., lives in Sarasota, Florida, where he practices as an individual, group, and Imago couples psychotherapist. His primary interest is in object relations psychoanalysis, with focus on the human person as a type of the Eastern Christian experience of the Trinity. He has published articles and conducted numerous workshops and retreats, and presents at conferences on the connection of human relationships to the Christian spiritual life. He has been married for forty years and counts his marriage a success story of the Imago vision.

Sophie Slade, Ph.D., is a clinical psychologist with a private practice in Montreal, Canada. She completed her doctorate at Concordia University, writing her dissertation on personality similarity and complementarity and relationship satisfaction in adult love relationships. In addition to conducting her private practice, she presents Imago trainings and workshops for couples and singles internationally in French and English, whenever possible accompanied by her husband, David. She is a coauthor of *Deepening the Conscious Self: An Advanced Toolbox for Working with Individuals, Couples and Groups,* a collection of resource materials for Imago therapists.

Ted Smith, D.Min. (deceased), had been a practicing Imago therapist since 1983, when he was one of the first Imago therapists trained by Harville Hendrix. He had a doctoral degree in pastoral counseling and practiced in New York City and Connecticut.

Joseph Zielinski, Ph.D., is a board certified clinical psychologist and a neuropsychologist in private practice in Cherry Hill, New Jersey. He is also a school psychologist in Burlington County Special Services School District, Mt. Holly, New Jersey. Dr. Zielinski is very active in the prescriptive authority movement for psychologists.

Index

A

Abandonment, 92
Abraham, K., 207
Adaptation, 81–82
Affect theory, 93–95; and assessment of intimacy, 97; basic tenets of, 92–105; and Behavior Change Requests, 100; and Container Exercises, 101; and Imago Relationship Therapy, 91–92; as process, 97–98; and safety and danger in Couples Dialogue, 98–99; and safety and danger in Positive Flooding, Caring Behaviors, and Surprises, 101–105
Affective responsiveness, 152
Albert the Great, 48
Almaas, A. H., 163, 169–171
Anxiety, 68–70
Aristotle, 142
Association: and healing dissociation, 39–41; and shift from individual to relational paradigm, 42–45; and wholeness and integrity, 41–42
Association for Imago Relationship Therapy, 24
Attachment, 32, 183
Atwood, G. E., 123, 141, 142, 145, 147, 151, 152, 174

B

Baca, B. J., 9, 201
Bach, J., 23
Bader, E., 92
Bailey, D., 92
Baptist Church, 14
Barbera, M. R., 8, 122

Basch, M. F., 93
Behavior Change Request, 17, 28, 79, 100, 132, 216
Belenky, M. F., 37
Bergman, S., 14, 157
Berit, 49, 58n2
Berne, E., 18
Berry, T., 3, 6
Blame, 76–77
Bollas, C., 124, 126, 127, 129
Bonding, 182–183
Boris, H., 203–207, 209
Bowen, M., 2, 64–90
Bowlby, J., 183
Brandschaft, B., 123, 147, 151, 152
Brown, D., 169
Buber, M., 4, 26, 27, 35, 37, 38, 41, 57
Buttrick, G. A., 49

C

Campbell, J., 146
Caring behaviors, 101–105
Carkhuff, R. R., 28
Casement, P., 125, 131
Center for Relationship Therapy (Dallas), 22
Chase, M., 148
Chestnut Lodge (Maryland), 148
Childhood: completing, 171–172; connection to marriage, 18–19; influences, 14–15; wounds, healing of, 214–215
Cleary, T., 168
Clinchy, B. M., 37, 38, 41
Clohesy, W. W., 42
Coach, therapist as, 31, 70–71, 73–74
Commitment scripts, 101–105

Complementarity, 72–74

Confrontation, 153

Connected relationship, 143

Connection: developing, 170; and empathy, 139–140; and empathy as connective tissue, 147; foundational, 180; ontology of, 25–26; relationships, individuals, consciousness and, 168–169; role of wounding in, 53–54

Connectional disturbance, 179

Connectivity: clinical and foundational, 179–181; experiential, 179; Imago as theory of, 189–191; meanings of, 178–181; new perspectives on, 191–192; ontological, 178–179; transitory, 179

Consciousness, relationships and, 166–168, 216–217

Container exercise, 17, 18, 21, 28, 75, 101, 216

Context, 64–65; multigenerational, 65–66

Contractual theory, 48

Core Energetics, 24, 25

Core scene, 201

Corrective relational experience, 131–132

Cosmogenesis, 4–5

Countertransference, 125, 129, 140. *See also* Transference

Couples Companion: Meditations and Exercises for Getting the Love You Want (Hendrix and Hunt), 24

Couples Dialogue, 5–7, 75, 79, 98–99, 128, 216; and empathy, 150–151; and mirroring, 148–149; and validation, 149–150

Couples Dialogue/Intentional Dialogue process, 24

Couples Therapy Manual (Hendrix), 88

Covenant: centrality of forgiveness in, 54–55; conscious marriage as, 48–58; contract *versus*, 48–52; definition of, 49; as dialogical relationship, 51–52; and differentiation, 54; features of, 52–56; in history and in Imago, 49–51; Hosea and Gomer symbolizing, 52; paradoxical quality of, 55–56; relational, 56–57; role of wounding in, 53–54

Culture and Psychology Reader, 44

D

Dallas Women's Foundation, 22

Darwin, C., 218, 219

David, King, 56

Dearman, A. J., 54

DeMaio, D., 23

Deprivation, 81–82

Descartes, R., 42, 43

De-selfing, 41

Desires, 203–204

Deuteronomy, 54

Dialogue: and covenant as dialogical relationship, 51–52; developing, 27–34; healing through, 130–131; and paradoxical problems, 29–31

Differentiation, 5–6, 54, 66–68

Differentness, 205–206

Disconnection, 179; effects of, 144–145; relationship nightmare as expression of, 193–200

Dissociation: and extreme separate knowing, 38–39; healing of, by association, 39–41

E

East Texas State University, 21–22

Edwards, D. G., 169

Ehrenberg, D., 126

Einfühlung, 41

Einstein, A., 44, 218

Eisler, M., 107

Elliott, R., 21, 22

Emotionality, 74–76

Empathy, 4, 40, 41, 128; avoidant *versus* useful, 152–155; boundaried *versus* unboundaried, 155–158; and connected relationship, 139–140; as connective tissue, 147; in Couples Dialogue, 150–151; dimensions of, 151–159; investigative *versus* bonding nature of, 151–152; responsiveness *versus* accountability in, 158–159

Enactment: by adults, in therapy, 124–125; description of, 124; *versus* imago match, 132–134; as opportunity for healing in psychotherapy, 125–126; by partners, in marriage, 126–127; understanding own role in, 128; as way of suffering in relationship, 127

Engler, J., 169

Engulfment, 92

Envy: as basis of conflict, 209; in couple relationships, 207; in power struggle, 203; self, 207–209; significance of, 206–212; six manifestations of, 210–212

Epistemology, 108

Erikson, E. H., 24

F

Fairbairn, W.R.D., 114, 124

Falcke, H., 58*n*2

False self, 169

Family patterns, 68–70

Family Systems Theory: and complementarity, 72–73; deprivation and adaptation in, 81–82; emotionality in, 74–76; focus of intervention in, 80–81; and individual responsibility, 78–80; mate selection in, 73; role of nature in, 71–72; shame and blame in, 76–77; and systemic theory, 64–71; and unresolved issues, 72

Ferris, T., 4

Filkin, D., 4

Forgiveness, 54–55

Freud, S., 2, 18, 65, 82, 122, 163, 207

G

Galileo, G., 218

Gendlin, E., 19

Genesis, 219

Genogram, 65

Gerson, R., 7, 8, 63, 65

Gestalt therapy, 16, 17, 19

Getting the Love You Want: A Guide for Couples (Hendrix), 7, 23

Gibson, J., 168

Gilligan, C., 3, 38, 46

Giving the Love That Heals (Hendrix), 215

Goldberg, A., 186–188

Goldberger, N. R., 37, 38

Gomer, 52–55

Goulding, M., 16

Goulding, R., 16

Greed, 204

Greenberg, J., 163, 169

Grostein, J., 205

H

Hadot, P., 169

Haley, J., 78

Haley, K., 2

Hannah, M. T., 6, 7, 9, 130, 131, 144, 193

Harding, S., 37

Harvard Bereavement Study, 183

Hawking, S., 4

Healing in the Relational Paradigm: The Imago Relationship Therapy Casebook (Luquet and Hannah), 7

Healing wounds, 130–131, 170–172, 213–217

Heisenberg, W., 165

Helping Couples Change (Stuart), 17, 20

Hendrix, H., 6, 7, 13, 63–67, 71–74, 77, 81, 88, 92, 98, 99, 123, 127, 132, 139, 140, 164, 169, 179, 192, 201–203, 208, 209, 213–216

Hendrix, R., 88

Heschel, A. J., 57

Hillers, D. R., 53, 57*n*1

Hittites, 49, 50, 53

Hoffman, M., 28

Hoffman, S., 90*n*3

Holding exercise, 28

Holding Time (Welch), 17

Holocaust, 213
Holt Publishers, 23
Hopes, 203–204
Hora, T., 169
Horney, K., 207
Hosea, 52–55
How Does Analysis Cure? (Kohut), 153
Hunt, H. L., 7, 35, 48, 213
Hunt, H. T., 168, 169
Husserl, E., 19

I

I and Thou (Buber), 4, 27
Idealizing transference, 183
Imago: definition of, 6; knowing and, 113; and object relations, 108–120; and power struggle, 202–206; as unconscious template for partner selection, 202
Imago match: enactment *versus,* 132–134; and relational healing, 128–129; as way of suffering in relationship, 127
Imago Relationship Therapy (IRT), 5–6; beginnings of, 13–17; evolution of, 17–24
In a Different Voice (Gilligan), 3
Institute for Imago Relationship Therapy (New York), 22
Integration, 82–83
Integrity, 41–42
Intentionality, 216–217
Intervention, 80–81
Intimacy, 65
Intimate edge, 126
Intrapsychic pathology, 163
Introjection, 202
I-Thou relationship, 4

J

James, W., 168
Jaworski, J., 213
Jordan, J. V., 3, 41, 139, 142, 156, 157, 165, 179
Jung, C. G., 17, 18
Jurgens, G., 21

K

Kant, I., 42
Kaplan, A. G., 3
Kaufman, G., 100
Kauter, K., 213
Keats, J., 46*n*2
Keeping the Love You Find: A Guide for Singles (Hendrix), 7, 23
Kelly, V. C., Jr., 97, 104
Kernberg, O., 205, 207
Kerr, M., 66, 71, 73, 74
Kierkegaard, S., 42
Klein, M., 203, 205, 210
Knight, G.A.F., 55
Knowing: extreme separate, 38–39; holistic, 114–120; and imago, 113; relationship, 108–120; separate *versus* connected, 37–38; theories about, 108–112; transformational stage of, 109–110; transitional stage of, 110–112
Kohut, H., 28, 41, 140, 147, 149, 150, 152–155, 160*n*2, 183, 185, 186
Kollman, M., 28, 132
Kuhn, T. S., 1

L

Lachkar, J., 207, 211
Landrine, H., 43–44, 46*n*3
"Law and Love in Jewish Theology" (Sherwin), 55
Levenson, J. D., 53
Linthorst, A. T., 169
Listening, 40
Lopez-Corvo, R., 207, 208
Lost self, 38, 132, 133
Love, P., 21
Lubac, H., 5
Luquet, W., 1, 6, 7, 218

M

Mahler, M., 24, 32, 179
Male relational dread, 157
Marriage: and childhood connection, 18–19; conscious, 48–58; understanding needs of, 20–21

Marrone, J. G., 130, 131
Mason, M., 9, 144, 193
Mason, R. C., 8, 9, 124, 126, 139, 144, 162–168, 171, 173, 174, 177, 193
Mate selection, 73–74
Mays, J. L., 55, 56
McGoldrick, M., 65
Meadows Foundation, 22
Merleau-Ponty, M., 19
Miller, J. B., 3, 143, 156
Minuchin, S., 2, 78
Mirroring, 17, 21, 24, 131; beyond, 27–28; in Couples Dialogue, 148–149; transference, 148, 183
Mitchell, S., 122–124, 126, 163, 169
Modern Dance/Movement therapy, 148
Moore, S., 147
Morrison, A., 207
Mutuality, 3, 4

N

Narcissism, 207
Narcissistic/Borderline Couple: A Psychoanalytic Perspective on Marital Treatment (Lachkar), 207
Nathanson, D. L., 92–97, 100, 101, 103
National Advisory Mental Health Council, 92
Nature, role of, 71–72
Negative capability, 40
New York Times, 23
Newton, I., 142
Nightmare, 193; anatomy of, 196; short-circuiting, 200; treating, 196–197. *See also* Relationship nightmare
No Exit process, 79

O

Old Testament, 49–53
Oprah Winfrey Show, 23

P

Palmer, P. F., 48

Paradigm: creational, 217–219; definition of, 1; in mental health, 1–6; relational, 1–4, 42–45
Parent-Child Dialogue, 99, 100, 128; and healing through specificity and corrective relational experiences, 131–132
Parkes, C. M., 183
Part-objects, 202
Pearson, P. T., 92
Peck, M. S., 105
Perkins School of Theology (Southern Methodist University), 13–15, 21
Perls, F. S., 18
Perry, W. G., 37
Personality, transcending, 170–171
Phenomenology, 19, 166–168
Pierrakos, J. C., 24, 25
Plumlee, S. R., 8, 108
Positive Flooding, 101–105
Power of Myth, The (Campbell), 146–147
Power struggle, 201; and envy, 203; and greed, 204; and hopes and desires, 203–204; imago and, 202–206; and sameness and differentness, 205–206; as unconscious process, 204–205
Projection, 132, 202; definition of, 135; as way of suffering in relationship, 127–128
Protoempathy, 32

R

Rage, 152–153
Reactivity, 66–68, 129–130
Reciprocal listening, 17
Relational healing: concepts for, 122–135; three ways of, 128–130; through dialogue, 130–131
Relationality: and cosmogenesis, 4–5; and covenant, 52–53; and Imago Relationship Therapy (IRT), 4–5; and relational paradigm, 2–4; theory of, 1–6

Relationship: and concept of no being outside of, 122–123; healing power of, 213–217; impact of, on individual, 141; influence of, on self, 143–144; as living laboratory, 35–46; power of, 142–143; primacy of, 163–166; three ways of suffering in, 127–128; as top priority, 146–147; traumatic events and, 145–146; as vehicle for growth, 5–6

Relationship nightmare, 144–145; clinical examples of, 197–199; definition of, 193–195; treating, 195–197. See also Nightmare

Relationships: being conscious and intentional in, 216–217; conscious, 79; couple problems beyond, 172–174; creational paradigm of, 217–219

Relaxed joyfulness, 143

Repetition compulsion, 214

Responsibility: individual, 78–80; personal, 215–216

Restoration of the Self, The (Kohut), 151

Road Less Traveled, The (Peck), 105

Robinson, H. W., 58n6

Robinson, J., 23

Rogers, A. G., 39

Rogers, C., 17, 19, 28, 140, 150

Romantic phase, 205

S

Safety, 92

Sameness, 205–206

Sandel, S., 148

Sandler, J., 124

Satir, V., 2

Sauls, M., 90n3

Scharff, D. E., 132, 163, 169, 202, 204, 205, 207, 211

Scharff, J. S., 132, 163, 169, 202, 204, 205, 207, 211

Schleifer, M., 215

Schnarch, D., 92, 129

Schoeck, H., 206, 208

Scholastic Period, 48

Schwaber, E., 129

Schweickart, P., 39, 40

Scotus, Duns, 48

Script theory, 95–97

Searles, H., 207

Self: and bonding, 182–183; discrete to expanded, 182–189; expanded connected, 186; false, 169; influence of relationship on, 143–144; lost, 38, 132, 133; referential versus indexical, 43–44; and transference, 183–184

Self psychology, 148, 152, 153, 179, 184

Self-empathy, 41

Self-focus, 78

Self-objects: clinical implications of, 187–189; notion of, 184; as pathology or necessity, 184–186

Senge, P. M., 44, 45

Separation, ontology of, 25

Shame, 76–77, 95, 100

Sheldrake, R., 164

Shem, S., 3

Sherwin, B. L., 55

Short-Term Couples Therapy: The Imago Model in Action (Luquet), 7

Shulkin, S., 125, 132

Sinaic Covenant, 49, 56

Slade, S., 9, 213

Smith, T., 8, 162

Socratic method, 37

Southeastern Transactional Analysis Association, 23

Southern Methodist University, 13–14

"Speech Is Silver, Silence Is Gold" (Schweickart), 39

Spillius, E., 207, 210

Splitting, 39, 202. See also Dissociation

St. Elizabeth's Hospital (Washington, D.C.), 148

St. John's Provincial Seminary, 48

Stark, M., 124, 125

Stern, D. N., 24, 143, 147

Stiver, I. P., 3

Stolorow, R. D., 123, 141, 142, 145, 147, 151, 152, 174

Stone Center for Women, 3, 8, 139–140, 143, 179

Stuart, R. B., 17, 20, 21

Sullivan, H. S., 24, 190, 191

Surprises, 101–105

Surrey, J. L., 3, 40, 44, 156, 185

Swimme, B., 3, 6

Symbiosis: role of, 32–34; theory of, 27–34

Synchronicity: The Inner Path of Leadership (Jaworski), 213

Systemic theory: anxiety and family patterns in, 68–70; differentiation and reactivity in, 66–68; importance of contest in, 64–65; and multigenerational context, 65–66; therapist as coach in, 70–71

T

Tarule, J. M., 37

Teilhard de Chardin, P., 3, 5

Thomas Aquinas, 48

Thorne, J., 22

Thorne, R., 22

Tillich, P., 18

Tolman, D. L., 39

Tomkins, S. S., 92–96, 105

Transactional Analysis, 16, 17

Transcendence, 170–172

Transference, 183–184

Truax, C. B., 28

Truth telling, 44–45

Twinship transference, 183

U

Ulricit, D., 90n3

V

Validation, 28; in Couples Dialogue, 149–150

Vaughan, F., 169

Vicarious introspection, 140

VISN cable network, 24

Vitality affects, 143

W

Walsh, R. N., 169

Watergate, 213

Wavacle, 44

Weiss, R., 183

Welch, M. G., 17

We-ness, 147

Whitaker, J., 2, 17, 19

Wholeness, 41–42

Wilber, K., 4, 169, 171

Wilber, T., 171

Winfrey, O., 23

Winnicott, D. W., 109

Women's Ways of Knowing (Belenky, Clinchy, Goldberger, and Tarule), 37–38

Wounds, 66, 77, 79, 81, 82, 169, 214–215; and connection, 53–54

Z

Zest, 143

Zielinski, J., 8, 91

Zimmerli, W., 49, 57n1, 58n3

Zohar, D., 44, 46n4

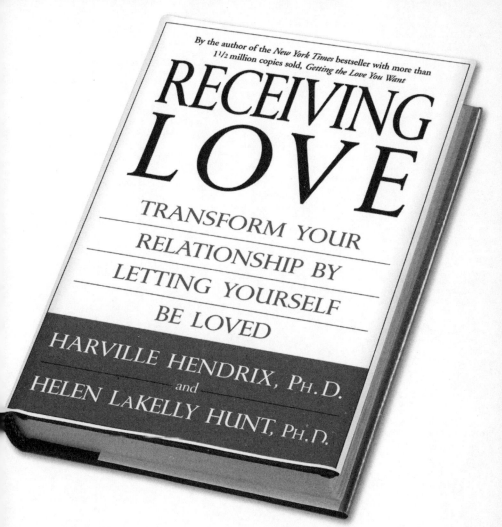